THE SERVICE INDUSTRIES

THE SERVICE INDUSTRIES

Strategy, Structure and Financial Performance

Derek F. Channon
Manchester Business School

First published 1978 by
THE MACMILLAN PRESS LTD
London and Basingstoke
Associated companies in Delhi
Dublin Hong Kong Johannesburg Lagos
Melbourne New York Singapore Tokyo

Printed in Hong Kong

British Library Cataloguing in Publication Data

Channon, Derek French
  The service industries.
    1. Service industries – Great Britain
    I. Title
    338.4'0941   HD9982.5

  ISBN 0–333–19807–7

TO MY PARENTS

Contents

List of Tables

List of Figures

Preface

The service industries as a sector of the economy are extraordinarily underresearched. Despite the fact that in the major developed economies of the world they are rapidly replacing or have replaced the manufacturing sector as the dominant source of employment they are still the cinderella industries of academics and politicians alike. Indeed, in some strange way, many opinion leaders see them as positively non-productive and are endeavouring to reverse the tide toward the manufacturing sector where the making of things is seen as somehow more honourable. Quite why this ethic prevails is difficult to understand while those who endeavour to reverse what appears to be an inexorable tide are likely to suffer the same fate as Canute.

The research reported in this book is therefore concerned with at least partially redressing the balance. It examines the strategic and structural development of the largest British service industry corporations and correlates these with the firms' financial performance. Funded by the Social Science Research Council, the work began in 1973 and continued over the next three years.

This book would not have been possible without the help and assistance of many people. First, the data itself was largely collected by my research assistants. A number have been associated with the project, some on a full time basis, others part time. At the beginning I was helped by Bruce Crowe who helped to design the package of data we eventually endeavoured to collect on each company. Mrs Helen Heerey was then responsible, during the mid-part of the project, for collecting together much of the data and beginning to shape it into a useable form. Finally, David Youngman helped to fill in some of the many gaps in the data and, in particular, was instrumental in improving our understanding of the major insurance companies.

Apart from those who were employed full time for periods on the project a number of MBA candidates at the Manchester Business School researched particular sectors of the service industries. The use of masters candidates for research purposes was well justified, and I am grateful for their diligence and effort. I have borrowed extensively on their dissertations in writing this book and, in particular, I single out Harry Chryssaphes for his research on the clearing banks; Ken Worthing for his study of the nationalised transport industries; Carmel Ryan for her study of non-food retailers; and Ian Milligan for his analysis of food retailing companies. I am also grateful to David Robinson who obtained an M.B.Sc. for his research of the merchant banks included in the population.

In addition to these detailed studies of specific industry sectors, a large number of individual case studies were prepared on companies. In the main these were prepared by MBA students as part of the corporate strategy programme at Manchester. There are too many involved to thank each individually, but specific studies are referenced in the text and to all concerned I express my appreciation.

The study could not have taken place at all without the great help received from many of the companies and their senior managements. There are no long established corporate records libraries in the United Kingdom and many companies generously gave their time and effort to help us accumulate records dating back to 1950. We were also kindly received by senior managers from many of the companies who generously provided us with details of their organisations and explained some of the intricacies of their industries. To those concerned we say thank you.

I should also like to thank many of my colleagues at Manchester who by their comments and constructive criticisms have substantially improved my thoughts. My secretary Mrs Sue Chapman has laboured diligently through the many drafts of the book and to her I express my gratitude. Finally, to my long-suffering wife, Ann, I apologise for the time taken up in writing which, but for her help, would have been required for more normal household duties.

Despite the many valuable contributions of others, the responsibility for the work and any errors or omissions contained in the argument are entirely my own.

Manchester, England   Derek F Channon
January 1978

1. Analysing the Post Industrial Society

In the post-war period the developed economies of the western world have witnessed a marked transformation of their industrial bases from a dominant dependence on manufacturing activity to the emergence of the service industry sector as the major source of employment. Despite this move to what has been called the Post Industrial Age, surprisingly perhaps there has been relatively little research into this sector of the economy. The primary emphasis has remained on the relatively declining area of manufacturing which has been the source of the majority of the theoretic concepts of business organisation and administration. Yet in many of the service industries such concepts are scarcely meaningful, for example the production function may not exist or the concept of 'sales' is unusable for no meaningful measure of it is applicable.

In an attempt to help redress this imbalance this book reports the findings of a major research study undertaken to investigate the strategy, structure and financial performance of each of the 100 largest service industry corporations in the United Kingdom over the period 1950–75. Further, it attempts to test the utility for the service industries of a number of concepts developed from experiences accumulated in the manufacturing sector, and to adapt or modify them where appropriate. In particular it seeks to examine the development of the corporations as unique individual business enterprises, rather than as is often done in analysing sectors such as banking and insurance, by aggregating the activities of the firms in these industries into a series of generalisations.

In the first chapter the background of the growth of the services sector is placed in context with a brief description of the development of the British economy. This is followed by a short description of the research methods used and defines the variables examined in the study. The second chapter describes the aggregate findings of the research. It outlines the trends in strategy and structure and the financial performance associated with the identifiable categories of each. Two basic strategic variables are examined namely the degree and type of product market or business area diversity and the degree of international activity. Structure is concerned with the traditional variable of the type of formal organisation adopted. In addition, the impact of leadership style is examined as a major structural variable, which is also related both to strategy and financial performance with interesting results.

The remaining chapters discuss in greater detail the strategic and structural evolution of the firms operating in major industry sectors covered by the study. Chapter 3 therefore, focusses upon the changes that have occurred among banks and other financial service institutions apart from insurance. This reveals the broad trend to increased diversification observable among the financial institutions which has led to a significant blurring of the traditional demarcation positions between the institutions and the emergence of broadly based multi-national, multi-service finance corporations.

Chapter 4 continues the examination of financial service institutions, focussing on the insurance sector. The insurance companies are subdivided according to the markets they serve and their ownership characteristics. Thus, the mutual life companies can be seen to have undergone only limited change, while the joint-stock composite companies have tended to diversify, especially in recent times, and to have moved substantially toward the multi-service mode adopted by the banks and other financial institutions.

Closely associated with the City of London are the shipping, merchanting and commodity trading companies and these are described in chapter 5. These firms, in most cases, trace their roots to the early development of the British Empire. The end of the British Empire in the post-war period forced many of these companies to undertake fundamental reappraisals of their strategy as decolonisation and growing local nationalism have changed their basic way of doing business. As a result not only have these firms tended to change their product market scope but they have been concurrently forced to relocate their asset base.

Chapter 6 covers some firms which also have connections with the City via the medium of property. This sector has experienced rapid growth in the post-war period and rising property values have led to forward integration by many insurance and banking institutions in order to gain a direct stake in property development. In addition to those organisations principally engaged in property the chapter also traces the evolution of the leading construction firms which have also, in the main, extended forward into property development. Finally, a number of firms engaged in the high growth leisure industries are included in this chapter since these companies either directly, or as a result of deliberate diversification, have developed property interests as part of their business portfolios.

Property also serves as a link to the retail and distribution companies which are discussed in chapter 7. These firms can be subdivided in several ways. Firstly, there are those firms principally engaged in food retailing while others operate primarily as non-food retailers. Secondly, there is a difference between those companies which are still managed largely by their founding families and those where professional managers are involved. The chapter traces the backgrounds of these different sub-groups and records and discusses their similarities and their differences.

The next two chapters examine the strategy and structure of the major public sector corporations. Although these organisations operate within an area of limited strategic choice they have nevertheless been subject to significant change. In part, such change has been brought about by environmental factors such as new technology, changing economics of scale and the like. In addition, a further major reason for organisational shifts in particular, has been almost continuous political intervention in both organisation and key strategic decision making, and the implications of this significant difference from normal private sector management are discussed at some length.

Finally in chapter 10 the process of strategic and structural change observed among service industry firms is reviewed. In addition to a discussion of a general pattern of change, a number of specific factors are considered in some detail including the role of acquisitions and certain aspects of leadership. The financial effects of certain strategic and structural changes are also reviewed. Finally the chapter concludes with a comparison of the similarities and differences observed between service and manufacturing industry firms.

TOWARD THE SERVICE ECONOMY

In all the major developed economies there has been in recent years a substantial shift in the balance between manufacturing industry and other areas of economic activity, but most importantly the service sector. The process of economic development itself can therefore be said to have developed in three main phases. In the first of these, the pre-industrial phase, agriculture provides the dominant means of employment. With the emergence of industrialisation a significant shift from the land occurs in order to man the new factories which in turn leads to a growth in urbanisation, as towns and cities develop around the centres of production.

Much more recently the industrial society, in turn, has begun to give way to the post-industrial phase where the locus of employment again shifts, this time with a relative decline in the importance of the secondary or manufacturing sector in line with a corresponding increase in the importance of the tertiary or services sector. This is illustrated in table 1.1 which shows the percentage distribution of both employment and gross domestic product (GDP) for a range of industrialised countries. As can be seen, in Spain and Italy the primary agricultural sector is still relatively important while in the United States and the United Kingdom the primary sector has been reduced almost to the limit. Moreover, in these latter two economies the process of industrial evolution has proceeded

Table 1.1   Employment and origin of GDP by sector, 1972, (%)

	UK	France	Germany	Italy	Spain	USA	Japan
Employment							
Primary Sector	1.9	12.9	7.5	18.0	27.7	4.3*	15.9*
Secondary Sector	44.4	40.3	50.4	43.8	37.2	31.0*	36.0*
Tertiary Sector	53.5	46.8	41.9	38.2	35.1	64.7*	48.1*
Origin of GDP							
Primary Sector	2.9	6.0*	2.9	8.0	12.8	3.0	6.0
Secondary Sector	42.7	48.4*	52.4	41.6	35.0	33.6	44.5*
Tertiary Sector	54.4	45.6*	44.6	50.4	52.2	63.4	49.6*

* 1971 Figures
Source: Hudson Institute Europe, *The United Kingdom in 1980*, Associated Business Programmes, 1974 p. 29.

furthest and the tertiary sector has already become the major area for both employment and contribution to GDP.

The situation in the United Kingdom is shown in further detail in tables 1.2 and 1.3 which indicate the changing pattern of employment by industry sector and the breakdown of gross domestic product respectively. Even by 1950 the numbers employed in service industries in the UK was high at 9.5m (43.2 per cent of total employment) compared with manufacturing industry which employed 8.5m (38.6 per cent). Over the next decade the importance of the service sector continued to grow and by 1960 the service businesses employed 11.8m or 52.5 per cent of the workforce and had overtaken manufacturing employment which actually increased slightly with the number employed rising to 9.0m or 40 per cent of the workforce. These changes were accompanied by a rundown of defence employment and especially the number of agricultural workers. Over the next decade and into the 1970s the main trend continued such that by 1974 the numbers employed in manufacturing had fallen to only 7.7m (34.6 per cent of the workforce) while the service sector continued to expand and by 1974 employed 12.3m or 55.1 per cent of the working population.

The growth trend of the service sector, however, has not been uniform, and in a number of industries employment has actually shown a significant decline. These changes are partially a result of changing technology as in retailing, where an initial post war boom led to an increase in sectoral employment which was later reversed with the advent of self service techniques. In building and contracting similar cyclical movement has occurred when, after an initial expansion to repair wartime damage, a decline in demand coupled with less labour intensive techniques has led to a reduction in employment.

A few industries, notably a number of those in the public sector have

Table 1.2   Industrial distribution of employment 1950–74[1] (thousands)

	1950	1955	1960	1965	1970	1974
Agriculture, Forestry and fishing	1197	1154	498	497	393	404
Mining and Quarrying	851	866	764	629	443	347
Manufacturing Industry	8471	9416	9001	9027	9075	7705
Service Industries:						
Building and Contracting	1448	1523	1607	1700	1469	1290
Gas, Electricity and Water	354	384	377	419	398	337
Transport and Communication	1802	1742	1691	1655	1625	1483
Distributive Trades	2610	2873	3355	3023	2761	2707
Insurance, Banking and Finance	452	493	564	645	977	1101
Hotels and Leisure	—*	900	830	874	745	1002
Professional Services	1597	1823	2184	2573	2903	3284
Miscellaneous Services	1275*	981	1216	1353	1149	1086
Public Administration and defence	1402	1322	1277	1338	1457	1551
Total all Industries and Services	22097	23447	22489	23621	22928	22297

Source: Department of Employment Statistics. *Includes hotels and leisure employment
1. Note these figures are drawn from somewhat different classification systems which have been periodically updated over time.

demonstrated consistent decline. The most obvious of these were the railways and the postal section of the Post Office which accounted for much of the decline in the transport and communications industry employment. Changing technology elsewhere in the public sector, in the gas and electricity industries, has also led to little growth or actual reductions in manpower, despite substantial growth in the overall demand for the products of these industries.

The most significant and consistent growth areas have been in the financial sector and in the provision of professional services. In this latter area there has been a major reallocation of resources into education and medicine which has led to notable growth in employment in these two industries. Other, smaller, professional services such accountancy, the law and research have also experienced some growth.

The only other sector of employment to grow in the post war period has been that of public administration. This reflects a growing bureaucratisation of society and, coupled with the large rise in employment in medicine and education, both of which are largely within the public sector, reveals the steady erosion of the private sector and the shrinking tax base available to support the growing burden of largely unproductive state services. These trends have begun to become recognised in the 1970s, albeit belatedly, and pressure is now being directed toward the rebuilding of the productive private sector base. Unfortunately perhaps, official attention is being primarily addressed to the re-establishment of the manufacturing sector, rather than encouraging the productive service industries, which have proved to be significant and useful contributors to the national economy.

The trends in GDP shown in table 1.3 reveal a pattern similar to that shown in employment. The percentage share of GDP coming from manufacturing activity has shown a steady decline since 1950 while that from the service industries in aggregate has similarly increased. Growth rates within the service sector have however varied sharply, with financial services, the gas industry, the tourist and leisure industries and professional services recording above average growth. Elsewhere experience has been mixed; in transportation for example a significant decline in the contribution from rail transport has been hidden to some extent by growth in road and air transportation. Similarly in the distributive trades, there has been rapid growth in the use of self service and the market share held by multiple retailers has increased in virtually all sectors at the expense largely, of small traders, many of whom have been eliminated.

While these trends reveal a significant rate of expansion among the service industries in general in terms of employment and GDP, the contribution made to the balance of trade reveals that the pattern of productive contribution to the economy is less widespread. Overall, the service sector has been a major positive contributor to Britain's international trade performance and the financial services sector in par-

Table 1.3 Gross Domestic Product by Industry, 1950–74 (million)

	1950	1955	1960	1965	1970	1974
Agriculture, Forestry and Fishing	610	801	915	1027	1241	2116
Mining and Quarrying	393	589	675	726	689	1021
Manufacturing Industry	4418	6168	8168	10624	14103	20645
Service Industries:						
Building and Contracting	624	977	1388	2153	2840	5645
Gas, Electricity and Water	251	401	617	1006	1401	2255
Transport and Communication	976	1418	1957	2629	3722	6648
Distributive Trades	1561	2150	2772	3605	4391	7003
Insurance, Banking and Finance	–	500	684	2092	3379	6750
Other Services	1389	1876	2567	3655	5205	8735
Public Health and Educational Services	346	566	907	1423	2321	4854
Public Administration and Defence	881	1011	1323	1812	2840	5312
Ownership of dwellings	448	557	902	1418	2848	4310
Gross Domestic Product at Factor Cost	11896	16801	22725	32153	44616	75294

Source: Central Statistical Office.

ticular has performed especially well. Although the City has traditionally had a net balance of payments surplus from insurance services and the like, international earnings from banking, broking and merchanting have increased dramatically from £67m to £253m over the decade to 1974. Overall the net contribution from the service industries 1964–73 increased from £186m to £947m, excluding the income from portfolio and direct investments from the private sector. Unfortunately over the same period the public sector invisible position worsened substantially, its deficit expanding from £550m to £985m. Nevertheless, Britain's overall invisible net trade balance expanded almost ten times over the decade from 1964, to reach £1165m by 1973.

Summarising, therefore, in the post war period the service industries have become increasingly important in all industrial economies as manufacturing industry reaches maturity and the developed countries move into the era of the post-industrial society. In the British and American economies this trend has proceded furthest and it is therefore, perhaps most appropriate to conduct an initial examination of the service sector in one of these two environments.

CONCEPTS AND DEFINITIONS

Models of corporate evolution

Research in manufacturing industry has revealed that definite patterns of corporate evolution can be distinguished which reflect the behaviour of most large corporations. As industrialisation proceded firms which had usually been created by individuals or groups of entrepreneurs began to expand, the first large scale private enterprises evolved usually being engaged in a single business or market activity. Often these emerging large corporations were formed by the amalgamation of a series of smaller similar concerns. These firms were also often vertically integrated and oriented toward the supply of primary sector products such as meat and tobacco in processed form, or the production of the essential building blocks of an industrial society, such as steel.

As a prerequisite to the development of the industry, the nineteenth century saw the growth of an infrastructure which enabled the transportation of goods and services to be conducted over wider areas. The birth of the railroads in particular, not only stimulated industrial development but provided the new, large firms with their earliest model of administrative structure, since the railways themselves had been forced to develop such systems by the very geographic separation which had led to their creation. The railways tended to adopt a form of organisation which divided the task of management along two basic dimensions, notably specialised functions such as sales, distribution and finance, and by geography.

Increasing size and complexity also led to the development of professional managers who were skilled in particular activities, such as accountancy and who were not owners of the businesses which they were charged with managing. Such men rapidly came to succeed the original entrepreneurs as the leaders of large corporations and so introduced the concept of continuity to the corporation. In a sense, the enterprise became an institution.

The growth of the large enterprise within the industrial society became a cause for widespread concern in many countries in the twentieth century. These firms have increasingly come to dominate the economies in which they operate and the introduction of professional managers brought about a relatively clear separation of ownership from control. Most recently this argument has been extended by some modern economists, notably Galbraith, who has claimed that while in the past the leadership of a firm was synonymous with entrepreneurial activity, in the modern corporation, built on technology and planning with ownership divorced from control, the entreprenueur no longer existed as an individual person.[1]

Galbraith argued that the entrepreneur had been replaced by a collective entity, the 'technostructure', which led to the development of group decision making. As a result the organisation became bureaucratic rather than entrepreneurial. The firm isolated itself from the uncertainties of the market by seeking to gain control over the environment in which it operated. Instead of the pursuit of the entrepreneurial concept of profit maximisation, the primary goals of the technostructure became survival and stability which were achieved by a continued expansion in size, measured by the growth of sales, and the achievement of a satisfactory level of earnings. While secondary objectives such as technical virtuosity and a rising dividend rate were also often present, these were permitted only subject to the condition that they did not conflict with the achievement of the primary goals.

Galbraith's concept of the large firm, therefore, suggests that it is one that seeks to integrate its functions in an effort to stabilise its environment, thereby achieving its goals of satisfactory financial returns and maximum size growth. This strategy did indeed seem to reflect that adopted by many early large firms which grew mainly by integration and by extending their sales to similar customer groups.

In his classic study of the development of large American enterprises however, Chandler noted two further important strategies.[2] He observed that growth also came as a result of a quest for new markets and sources of supply in new areas, or from the development of new markets by the introduction of new products to meet the needs of new customer groups.

The adoption of these two alternative strategies of geographic and product diversification resulted in the creation of new administrative problems. Initially, the firms adopting such policies endeavoured to continue managing with a traditional functional form of organisation or by the creation of a loosely knit holding company, where distant or product diversified elements of the corporation were permitted to act as virtually autonomous subsidiaries, with few or no central controls or methods of coordination. However, continued growth in size, complexity and information flows placed an increasingly intolerable strain on the functional and holding company forms of organisation, especially at the corporate management level. As a result, in the 1920s a new administrative form began to emerge in a few innovative organisations, most notably E. I. Du Pont de Nemours and the General Motors Corporation.[3]

This administrative structure subdivided the firm into a series of quasi-autonomous divisions. There were four main hierarchical levels stated by Chandler. Firstly, at the centre was a general office where the top general officers of the corporation, together with staff specialists, coordinated, appraised and planned goals and policies and allocated resources to the divisions. Each division which was largely self-contained, handled a major product line or was responsible for the firm's activities in a particular region. The divisions, in turn, also contained a central office responsible for the general management of the activities of each division, and were subdivided into specialised functional departments. Each of these departments, then, coordinated, appraised and planned for a number of field units. These units were responsible for the management of a works, branch office, sales territory and the like.

In the field units the management was primarily responsible for supervising day to day activities. The departmental and divisional offices were concerned, to some extent, with the long term aspects of their own division activities but in the main were involved in tactical, operational decisions. The central corporate office conducted broad strategic or entrepreneurial decisions, affecting the corporation as a whole. The adoption of this form of organisation therefore, permitted some reestablishment of an entrepreneurial role at the top level of the diversified firm. The general executives in the central office had no specific commitment to any one activity, although in practice the emergence of a top management cadre, in many firms drawn from a key division, has tended to lead to bias in a number of cases. In theory, however, the commitment of this central office group to the enterprise as a whole enabled it to treat the quasi-autonomous divisions as a portfolio of businesses which could be bought or sold, and starved or fed with resources, according to the overall strategy adopted for the firm.

This structure conceivably permitted the firm to transfer its resources to the most profitable areas or divisions, and to the division general managers of proven ability. Further, the development of general management skills at a number of points within the organisation provided the initial resource required to permit the addition of new activities. Moreover, a spirit of inter-divisional competition was encouraged, since resources were allocated on the basis of divisional performance. Thus, in order to obtain the desired share of limited resources, a divisional management had to demonstrate that its claim overrode those of other divisions.

Diversification has become the dominant strategy among most large manufacturing corporations in the developed western economies. In the United States a new breed of company, the conglomerate, emerged in the post war period; such firms grew rapidly by a process of acquisition, into large organisations with little or no inter-divisional dependencies. For most large corporations however, diversification by both geography and product has been a gradual process. Those organisations engaged in technologies such as chemical or electrical engineering provided a natural research base for the development of new products which extended those firms quickly into a series of related product markets. For other companies, with a less fertile technological base, acquisition has proved a more significant route to gaining new market entries. By 1967, it has been estimated that 86 per cent of the largest 500 manufacturing industry based firms in the United States were at least partially diversified, and furthermore, were managed with some variant of a divisional organisation.[4] A number of other studies have demonstrated that similar trends are taking place in each of the major European economies, although the rate of change has been somewhat less than that experienced in the United States.[5]

The widespread observation of the move toward a diversified enterprise has led to the development of a basic evolutionary theory of corporate development. In its original form, proposed by Bruce R. Scott,[6] the firm was seen to evolve from its early origins, when the founding entrepreneur was engaged in all aspects of operations and decision making, firstly, into a relatively undiversified or integrated system. This type of firm, where the main interactions took place within the corporation rather than with the external environment, could be treated essentially as a closed system. Such firms tended to organise the task of management into a series of specialised functions, with overall corporate coordination taking place in the office of the chief executive and the main board. As such firms diversified, however, new activities were added which changed the basis of corporate transactions such that each of the quasi-autonomous divisions interacted primarily with its external environment rather than with other internal divisions. Such firms were more akin to open systems and as a result of their diversity were usually managed with a divisional form of organisation.

Strategic and structural variables
The present research focusses upon examining the development of the major service industry corporations in the United Kingdom. It seeks to describe their strategies and organisations and to compare the differences in financial performance associated with each. The research endeavours to make use of some tools developed for similar studies in manufacturing industry modifying these where necessary in order to better cater for the managerial needs of the service industry firms. In addition, the importance

of a number of new strategic and structural variables is examined in order to understand their importance in the process of corporate development. In this way, therefore, it is hoped to gain a better understanding of the conditions of corporate life in the key sector of the post industrial economy.

The Scott model of corporate development has subsequently been extended to account for the notable differences which can be distinguished between firms operating with divisional forms of organisation. Firstly, Wrigley[7] observed that both the type and degree of product market diversification significantly modified the level of decision making autonomy permitted to divisional management. Secondly, Stopford[8], Franko[9] and others observed that both the degree of geographic and product diversity influenced the make-up of divisional structures in firms which had developed international operations. These two factors were therefore, examined in detail as key strategic variables for analysis. The precise definitions used to measure each are set out below. In addition one further factor was observed to be of particular importance in the process of strategic change. Many companies used acquisition as a major mechanism for change and the type and rate of acquisitions undertaken therefore formed a third strategic variable for analysis.

The relationship between strategy and structure was a fundamental area for examination. The categorisation of formal structure and comparison with the strategic variables was therefore naturally undertaken. In addition the research examined in detail the function of leadership, which was also categorised. Apart from the role of individuals however, the composition of the boards of directors as a whole of the companies researched was also studied. In particular the research focussed upon changes in board composition as an element of strategic and structural change but where it was found to be important, kinship relationships, socio-economic background and cross directorships with other organisations were also examined.

The effect of product diversification

Wrigley was able to discover four major strategic categories of large firms which were differentiated by their degree of diversification and the related nature of the product market activities in which the firm was engaged. A slightly modified version of these categories was used as a starting point for classifying the product market strategies of service industry firms. These categories were defined as follows: –

Single Business	firms which grew by the expansion of one business activity so that at least 95 per cent of sales lay within this single business area.
Dominant Business	firms which grew primarily by the expansion of one main product line

but which in addition had added other business activities making up 30 per cent or less of the total sales or its equivalent. These secondary activities might be related to the primary activity as for example with the petro-chemical interests of an oil company or unrelated as say the cosmetics interests of a tobacco company.

Related Businesses   firms which grew by expansion by means of entry into related markets, by the use of related technology, by related vertical activities or some combinations of these strategies such that no one business area accounted for 70 per cent of the total corporate sales or its equivalent.

Unrelated Businesses   firms which grew by expansion (usually by acquisition) into new markets and new technologies unrelated to the firm's original business so that no one business area accounted for 70 per cent of total corporate sales or its equivalent.

The effect of international operations

In addition to diversifying into new business areas, as most large firms expand so they tend to develop overseas operations. Detailed breakdowns of the location of the interests of most of the service companies were not available on a longitudinal basis. Nevertheless, the data was available for later years and the relationships between the level of international activity and both structure and financial performance were therefore explored. Companies were classified into one of three basic categories according to the level of overseas sales (or equivalent) in 1974. The three categories concerned were defined as follows: –

High International activity   where 40 per cent or more of corporate sales were generated from international operations.

Medium International activity   where more than 10 per cent but less than 40 per cent of corporate sales (or equivalent) were generated from international operations.

Low International activity   where 10 per cent or less of corporate sales were generated from international operations.

The effect of acquisitions

One final strategic decision area was analysed in some depth. It was found that acquisition had been a major mechanism for strategic change and data was systematically collected on the acquisitions undertaken by the service industry firms. This data was classified in two ways. Firstly, acquisitions were categorised by product market type into four categories which are defined below: –

Horizontal (H)	the extension of the same range of products or services to the same basic customer group.
Integrated (I)	The extension of a business by forward integration toward the market place or backward to sources of supply.
Related (R)	diversification either by the addition of related products selling to an established customer group or by the extension of the existing services to new customer groups.
Conglomerate (C)	the addition of new businesses to service markets which have no relationship to the firm's existing activities.

Secondly, it was found that the rate of making acquisitions varied considerably from company to company. For some organisations acquisition was virtually an integral ongoing feature of their strategy while at the other extreme some firms grew entirely by internal development. In order to differentiate between these extremes three different categories of acquisition strategies were determined empirically and were defined as follows: –

Aggressive acquirers	where the number of acquisitions undertaken in the decade from 1964–74 was 10 or more.
Moderate acquirers	where the number of acquisitions undertaken in the decade from 1964–74 was more than 3 but less than 10.
Passive acquirers	where the number of acquisitions undertaken in the decade from 1964–74 was 3 or less.

Problems of strategic analysis

In practice it was found that most service industry firms could be classified using these simple strategic categories although the method was not wholly without problems. Firstly, in a number of industries, turnover or sales revenue was not a meaningful measure of size. This was especially true in banking, both among the clearing and overseas banks as well as among merchant banks. To some extent types of diversification could be measured by the use of surrogates, such as premium income in the case of insurance and loans and advances in the case of banks. Alternatively the use of percentage asset base devoted to specific activities could be used, especially where registered subsidiary companies were involved. That significant diversification did occur in banking becomes clear in chapter 3, but the measures used are not entirely comparable with those adopted in those situations where sales revenue figures were available.

Apart from the technical problem associated with banking, ambiguity arose in the classification of companies which provided no data on the breakdown of their activities prior to the introduction of a statutory requirement in 1967. A problem also occurred in insurance and property where turnover again was not a relevant measure. In each of these cases, however, the solution was not difficult in practice since in the main the degree of diversification was clearly lower than the related business category. Property companies which did nothing other than property development were readily classifiable while for insurance companies, annual premium income proved a satisfactory surrogate for turnover.

A more serious problem occurred with two groups of companies which were very different from the manufacturing sector. The first of these were the colonial merchants which operated a unique strategy which could have been classified as related-linked. In the event, the significant differences in the nature of the businesses these firms operated led them to be classified as conglomerate as early as 1950. In later years, as the linkages between their disparate activities were weakened due, usually, to disproportional growth rates, they became more clearly conglomerate although geographic relationships were still common between the activities.

Secondly, the distributive trades also posed a classification problem. In some cases retailing firms had clearly diversified into quite different forms of retailing, such moves were treated as related diversification although this is not wholly satisfactory since it is like saying that all manufacturing activities should be treated as related which they are clearly not.

The classification of formal organisation structure

Associated with each of the strategic product market categories named by Wrigley were distinctively different organisations. The single business firms were usually managed with a functional form of organisation. The remaining three categories all tended to operate variations of the divisional form of organisation, however measurable differences could be observed between these as shown in table 1.4. In dominant business firms the dominant division itself tended to receive substantial operational involve-

Table 1.4 Multidivisional Firms—Organisation Models

Characteristics	Divisional Category		
	Dominant Business	Related Business	Unrelated Business
Diversification	Dominant Product	Two or more related Product lines	Two or more unrelated Product lines
Product Flow	Mixed System Dominant Area Integrated Other Areas Open System	Open System with lines to Corporate office Some units linked	Open System Divisions Completely separate
Corporate Management and Staff	Corporate large specialised staff for Dominant Product	Corporate large specialised staff related to core skills	Corporate small staff Control & Legal only
Organisation	Dominant Area Weak Divisional or Functional Other Areas Divisional	Product Division plus service Departments	Product Division
Divisional	Dominant Area Routine Operation Other Area Product Strategy	Product Strategy	Product Strategy plus supplies
Resource Allocation	Dominant Area Balance Between Units Other Area ROI	ROI	ROI
Control Performance	Dominant Area ROI Growth Market Share Costs Other Area ROI	ROI Growth Market Share	ROI Growth

Source: L Wrigley, op cit, pp vi–32.

ment from top management and was usually organised on a functional basis. The central office in such firms was large in order to coordinate operations in the major division. In the area of limited diversification found in such firms, however, the degree of autonomy permitted divisional management was high when these interests were not highly interrelated with the dominant business.

Related business firms also tended to operate with relatively large central offices. Such head office departments, however, were seldom directly involved in the operational management of the divisions but rather ensured adequate coordination of interdependent activities between the divisions. By contrast, unrelated business firms were coordinated on a financial and control system basis. Such firms tended to have only a small financially oriented central office. However, central management did play an important role in deciding the make up of the strategic portfolio of businesses in a number of such companies. At the division level, relatively high levels of autonomy were permitted, since inter-divisional dependence in conglomerates was kept deliberately low.

Overseas manufacturing involvement was shown by Stopford to also be a significant determinant of organisation. Initially, overseas operations tended to be grouped together into an international division but as both overseas size, in terms of sales, and product diversity increased, this division broke down to be replaced by one of three multi-divisional variants. A relationship appeared to exist between organisation, the degree of overseas product range diversity and the relative size of international operations. Low product diversity, coupled with a significant volume of overseas sales, tended to lead to the adoption of a structure based on geographic or area divisions. Growth in overseas sales, coupled with significant product diversity led initially to the formation of worldwide product divisions. However, when growth and product diversity reached a certain level, determined by Stopford as an empirical boundary condition, this led to the formation of a 'grid' structure where conflicting product and geographical demands required central coordination of function, product and geographic activities. Empirical evidence suggests that geographic differentiation is increasingly the key determinant of international structure especially among American corporations, where the emergence of the regional headquarters organisation provides a mechanism for introducing a local head office to coordinate local national operations. The international organisations of service industry firms were therefore examined as a specific series of sub categories of the main structural forms discussed below.

Three basic forms of formal organisation were therefore categorised from studies of manufacturing industry. These were also used for the analysis of the service industry companies and are defined below: –

Functional Structure   in this form the firm was subdivided

	into a series of specialised functions, culminating in the office of the chief executive who performed the role of coordinator and general manager of all the individual functions.
Holding Company Structure	in this form the firm was subdivided into one of two basic structures namely:
a) *Functional holding company*	where semi-autonomous subsidiaries were grafted onto the basic functional organisation.
b) *Holding company*	which was composed of a system of semi-autonomous subsidiaries, held together only as a corporate legal entity.
Multi-divisional Structure	in this organisation the firm was sub-divided into a series of autonomous multi-function divisions responsible for operations, but with a general office which serviced and monitored their performance. The multidivision structure can be further subdivided into a series of sub categories usually related to the degree and type of international operation conducted by the firm. These major subcategories are outlined below:
a) *Geographic Divisional*	(MG) in which divisions are organised regionally.
b) *Product Divisional*	(MP) in which divisions are organised by product market area.
c) *Mixed Divisional*	(MM) in which there is a combination of geographic area and product based divisions.

All the three basic organisation forms could be seen among the service industry companies and in addition there were examples of each of the holding company variants and all the main divisional sub-categories. However, there were also a significant number of structures which could not be readily categorised using the suggested descriptions. A few of these firms were unique hybrids such as that of the co-operative movement, the Co-operative Wholesale Society and the John Lewis Partnership. More important was the relatively frequent appearance of another structure which was designated the *critical function* structure.

The critical function structure

This organisation form was a hybrid incorporating many elements of the divisional system but also being functional in at least one area. Thus in retailing, it was common for stores to be grouped into geographic profit centres, while in insurance, certain product areas and geographic areas could be similarly treated. Furthermore, the very nature of the task assigned to such units meant that they had to be autonomous on an operating, although not strategic, level. At the same time these quasi-divisions did not have complete control over all aspects of their operations as certain critical activities were treated as centralised 'functions'. These functions were not usually critical in manufacturing firms[10] and included activities such as the central buying function in retailing or the investment function in insurance. For many service firms such functions required centralised management, due to their specialised and crucial nature and despite the fact that their presence tended to make the measurement of divisional profit centres the more difficult. In one respect a common critical function was observed as emerging in both service and manufacturing firms, namely the central treasury management function in multinational corporations.[11] The relative frequency with which this structure was encountered led it to be separately categorised. The critical function structure is therefore defined below and illustrated in Figure 1.1.

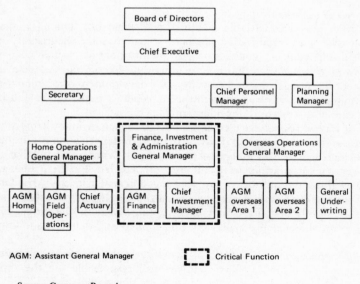

AGM: Assistant General Manager   Critical Function

Source: Company Records

Figure 1.1   Critical Function Composite Insurance Company Structure

Critical Function   In this organisation form the structure
was subdivided into a series of geo-
graphic or product based operating
units which were semi-profit accountable. However, one or more critical
functions were fully centralised and
outside the responsibility of the operating units making full profit account-
ability unrealistic.

In the main critical function structures were found associated with
geographic operating units as for example in retailing and banking. In
insurance, sub-unit responsibilities were usually product based or some
combination of product and geography. In addition the critical function
structure was also found in combination with the holding company
structure. Thus for example the organisation of the clearing banks for
much of the 1960s consisted of a critical function regional hybrid for the
domestic banking activities while interests in other financial service
subsidiaries, engaged in credit finance and the like, were not coordinated
and treated on a holding company basis. With the introduction of a critical
function structure it was possible with a few exceptions to classify the
service industries into the four basic structural categories defined.

The role of leadership
A further structural variable examined was leadership. The top management role in an organisation has been stated by some theorists to be of
critical importance[12] while for others, organisations are seen as coalitions
of power groups[13] such that no one individual has a dominant role. This
concept was tested since earlier study of the development of manufacturing
firms indicated that leadership did seem to play a particular role in both
strategic and structural development[14].

The largest 100 service companies proved to include many firms still led
by a founding entrepreneur. Bearing in mind the length of time it normally
takes for a firm to grow to this size it seemed somewhat surprising that 21 of
the service corporations were still entrepreneur led. Further, there were
also a substantial number of firms managed at senior levels by the family
descendants of a founding entrepreneur although this did not usually mean
that the family held a majority of the voting shares in such firms. Three
categories of leadership type were thus named and defined as follows: –

Entrepreneurial   firms where the organisation's founder
was still responsible for the critical
strategic decisions.
Note: this definition is somewhat more
ambiguous than desired, but in some

cases a figurehead chairman had been introduced and the senior management job was that of managing director. This position was reversed in other cases. Also in two cases the founding entrepreneur had taken the position of life president and occupied neither the chairmanship nor chief executive position.

Family   firms where the top management job of chairman and/or chief executive was held by direct descendants of the company's founder or founders.

Professional   firms where the top management positions of chairman and chief executive had passed to professional managers which had no lineal descendancy to the company's founder.

The analysis of financial performance

In addition to establishing patterns of strategy and structure in the service corporations, the research also tested to see if particular categories of these variables produced significantly different economic performance. This followed the work of Richard Rumelt at the Harvard Business School who conducted a number of such tests on a sample of manufacturing firms drawn from the Fortune 500 for which Compustat financial statistics were available.[15]

Using this data base Rumelt examined a series of ten financial performance results against product market strategy and formal organisation variables similar to those defined above.

Although in principle a similar form of analysis was conducted on the service companies, for a number of reasons it differed in detail from that conducted by Rumelt on U.S. corporations. The major reasons for the differences in treatment were as follows:

1. Sales was not a suitable measure for many service industry firms thus although sales growth was calculated in some cases a substitute value was actually adopted.
2. A large number of the companies were not suitable for examination for earnings per share since they did not have shareholders in a conventional sense. These companies included the public sector corporations and mutual insurance companies. These firms were therefore not included in much of the financial analysis.
3. Performance measurement of clearing and merchant banks and joint stock insurance companies was substantially different from con-

ventional companies. For example, until 1969 the banks did not disclose their overall profitability, merely giving a figure for after tax profits while undeclared sums were placed to inner reserves. In insurance, performance tended to be related to expense ratios rather than return on assets or the like. As a result, therefore, companies in these industries were excluded from much of the financial analysis where the measures used were not relevant.

4. In a number of service corporations, especially in property and property related concerns, earnings per share was a measure much less meaningful than assets per share. In addition to a growth in earnings per share variable (geps) therefore, growth in assets per share (gaps) was also calculated and a straightforward overall growth of assets (gassets) term was also evaluated.

5. Rumelt in his analysis took only three points of measurement in 1949, 1959 and 1969. In his calculations of the value of each of his variables, therefore, he takes only those companies which have remained unchanged in a specific strategic and/or structural category throughout an entire decade. In the service industry research the greater depth of detail made it possible to consider strategic and structural variables at shorter intervals. Each observation was, therefore, taken from the time when a corporation changed category.

6. The experience with British companies leads us to seriously challenge one of Rumelt's basic assumptions that earnings per share growth rates (and by imputation assets per share growth) can be treated as a simple log linear function thus:

$$\text{Log } (\text{eps}_t) = A + (\text{geps})t + E_t$$

Where geps is the uniform annual growth rate, t is an integer that measures time in years and E is the annual deviation from the uniform growth model.

This model appeared to hold only in cases of extreme stability where both strategy and structure had been established for a substantial period as in the case of some retail concerns. Unfortunately the environment in which firms operated appeared to be increasingly turbulent resulting in much more rapid change which, in some cases, could be described as discontinuous. In many situations, therefore, long-term trend lines appeared to be not only interrupted by category changes, but even permanently changed.

In addition, where new corporations had entered the ranks of the top 100 due to exceptionally rapid growth there was no expected evidence of a Gompertz type growth function with growth rates declining as maturity was reached.

Although a log linear function was assumed, therefore, in our calculations of the growth variables, experience in its use led to some dissatisfaction with its simplicity and explanatory power.

7. Industry differences, although briefly considered in Rumelt's analysis, are not strongly dealt with. As mentioned, financial analysis of the service corporations threw some of these differences into stark relief since a number of the normal financial variables are meaningless in some service industries. This makes a number of cross industry comparisons impossible and others remaining are usually crude. Further, it makes data aggregation somewhat dangerous on the one hand while interfirm comparison within an industry is also difficult due to small sample size and also the difficulties inherent in placing firms within specific 'industries' as they become more diversified.

Nevertheless, interfirm comparisons were made within broad industry based groups, especially in insurance and banking, where data aggregation was not relevant. Here, therefore, we were less concerned with seeking specific correlations, but rather looking for meaningful indicators of significant differences.

Rumelt's argument that since strategy and industry are clearly interrelated and that industry strategies are insufficiently heterogeneous to permit controlled comparison holds for the service industries. Thus most of the strategy related performance differences are probably due to industry differences, but the two effects are inseparable. It was not, therefore, possible to 'correct' data on performance for industry without at the same time eliminating the effects of diversification strategy. As Rumelt observes, therefore, a strict normative interpretation of performance difference is in general somewhat questionable, but can be considered as indicative.

One further problem which has become of increased importance is that of inflation. Again the data has not been corrected and the indicative results described in the following chapters could be usefully reinterpreted, with attempts made to modify the data to allow for inflationary change. Some limited efforts were made to treat the data for inflation, however, with the result that the values of the financial variables tended to be reduced but the direction and relative values of one category with another tended to remain the same.

For the reasons given the financial analysis conducted on the service industry companies therefore differed somewhat from that conducted by Rumelt. In all, 6 key financial variables were considered, namely: –

GAPS:	Growth rate in assets per share.
GEPS:	Growth rate in earnings per share.
RBIT:	Return on capital before interest and taxes as an annual year on year average.
RAT:	Return on capital after tax taken as an annual year on year average.
GSALES:	Growth rate in group sales turnover.
GASSETS:	Growth rate in group net assets.

While the research was conducted over the period from 1950 in the event this proved relatively impracticable for financial analysis. This was due in particular to the tax change in 1964 to corporation tax. This change made a substantial difference to the measurement of post tax earnings and hence earnings per share. As a result a decision was taken to concentrate the financial analysis on the shorter period 1964–74.

The research method

The strategic, structural and financial histories of the largest 100 service industry companies taken from the Times 1000[16] were built up over the period 1950–74. There was a marginal problem at the earliest stage of the research when actually deciding on the largest 100 firms since, unlike in the manufacturing sector, no single characteristic of size can be used for classification. In the event, three measures of size were used, net assets, sales turnover and number of employees and while the great majority of the firms examined would clearly be selected on all these criteria, there are a limited number of cases where some question could be raised. For example, despite their very high turnover figures, the discount houses were not included due to their low capital base and small number of employees.

The data on each of the selected firms was built up primarily from published sources and in particular from annual reports. These were supplemented by many other sources, including company magazines and newspapers, magazine articles and case histories, company histories, McCarthy press clippings, brokers reports and the like. Although not always comprehensively available, the basic data collected for each year for each company is set out below: –

  i)   Business activity broken down by product line and geography in terms of sales, profitability and assets.
  ii)   Board composition.
  iii) Board emoluments.
  iv)   Other directorships.
  v)   Directors shareholdings.
  vi)   Details of mergers and acquisitions including price paid, product market classification, and location.
  vii) New subsidiaries formed by product classification, location and ownership.
  viii) Subsidiaries terminated and disposed of by product area, geography and price.
  ix)   Businesses started and discontinued.
  x)   Consultants used, including nature of assignment.
  xi)   Major policy statements.
  xii) Geographic location of activities.
  xiii) Organisation form.
  xiv) Full financial details of profit and loss and balance sheet statements.

In addition, to supplement the published source material and to validate its findings, structured interviews were conducted with directors or senior executives of more than half of the companies. Further, detailed case studies were constructed for over 50 of the companies. This volume, therefore, describes in aggregate form only a small amount of the data collected, its purpose being to extract a number of the broad generalisations discernible from the study.

Summary

This chapter has outlined the trend toward the emergence of the service sector as the major component of the national economic base in the post industrial society. Further, it has examined patterns of corporate evolution which have been categorised largely from observations of the development of major manufacturing corporations. From the first of these discussions a need to examine the pattern of strategy and structure in service industry firms was developed and from the second a number of specific variables emerged which provided part of the method of analysis.

Based upon meaningful categories established in manufacturing concerns, classification systems were defined for the analysis of corporate strategies by their degree and type of diversification and by their level of international activity. In addition, in view of their importance as a mechanism for strategic change, acquisitions were treated as a third strategy variable, and classified both by type and by the rate at which they were undertaken by particular firms.

Two key structural variables were also categorised and defined. The first of these, the formal organisation of the firm, built upon concepts established from research into manufacturing companies, but a new category was added with specific relevance to service industry firms. The second category of corporate leadership was subdivided into three classes based essentially upon the pattern of ownership or proprietership of the company.

The financial performance of the firm over time provided a third class of variable against which both structural and strategic variables could be correlated. In a similar, but somewhat different manner from earlier work in the manufacturing sector, a series of six meaningful financial variables were established to measure the performance of service industry firms.

Finally, the chapter concluded with a brief review of the manner of data collection and an outline of the type of information actually gathered on each firm. While this was not wholly available in all cases, in the main a large amount of data was accumulated from a wide variety of published sources, this being supplemented in over half the companies by structured interviews and the construction of detailed cases describing individual concerns.

2. Strategy Structure and Financial Performance

This chapter presents the results obtained from categorising the service industry firms by the strategic and structural variables defined in the previous chapter. The changing pattern of diversification exhibited by the largest 100 service industry firms is shown in table 2.1. This divides the companies by the dominant industry sector in which they operate and assigns each to a particular category of diversification for successive 5 year periods from 1950–74.

The data clearly reveals that in many companies, and especially those involved in financial services, there has been a clear trend toward an increase in diversification over time. While this process began during the 1950s among the clearing banks and insurance companies, the pace of change has accelerated rapidly since the late 1960s. Although causality can seldom be perfectly demonstrated as shown in chapter 3, there was a series of events which took place in 1968 which signalled a need for strategic change. These events included an official change of attitude toward industry concentration, a growing need to develop international services to compete with the leading American commercial banks, and an increase in competitive pressure from other financial institutions in the United Kingdom. As a result both the merchant banks and clearing banks have diversified into related financial services, and expanded overseas. In 1950, each main type of financial institution occupied a relatively distinct position in the overall market for credit. Thus, the clearing banks were essentially operators of widespread branch banking networks concerned with short term deposits and loans, while the merchant banks were small, highly personalised, often family dominated institutions operating mainly in the medium and long term capital market, as wholesale bankers and investment managers. Diversification has led to each type of institution moving into areas traditionally held by the other, such that the traditional demarcation lines have been largely blurred. This phenomenon of new competitors emerging from new market entries occurs in several sectors of the service industries where in many cases barriers to entry are relatively low.

Table 2.1 Frequency of Diversification Strategy by Industry, 1950–74[1]

	1950				1955				1960				1965				1970				1974			
	S	D	R	U	S	D	R	U	S	D	R	U	S	D	R	U	S	D	R	U	S	D	R	U
Clearing Banks[2]	4	–	–	–	1	3	–	–	–	4	–	–	–	4	–	–	–	2	6	–	–	1	7	–
Merchant Banks	–	3	–	–	–	3	–	–	–	4	1	–	–	4	2	–	–	–	6	–	–	–	6	–
Other Financial	1	3	–	–	1	3	–	–	1	3	–	–	–	5	1	1	–	3	3	1	–	2	3	2
Insurance	11	5	5	–	10	5	6	–	9	6	7	–	9	6	7	–	9	5	9	–	9	4	10	–
Property	1	–	–	–	3	–	–	–	4	–	–	–	4	–	–	–	3	1	–	–	3	1	–	–
Hotel & Leisure	1	–	–	–	1	–	–	–	–	1	–	–	–	1	1	–	–	1	2	–	–	–	2	1
Construction	–	–	3	–	–	–	4	–	–	–	4	–	–	–	5	–	–	–	5	–	–	–	5	–
Food Retailing	–	2	–	–	–	2	–	–	–	2	1	–	–	1	3	–	1	–	4	–	1	2	4	–
Non Food Retailing	3	7	1	–	3	6	1	2	3	6	1	2	2	7	1	2	2	4	4	2	2	2	6	2
Commodity Trading	1	1	–	1	1	1	–	1	1	1	–	1	–	2	–	1	–	1	1	1	–	–	2	1
Colonial Merchants	–	1	–	2	–	1	–	2	–	1	–	3	–	–	1	3	–	–	1	3	–	–	1	3
Nationalised Sector[3]	2	3	2	–	2	4	2	–	1	5	2	–	–	7	2	–	1	7	2	–	1	6	2	–
Miscellaneous	1	3	1	1	1	3	1	1	–	4	–	3	–	4	1	4	–	2	2	6	–	–	–	10

[1] Increase in row totals reflects new companies joining the sample population.

[2] Includes overseas banks.

[3]This column is not strictly comparable due to major structural shifts within a macro set of industries in particular land based transportation.

Key: S = single business: D = dominant business: R = related business: U = unrelated business

There has also been some increase in the degree of diversification exhibited by the insurance companies, although here the rate of change has been much lower. The insurance companies divide importantly according to ownership, between the mutual concerns which are almost all engaged only in the whole life market, and the joint stock companies which are generally diversified, composite insurance groups. The mutual companies have few direct external threats to spur them to undertake strategic change and in particular they cannot be acquired, their share capital being owned by their policy holders. Largely as a result, with few exceptions, mutual insurance companies have remained relatively unchanged strategically. By contrast a number of the composite groups have chosen to diversify both by geography and by product line, developing both new areas of insurance business at home and overseas. Moreover in recent times a number of these companies have also integrated forward into other areas of the financial services and into property development.

The remaining financial service industry firms were composed of two sorts. Firstly, there were a number of relatively specialised concerns such as the credit finance companies. These concerns had not diversified significantly from their traditional activities, although legal changes in the credit market in the early 1970s had led them to adopt banking status. This in turn, led them to extend into secondary banking especially for property lending, a move which was ultimately seriously to jeopardise their long term viability. The remaining firms had either a relatively short history, being created by entrepreneurs, or had extended their financial service activities by a process of acquisition. Such diversification moves also date to around the same time as the strategic changes undertaken by the main banks. By 1974 two of these companies had diversified so far as to be reclassified as conglomerates.

By contrast the firms engaged in property development had remained remarkably stable. Many property companies have been created post war, and in terms of numbers of employees are relatively small. However, the assets they control are often very large, and indeed the key measure for performance in the property sector is perhaps the growth in assets per share, rather than earnings. Partially in order to remain small, in terms of employee numbers, as well as finding property development itself to be an extremely attractive area for investment, property companies have been able to fulfil their objectives largely without diversifying into other businesses. There has, however, been a limited degree of overseas investment.

A further fast growing sector has been the hotel and leisure industry where the small number of companies examined have largely emerged in the post war period, two strongly connected with hotels and catering, while the last has emerged following changes in the gaming laws in the UK. The hotel and leisure industry firms have diversified substantially to embrace a variety of leisure activities and in the case of Grand Metropolitan and Lex

Service Group acquisitions have led to the creation of conglomerates.

Shipping companies have also diversified rapidly since the end of the 1960s. At this time the purchase of Cunard by Trafalgar House Investments awakened the remaining shipping companies to a threat from corporate raiders, anxious to obtain the benefit of their asset situations and taxation saving depreciation allowances. After a poor financial performance for much of the post war period therefore, the shipping companies diversified rapidly by making large, usually conglomerate, acquisitions, in the early 1970s so as to reduce this threat.

The construction companies have traditionally operated a diversified strategy although individual firms have extended their operations from relatively specialised bases toward larger civil engineering contracting. The most common diversification moves evident in construction companies, however, have been the trends toward increased integration, backward into the production of construction materials and forward into property development, coupled with diversification outside the United Kingdom.

Retailing companies have exhibited strategies with both low and high levels of diversification, although relatively few have moved far outside of retailing. The companies which have not diversified significantly tend to be those which are family managed such as Sainsbury and Marks and Spencer, where the early adoption of a successful retail formula has made diversification relatively superfluous. Certainly such firms have changed in terms of their geographic coverage, the range of merchandise offered and the size and type of store operated. Such changes, however, have been essentially evolutionary rather than revolutionary.

By contrast a number of store groups have diversified aggressively and almost wholly by acquisition. Such firms have tended to be entrepreneur led, such as Great Universal Stores, or professionally managed concerns where a traditional retail formula has been found to be in need of transformation as with the Burton Group. Overall, the multiple retailing groups have seen their market share expand significantly in the post war period, but as competition with the small retailer has changed toward serious competition between multiple store groups, product diversification has tended to become more important than domestic geographic expansion. As a result, as in banking, traditional demarcations such as those between food and non-food retailing have tended to break down. The retailers however, have been very slow to attempt international expansion, although a few had begun to pursue such a strategy by the mid 1970s.

Companies engaged in commodity trading have also demonstrated a tendency to diversify with again the rate of transformation accelerating from the end of the 1960s. These firms are closely related to the banking and financial services concerns, and in the case for example, of Guinness Peat diversification has actually taken the form of a move into merchant banking.

The colonial merchants are a relatively unusual group of companies. They were usually founded in the nineteenth century as an adjunct to the creation of the British Empire. In the post colonial era after the second world war these firms lost their essential raison d'etre of providing a trading route between Britain and its colonies. Usually formed around a specific agricultural commodity, the colonial merchants diversified by adding vertical activities such as shipping, insurance broking, colonial shopkeeping and the like. These firms were therefore early diversifiers but there was usually a clear relationship between the activities. After decolonisation the colonial merchants often built their disparate, but integrated, activities into a series of independent operations as well as extending into more stable political environments. As a result therefore these organisations were nearly all categorised as conglomerates by 1974.

The public sector companies have remained basically stable in terms of their strategies. This has usually been as a direct result of the constraints placed upon them in their vesting legislation. Strategic change has occurred, but usually as a result of technological change which has perhaps severely affected the economics of the industry. Most importantly, however, the nature of a number of the public sector companies have been fundamentally changed from time to time as a result of political intervention which has led to transformation largely for ideological reasons.

The final group of companies do not readily fit into any specific industry category. Most were created in the post war period, usually by individual entrepreneurs and have expanded rapidly by acquisition. By 1974 all these firms were engaged in a wide variety of activities mainly in the service sector, but in some cases in manufacturing, which were so disparate the firms were classified as conglomerates.

THE EVOLUTION OF STRATEGY AND STRUCTURE

The results of assigning the companies into the strategic categories and the number in each category with each of the major forms of organisation are shown in table 2.2. Further, table 2.3 illustrates the strategic and structural evolution of the service industry firms over the period. In 1950 the service industry corporations were largely engaged in businesses with at most a limited degree of diversification. In toto 75 per cent of the population could be placed within the single or dominant business categories each of which contained a roughly similar number of firms. Where diversification occurred it was usually into related activities, although there were a few conglomerates made up of colonial merchants and the cooperative movement, with its wide range of service and manufacturing interests.

The multidivisional form of organisation was virtually unknown in the service industries in 1950, the only company with such a system of

Table 2.2 Service Industry Diversification Strategy and Structure Relations, 1950–74¹

Diversification Strategy	1950				1955				1960				1965				1970				1974			
	F	CF	HC	M	F	CF	HC	M	F	CF	HC	M	F	CF	HC	M	F	CF	HC	M	F	CF	HC	M
Single Business	21	3	1	–	16	2	5	–	13	2	4	–	13	1	1	–	13	1	2	–	13	1	2	–
Dominant Business	15	1	12	–	18	1	12	–	13	3	20	1	12	4	23	2	5	7	9	5	4	5	3	4
Related Business	7	–	4	1	4	4	5	1	5	4	6	1	5	4	11	4	4	8	18	15	1	11	13	23
Unrelated Business	–	–	4	–	–	–	5	1	–	–	8	1	–	–	9	2	–	–	8	5	–	–	9	10
Total	43	4	21	1	38	7	27	2	31	9	38	3	30	9	44	8	22	16	37	25	18	17	27	37

¹ increase in column totals for different time periods due to new entrants joining the population.

Key: F = functional structure, CF = critical function, HC = holding company, M = multidivisional

management being Sir Isaac Wolfson's Great Universal Stores (GUS) Group.

Wolfson had in fact discovered this form of organisation from his close observation of the American retail giant, Sears Roebuck, which was one of the pioneers of the multidivisional structure.[1] Sears, in conjunction with outside consultants was perhaps the first diversified retailing firm to adopt such a corporate form. Moreover, the consultants who evolved the structure in conjunction with Sears were to provide the founders of McKinsey and Company, which was later to be largely responsible for the distribution of the divisional structure around the world.[2]

Wolfson who had been building in Britain a diversified retailing and catalogue selling company similar to Sears brought a version of the American company's structure to the UK. This new organisation was actually an early form of the critical function structure since buying was gradually highly centralised. Initially, however, the significant differences between the early GUS retailing activities permitted a product based divisional system to be introduced, each division having its own buying department.

The principal organisational forms found among the service industry firms in 1950 were functional and holding company systems. Most single business firms, and a substantial number of dominant business concerns, were managed with a functional structure, although geographic sub-division below the main functional split, was common for the distribution function in public utilities and retailing. Diversification had usually occurred by the purchase of related activities and these tended to be managed as separate legal entities, control being maintained by the classic holding company pattern of overlapping board membership. In clearing banking and insurance, main board composition was usually wholly non-executive with no members of the executive management group participating. In merchant banking, on the other hand, partnerships were common in those firms where a traditional family ownership/management system prevailed. Although not wholly accurate this type of structure has been categorised as functional.

The late 1950s provided a fruitful period for the evolution of property and property-related acquisitive conglomerate companies and during this time a number of the entrepreneur led concerns came into being. Among the companies already in existence in 1950 a slow, gradual process of diversification took place notably in banking, but in the main strategies remained relatively stable.

Organisation structures also saw little change, although holding companies became the largest single form as expansion by acquisition took place. Further, early versions of the critical function structure, with subunits becoming profit accountable, emerged toward the end of the period, while insurance companies began to add their own professional investment management departments to existing functional organisations. The

Table 2.3   Service Industry Diversification Strategy and Structure Evolution 1950–74
(% Distribution)

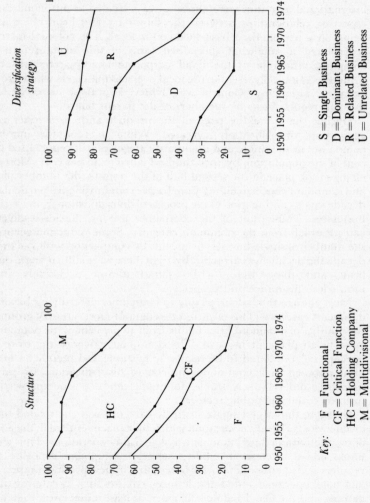

Key: F = Functional
          CF = Critical Function
          HC = Holding Company
          M = Multidivisional

S = Single Business
D = Dominant Business
R = Related Business
U = Unrelated Business

multidivision structure remained virtually unknown with only 3 of the 81 companies observed having adopted it, each of these being diversified retailers.

Overseas operations tended to be limited, except for the trading companies, and where these existed they were usually based on the old Empire territories and, in particular, the White Commonwealth. These international activities were almost always treated as autonomous, with reporting relationships between the subsidiary and head office usually being on a personalised basis at director level. The colonial merchants represented a somewhat specialised form of this structure. In these companies the role of the small corporate headquarters was to act primarily as a supply agent to the local overseas managers who were given extensive autonomy. Control was achieved in these concerns largely through regular visits by members of the parent board.

During the 1960s the pace of the product and, to a lesser extent, geographic diversification increased. While in 1960 the number of companies in the single and dominant categories still represented 69 per cent of the population, by 1970 this had fallen to 42 per cent. Most of this change took place in the second half of the decade, the number of single and dominant concerns falling from 62 per cent in 1965. In particular, the decade saw a continuation of the process of diversification from specialised businesses. Thus, most of the companies leaving the lesser diversified categories left from the dominant category. Some reduction occurred in the number of single business firms, but by comparison with the previous decade the decline was arrested. By 1970 there were still 16 single business firms and these were to be found almost exclusively in two industries – insurance and property.

Most change thus occurred due to companies diversifying beyond the dominant category. This occurred throughout most industry groups with the number of dominant firms falling from 46 per cent of the population in 1960 to 26 per cent in 1970. The dominant category therefore could perhaps be considered to be relatively unstable and merely an artificial limit imposed in a continuous process of diversification. In only two industries did relatively stable dominant product concerns persist – in insurance and the public sector.

By 1970, the largest single strategic category was the related business group. Most of the diversification which took place resulted in the addition of new activities related in some way to existing operations. Thus clearing banks added interests in credit finance, leasing, and factoring, many retailers added either new forms of retailing or new product market areas, and hotel operators added new leisure activities such as catering, motels, gaming and the like. In almost all cases, at least initial entry to new fields was gained by acquisition, and most of the companies which changed category during the late 1960s did so as a result of extensive acquisition programmes.

The number of conglomerates present in the population by 1970 had changed little over the decade, remaining at around 10 per cent. In terms of actual numbers, three new firms joined the group during the 1960s. Two of these concerns, Slater Walker Securities and Lonrho enjoyed explosive growth during the late 1960s as a result of acquisitions rather like those made by Sears Holdings and similar firms in the late 1950s, when again stock market capitalisations were below asset valuations.

In line with increased diversification there was a growing number of firms adopting a multidivisional organisation during the 1960s, although this was mainly due to new entrants to the population. However, from 1965 there was a gradual awareness that structures were in need of redesign, and many companies turned to outside consultants for help. For most this meant the adoption of a multidivision organisation and 25 per cent of the population had accepted this structure by 1970. The structure was always found associated with a degree of diversity, none of the single business firms having such a structure, and was most common among the related and new acquisitive conglomerate companies.

In addition to the increase in the number of multidivisional structures the period saw an accelerating decline in the number of holding companies. In most cases this coincided with increasing numbers of multidivisional firms, but for some companies the change was to a critical function organisation. This structure began to emerge in significant numbers by 1970, being adopted by 16 per cent of the population. The composite insurance companies, in particular, began to adopt the partial profit centred structure by subdividing their domestic marketing and actuarial activities by product and adding an international division to supervise overseas activity, while at the same time building up their central investment management departments and adding separate property investment sections.

During the 1970s the same trends observed in the latter half of the 1960s have tended to continue, at least until the great bear market of 1974–5. By 1974 the number of dominant business firms had fallen to 16 of which 10 were either insurance companies or in the public sector. In contrast the single business concerns remained virtually unchanged and still numbered 16. The fall of the property market in 1973, however, was indicative that this situation might not persist indefinitely. As the interests of the insurance companies in direct property investments increased and the same institutions came for the first time under direct competitive attack from the diversifying bank sector there were signs that the insurers might move to acquire control, rather than investment stakes, in major property firms. Further, diversification directly into the banking area also seemed a longer term possibility, as an alternative to investment stakes in companies such as finance houses, secondary banks and the like.

As the dominant business group continued to decline the number of related business firms continued to expand. By 1974, nearly 50 per cent of the service companies were diversified into areas related to one another. Nevertheless, there were clear signs that diversification would continue and a further 6 companies had been reclassified as conglomerates. Further, relationships between activities, especially in the financial sector, were becoming increasingly tenuous and a number of the firms involved clearly announced to the researchers that they intended to become 'financial service conglomerates'.

International strategies changed, too, from the late 1960s and in the early 1970s the trend of new investment was strongly toward the developed countries. Banking and financial services both exhibited significant international growth away from the former Empire territories and toward the series of emerging financial centres around the world. The construction companies, too, had expanded their overseas operations, partly because of the opportunities offered for new large contracts in developing countries such as the oil producing nations and partly to escape the politically induced uncertainty in the domestic demand for construction. Retail concerns, by contrast, were notably slow in pursuing an international strategy, although there were signs that by the mid 1970s a number of such firms were beginning to seriously investigate overseas opportunities.

The trend to the multidivisional organisation continued rapidly, and by 1974 37 per cent of the service firms had adopted this structure. The multidivision form usually replaced a loose holding company system. In the main the new structures tended to be combinations of geographic and product divisional forms, overseas activities usually being grouped into an international division which in turn was subdivided by geography, rather than a more complex matrix organisation. Where product diversification was limited geographic considerations were important in organisation design and such subdivisions were the normal method of developing semi-autonomous profit centres in critical function divisional hybrid structures. Conventional functional structures were still present in 18 firms in 1974 these being largely single business firms.

The impact of international strategy

It was not possible to conduct a full longitudinal analysis of international activity over the period since 1950. However, data was available for the latest period for some 65 companies on their level of overseas activities as measured by sales.[3] The nationalised industries were deliberately omitted since it was considered that in the main their strategic choice was constrained, although the National Freight Corporation did actually have a relatively aggressive European expansion strategy, and British Airways would qualify as a high overseas sales corporation. The 65 companies were empirically divided into the three categories of activity level, defined in chapter 1. Using these cut off points the relationship between the level of international activity and organisation is illustrated in table 2.4.

Low levels of international activity tended to be the only condition

Table 2.4   *Relationship between International Strategy and Structure*

Structure	Level of Overseas Sales			Total
	Lo <10%	Med 10–40%	Hi > 40%	
F	12	2	–	14
CF	3	6	4	13
HC	5	3	6	14
M	12	5	7	24
Total	32	16	17	65

Key: F=functional,   CF=critical function,
      HC=holding company,   M=multidivisional.

under which a functional structure was workable and as international activity increased, of necessity, it required the addition of separate management activities leading to the adoption of a more complex structure. Nevertheless, a significant number of multidivisional firms had not expanded overseas to a substantial degree implying perhaps that domestic product diversification is a preferred strategic expansion route to overseas operations.

High levels of overseas activity were usually managed with a divisional or holding company structure, although a few insurance companies operated a critical function organisation with overseas operations being controlled as semiautonomous units, but with investment management centralised. Overseas holding companies tended to be of the mother-daughter variety, where subsidiaries, often of long standing, were allowed substantial autonomy subject to a personalised system of control implemented by frequent visits at board level from and to the parent company. The divisional structures tended to be of relatively recent origin, and in most cases had not progressed beyond an international division stage which in turn was usually divided geographically. Where further sub-division had occurred, overseas activities were usually grouped into area based divisions rather than world wide product or other alternative systems.

The relationship between international activity and diversification strategy is shown in table 2.5. This shows that high levels of overseas activity usually go hand in hand with high product diversity, almost all the high international activity companies being diversified related or con-glomerate business companies. Similarly no single business company had significant overseas operations and most dominant business concerns were also primarily concerned with domestic activities.

The single business firms for the most part were the mutual life insurance

Table 2.5 Relationship between International Strategy and Product Diversity

Product Diversity	Level of Overseas Sales			Total
	Lo <10%	Med 10–40%	Hi >40%	
S	12	–	–	12
D	4	2	1	7
R	14	9	8	31
U	2	5	8	15
Total	32	16	17	65

Key: S=single Business,   D=dominant business,
R=related businesses,   U=unrelated businesses

companies, which had traditionally maintained a particularly conservative attitude to both product and geographic diversification. By
comparison, the composite insurers were often especially active overseas
although usually in a relatively limited number of countries, with
specialisation occurring in North America and more recently, western
Europe.

Apart from a number of the composite insurance companies the largest
single group of high international activity firms were the colonial
merchants and commodity traders. However, these firms had almost
adopted a strategy of international retrenchment in recent years, with-
drawing assets from politically vulnerable or low growth regions and
redistributing them to more promising or stable markets, the most
important of which was the UK. Deliberate overseas expansion strategies
were most common among the medium international activity level firms
which were engaged in building and construction, hotels and leisure and
banking and finance services. These businesses, which had usually begun
to diversify domestically, had concurrently, or shortly after, also began to
expand their principal activities overseas. This strategy had been pursued
usually with great speed, with investments being concentrated in the
developed regions of western Europe and North America or other high
growth countries.

Strategy, structure and financial performance
Six key financial variables were studied for the service industry firms. Not
all these variables were available for all firms and in some cases they were
not appropriate at all. In all, financial data was available on average for
about 65 companies, the number varying slightly for particular financial
variables. Notable exceptions from the financial analysis were the
insurance companies, where most of the terms under consideration were

not relevant, a number of the merchant banks for which adequate data was not available, and the public sector firms, where again a number of the terms were strictly not meaningful either in view of the fact that what was being measured varied considerably due to organisational change, or aspects such as capital structure changes and factors like debt write offs or similar actions severely affected the basis of measurement. In addition the raw data collected from the remaining firms was not corrected for inflation nor were changes in accounting treatment taken into account. Tax changes were found to have a major impact and as a result data was only used for the period since 1964 to eliminate the problems caused by the change to corporation tax. The results obtained, therefore, are relatively crude and should only be treated as indicative. Nevertheless a number of interesting and at times surprising findings did materialise.

The impact of product diversification
Differing financial performances for alternative strategies have been hypothesised by a number of writers on manufacturing firms and although most attempts at matching degree of diversification and financial performance have been inconclusive,[4] Rumelt has recently established a number of such relationships for both diversification and structural variables,[5] similar to those defined in chapter 1 and used throughout the present research.

Rumelt's analysis of the main strategic categories revealed that significant differences in financial performance did exist for major US manufacturing firms according to their degree and type of product market diversification. In particular he noted that the variables providing the best measures of economic efficiency namely return on equity, return on capital and price earnings ratio were strongly related to diversification strategy. Moreover, Rumelt's results showed a high degree of consistency. Thus strategies associated with high profitability tended also to be associated with high growth rates, lower amounts of variability and higher price earnings multiples. As a result Rumelt was able to observe three clusters of strategies yielding high, medium and low economic performance.

These strategies, which were discovered by subgrouping the main strategic categories, were heterogeneous. This therefore, suggested performance did not vary smoothly with the degree of diversity. Rather two 'losing strategies' stood out namely the strategy of the dominant business, vertically integrated, concern and that of the 'passive' rather than the acquisitive conglomerate.

The financial performance results of the service industry firms by strategic category are shown in table 2.6. High significance levels were not observed in many cases, although significant differences did occur between the strategic categories which were not divided into more detailed sub categories. Broadly speaking the results were very similar in direction to those observed by Rumelt in American manufacturing companies. The

Table 2.6   Financial Characteristics of Product Diversification Strategy

		S	D	R	U	Avg.	F
GEPS	Mean	25.5	11.3	22.1	19.7	18.8	1.72
	t	0.951	−1.623	0.678	− 0.053		
	α	0.20	0.10	0.25	—	—	—
GAPS	Mean	27.0	9.4	18.0	14.0	14.76	3.3
	t	1.982	−1.472	0.780	−1.091		
	α	0.05	0.10	0.25	0.15		0.05
RBIT	Mean	14.21	13.60	18.81	16.09	16.2	2.13
	t	−0.758	1.283	1.451	−.062		
	α	0.10	0.10	0.10	—		0.10
RAT	Mean	6.4	5.9	8.9	6.3	7.2	2.17
	t	−0.441	−1.098	1.523	−0.731		
	α	—	0.15	0.10	0.25		0.10
G SALES	Mean	18.61	19.52	27.33	22.75	20.69	1.71
	t	−0.235	−0.232	1.670	0.400		
	α	—	—	0.05	—		—
G ASSETS	Mean	20.54	16.37	24.44	28.28	22.66	2.00
	t	−0.281	−1.608	0.510	1.177		
	α	—	0.10	—	0.15		—

Note: The *t* statistics here test the difference between an estimated category mean and the overall mean. The F statistic tests for equality of all category means and the significance level is shown for each financial variable below the corresponding F value. α measures the significance of respective *t* ratios.

Key S = single business; D = dominant business; R = related business; U = unrelated business

dominant business category, although largely a transitory phase for the majority of the service industry firms, stood out as having an inferior economic performance on almost all measures. Only in absolute sales growth rate do the dominant product companies not underperform, and, since the single business firms' sales performances are skewed due to the presence of the property firms, this does not seem surprising and the difference in fact is too small to be significant.

Unrelated businesses, although not as poor as dominant strategies, also exhibit inferior economic performance along a number of financial dimensions, although they do achieve relatively high absolute growth rates in sales and assets. This growth, however, is not readily converted to growth in earnings or assets per share, due in part to the use of paper for making acquisitions. The conglomerates performed relatively well in terms of return on capital both before and after tax and interest, although the results for the single business firms, which show a similar performance, are affected by the pursuit of assets growth as a key criterion for success among property companies.

The two most successful strategies appear to be in the single business and related diversified categories, with diversified firms seeming to be marginally superior. This adds some weight to the hypothesis that firms seek to escape from a business area with declining prospects by the process of diversification, but while a specific business has good prospects, diversification possibly offers a less attractive course. Further, for those firms which do decide to diversify, moves into areas related to the original business or building upon skills developed in this activity would seem to have more chance of success than ventures into unrelated businesses.

The addition of the nationalised sector to the financial analysis would have tended to enhance these findings. The public sector firms operated predominantly dominant business strategies and had the worst economic performance of all industry groups, although only in return on capital were the financial measures strictly comparable.

The effect of industry sector performance
In view of the fact that alternative strategies did appear to give different financial results it seemed relevant to try and correct the data for the effect of varying industry performance. This proved difficult since specific strategies tended to be associated with particular industries and it was thus not possible to differentiate adequately between the two effects. Only in the insurance industry was there a spectrum of strategies covering most of the major strategic categories, but in this industry many of the financial variables were not relevant or available.

Apart from the public sector companies, which as a group reported an extremely low rate of return on capital before interest and taxes and a negative average rate of return after tax, other low return industries were shipping, property and insurance. The low returns achieved in the public sector were to a large extent beyond the control of management, being induced by political decisions made with little regard for commercial considerations. In addition, capital structures made up largely of debt meant that increasing post tax losses had been recorded by many nationalised firms in recent years. These firms, however, also represented the classic low performing, dominant business pattern with a high fixed capital to sales ratio, high labour content and an undifferentiable product.

As a group the insurance companies were also poor performers in terms of return on capital, although in part their actual performance was obscured by uncertainty as to their true surpluses generated due to actuarial conservatism. The shipping companies were therefore the nearest match to the low performing public sector corporations. These firms were also high capital users and until the late 1960s had conservative and traditional management, which at least in part appears to have led to

their poor performance. The final group of low return businesses were
engaged in property development. These firms were expected to show a
low return on capital since performance was really measured in terms of
asset growth as the value of property increased. Thus the poor return on
capital was compensated for by a high growth rate in assets per share.

The highest performing companies were engaged in banking and
retailing. In terms of high growth, acquisitive conglomerates and
commodity traders had also performed well, reflecting to a degree, their
relatively high gearing. The asset concentration of the acquisitive
conglomerates and also of the hotel and leisure concerns reflected their
similarity to the property companies. By contrast, growth in assets per
share among retailers reflected in most cases their lack of concern for
property, demonstrating the rapid growth in sale and leaseback during the
1960s. The construction companies, too, had tended to enter property
development having seen the rapid growth and success of the developers,
and this trend too is reflected in their relatively high growth in assets per
share.

The modest performing industries were mainly the highly diversified,
passive conglomerates and colonial merchants which, in terms of their
depth of product market coverage, tended to be rather similar. The
miscellaneous financial companies which were very late diversifiers like the
finance houses and insurance brokers were also modest performers. These
concerns tended to be at a natural economic disadvantage to the banks in
that their diversification was in large part a reaction to competitive threats
from the banks. In all of the modest performing industries it was notable
that few had undertaken organisation reconstructions despite their
diversification, and most tended to still be managed with holding company
structures.

The impact of geographic diversity

For 42 companies it was possible to relate their financial performance to
their level of overseas sales (or equivalent) activity. These results are shown
in table 2.7. The results are not strongly significant between the three
categories of activity used to segment the sample. However a particular
interesting trend which appears reasonably significant is the apparent
decline in return on capital with increasing levels of overseas activity. This
appears to be true for returns both before and after tax but the impact of
international taxation appears to enhance the effect. Like product
diversification, therefore, geographic diversification appears to take place
when high quality domestic opportunities in the firm's original business
area are no longer available, a tendency supported by the earlier result in
table 2.5 which indicated that product and geographic diversification
tended to occur together.

High rates of overseas sales also do not seem to have led to a marked
superiority in growth rates of either sales or assets, despite the steady

Table 2.7   *Financial Characteristics of International Activity Level*

		Level of Overseas Sales				
		LO (>10%)	MED (10 – 40%)	HI (<40%)	Average	F
GEPS	Mean	19.22	12.18	16.34	16.49	
	t	1.123	−1.568	−0.061		2.956
	α	0.15	0.10	–		0.10
GAPS	Mean	14.82	12.83	10.83	13.01	
	t	0.800	−0.106	−0.977		1.135
	α	0.25	–	0.20		–
RBIT	Mean	21.26	20.39	16.29	19.30	
	t	0.797	0.334	−1.304		1.673
	α	0.25	–	0.10		–
RAT	Mean	10.99	7.42	6.52	8.75	
	t	1.952	−0.953	−1.858		5.565
	α	0.05	0.20	0.05		0.01
G SALES	Mean	19.29	24.14	21.81	21.28	
	t	−0.523	0.513	0.114		0.585
	α	–	–	–		
G ASSETS	Mean	19.83	21.22	22.81	21.12	
	t	−0.327	0.016	0.359		0.247
	α	–	–	–		–

decline in sterling relative to other currencies. There are slight improvements in these variables as international activity increases but the results are not significant. Further, in terms of assets and earnings per share the results indicate that high levels of international activity actually result in inferior performance. This is, of course, in large measure an industry effect, since it is the retailing and property companies which have not diversified overseas. The UK clearing banks illustrate that within an industry the effect of an international strategy can be marked. Barclays Bank, for example, has adopted a relatively aggressive international strategy, building up its overseas deposit base and branch network. By contrast, the Midland Bank, in particular, has pursued an essentially domestic strategy, relying upon consortium participations to develop its international position. As a result Barclays growth rate in recent years has significantly outpaced that of the Midland, which has suffered more from the declining international value of its largely sterling deposit base.

The impact of organisation structure

The effect of organisation structure on financial performance is shown in table 2.8. Differences between three basic structures were tested namely functional (including critical function), holding company and multi-divisional organisations. The results indicate that significant differences can be observed between the various structural forms for almost all the financial variables.

Table 2.8   Financial Characteristics of Structural variables

		F	HC	M	Average	F
GEPS	Mean	19.22	10.01	32.39	19.33	
	t	−0.115	−2.473	2.754		8.82
	α	−	.01	.005		0.01
GAPS	Mean	15.38	9.41	14.40	12.11	
	t	1.07	−1.46	1.06		3.16
	α	0.15	0.10	0.15		0.05
RBIT	Mean	18.22	14.71	16.23	15.71	
	t	0.799	−0.563	0.219		0.649
	α	0.25	−	−		−
RAT	Mean	9.01	6.23	8.71	7.51	
	t	0.88	−1.26	1.01		2.39
	α	0.20	0.15	0.20		0.10
G SALES	Mean	14.6	16.0	30.62	21.44	
	t	−1.378	−1.924	2.649		11.58
	α	0.10	0.05	0.005		0.01
G ASSETS	Mean	14.06	15.99	32.57	22.01	
	t	−1.259	−1.850	2.758		11.41
	α	0.15	0.05	0.005		0.01

Key F = functional structure: HC = holding company: M = multidivisional

The best rates of return both before and after tax were achieved by the functional and critical function companies. This represents a finding slightly different from Rumelt's study of US manufacturing firms where the multidivisional structure proved superior along every dimension. The reason for the difference, is perhaps, that these structures were normally associated with successful businesses, where the critical function structure in particular, was seen as an alternative to the multidivisional form. The functional structure also had the best assets per share growth performance – a result which can be largely attributed to the property companies where assets per share was the critical indicator of success.

The multidivision structure firms exhibited clearly superior growth rates in both absolute sales and assets, in addition to earnings per share. Thus, while the critical function and functional structures are adequate for efficiently managing relatively slower growth companies, high growth, which tends to be spread over a wider variety of businesses and often involves a substantial element of acquisition, seemed to require a divisional form, allowing more executives to be involved in the management process.

The holding company structure was clearly inferior on all counts, implying that an adequate degree of central management direction is needed to achieve the desired effects from mergers and acquisitions in particular. This result also indicates why perhaps the performance of diversified companies is so variable, since among the service industry firms relatively few had adopted a divisional organisation.

The impact of leadership

The need for adequate central strategic direction is also indicated by an analysis of the structural variable of leadership. The results for the three classes of leadership defined in chapter 1 are shown in table 2.9.[6] Significant differences between the categories are obtained for most of the variables but especially those concerned with growth. It is not altogether surprising perhaps, for entrepreneurial firms to record a superior growth record, since to have reached the ranks of the top 100 service firms within the lifetime of the founder high growth has clearly occurred. The entrepreneurs also achieve superior performance in earnings per share, assets per share and return on capital both before and after tax and with the exception of the rate of return on capital after tax the difference between this performance and the average is significant. Similarly, in all dimensions the worst performances are achieved by professional management led concerns with, again, significant differences from the average being observed in all cases except return on capital after tax, although the significant levels in this case are not as high. Family-managed companies perform near or slightly below the average. The test to see if meaningful differences can be observed between the three categories of leadership shows significant results in four of the six variables, the exceptions being in the two measures of rate of return on capital. In each of the four measures of growth, however, significant differences between leadership types are observed with entrepreneurial leadership being substantially superior to family leadership, which in turn tends to perform better than professional management.

While entrepreneur led firms outperform all others they are followed by family managed companies. This is a somewhat surprising finding since

Table 2.9   Financial Characteristics of Leadership Categories

		Entre-preneurial	Family	Pro-fessional	Average	F
GEPS	Mean	28.54	15.78	15.49	19.91	
	t	1.716	−0.857	−1.034		2.933
	$\bar{\alpha}$	0.05	0.20	0.20		0.10
GAPS	Mean	22.46	14.59	10.75	15.47	
	t	2.157	−0.221	−1.600		5.542
	$\bar{\alpha}$	0.025	−	0.10		0.01
RBIT	Mean	21.66	17.01	16.06	17.95	
	t	0.864	− 0.279	− 0.739		1.065
	$\bar{\alpha}$	0.20	−	0.25		−
RAT	Mean	9.360	8.105	7.607	8.351	
	t	0.493	−0.117	−0.476		0.372
	$\bar{\alpha}$	−	−	−	−	
G SALES	Mean	34.24	18.71	16.22	22.30	
	t	2.137	− 0.686	−1.689		7.347
	$\bar{\alpha}$	0.025	0.25	0.05		0.01
G ASSETS	Mean	41.94	17.09	15.37	24.08	
	t	2.564	−1.025	−1.880		11.41
	$\bar{\alpha}$	0.01	0.20	0.05		0.01

there would not necessarily seem to be any good reason why family managements should outperform professional management. One explanation is that a direct equity stake is a significant motivator to superior performance. It was not possible to fully test this hypothesis although an analysis of shareholdings by the boards of professionally managed firms was conducted and some indication that superior performance was associated with higher values of shareholding did emerge. A further explanation which can be offered is that professional management is only normally introduced after an entrepreneur has retired or his family has run out of suitable successors. As a result many professional managements can be seen to perform a maintenance task, seldom modifying the traditional strategy until external forces make change essential.

The relationships between leadership style and the strategic categories of product diversity and international activity are shown in tables 2.10 and 2.11. In terms of product market strategy, the entrepreneur led firms carefully avoid the dominant business category, only 5 per cent of such firms being so classified, compared with 17 per cent of professionally managed concerns and 13 per cent of family run businesses. Ten per cent of

Table 2.10   Relationship between Product Market Strategy and Leadership
Type

| Strategy | Leadership Type | | | Total |
	E	F	P	
S	2	2	2	6
D	1	2	5	.8
R	9	8	17	34
C	8	3	5	16
Total	20	15	29	64

Key S = single business: D = dominant business: R = related business:
U = unrelated business: E = entrepreneurial: F = family P = professional

Table 2.11   Relationship between International Activity and Leadership Type

| Level of Overseas Sales | Leadership Type | | | Total |
	E	F	P	
Hi	3	2	6	11
Med	5	3	3	11
Lo	5	4	10	19
Total	13	9	19	41

Key E = entrepreneurial: F = family: P = professional

entrepreneur led firms are single business operations, however. The
entrepeneur led firms, like each of the other leadership categories are in the
main diversified, but by comparison with the other categories a surprisingly large 40 per cent are conglomerate businesses. Such companies,
however, tend to be far from passive and are generally aggressive
acquirers, a strategy shown in chapter 10 to be coupled with relative
financial success.

   Leadership patterns are, however, not evenly distributed by industry.
Property, construction and leisure are industries dominated by entrepreneurs who have also been active in the development of conglomerates
and newer areas of financial services. Family managements are
still strong in retailing, in a number of merchant banks, and have only
recently been replaced in commodity trading and most of the shipping and
colonial merchanting companies. Professional managements dominate in
insurance, clearing banking and certain other financial service areas.

However, there remains a group of traditional banking families which no longer necessarily run their own banks but rather have become professional managers, thus many of the senior executives of the clearing banks are descendants of such families, this being especially true for example in Barclays. Elsewhere professional managements are strong in non-food retailing and have relatively recently replaced family managements in the shipping and colonial merchant groups.

Internationally the differences between the categories are less marked although there is a tendency for more entrepreneur led firms to have developed international operations, 61 per cent having either moderate or high levels of overseas sales. By contrast 53 per cent of professionally managed firms had less than 10 per cent of their sales overseas while family managed concerns were somewhere between the two extremes.

Further interesting differences between entrepreneurs and other managerial groups can be observed in their socio-demographic backgrounds. These are indicated in table 2.12 which gives details of the socio-demographic characteristics of company chairmen from each of the three corporate leadership variants and in addition, separate details were obtained for the chairmen of nationalised enterprises. From 'Who's Who' biographical details were available on the chairmen of 81 companies. It was notable that details on the chairmen of a number of entrepreneur led companies were *not* available. This indicates, perhaps, that these individuals, despite running major corporations, were not perceived as important persons within society, at least as defined by 'Who's Who'.

By comparison with the chairmen of other types of company, entrepreneurs are notably different. In general the majority have neither been to public school nor grammar school, but rather have either been to a secondary modern school or were educated outside the United Kingdom. It is noticeable that the chairmen of a few entrepreneur led firms went to Eton. These actually make the results somewhat misleading, since except in one such case, the entrepreneur fills the role of the chief executive officer, and a non-executive chairman has been appointed, having the archetypal British elitist background, usually consisting of Eton, Oxford or Cambridge and the Guards.

In tertiary education, most entrepreneurs again differ from the normal senior executive background. The majority have no tertiary education at all, very few attended the elite institutions of Oxford and Cambridge and most of those with tertiary education obtained it outside the United Kingdom.

Similarly with military service. The majority of entrepreneurs were not members of the armed forces despite their relatively advanced age and of those who were, virtually none were officers. This is an interesting divergence and perhaps indicates that business leadership requires some skills different from military leadership, alternatively the selection methods for officers do not duly recognise certain leadership skills!

Table 2.12   Characteristics of Service Corporation Chairmen

	Entre-preneur-ial (n = 15)	Family (n = 13)	Pro-fessional (n = 45)	Nationalised (n = 8)	Total (n = 81)
Average age	63	59	62	57	62
Secondary Education (%)					
Grammar School	13	15	24	38	22
Eton	20	38	22	–	22
Other Public School	13	38	51	52	43
Other	53	8	3	–	12
Tertiary Education (%)					
Oxford	7	15	22	13	17
Cambridge	7	62	24	50	30
Chartered Accountancy	7	–	11	–	7
Other Tertiary	27	–	19	25	18
No Tertiary	53	23	24	13	28
Military Service (%)					
Guards	7	8	11	–	7
Other Army	19	31	36	25	24
RAF	7	–	7	–	5
RN	–	8	7	25	13
No Military Service	67	54	44	50	51
London Club Memberships					
Brooks	–	3	12	–	15
Bucks	1	2	1	–	4
Carlton	–	–	3	1	4
MCC	–	1	7	1	9
Royal Automobile	2	–	2	–	4
Whites	–	1	7	–	8
Oriental	–	2	2	–	4
Others	4	15	28	6	53
Average No. of Memberships	0.5	1.85	1.41	1	1.23

Source: *Whos Who.*

Companies led by professional managers tend to have chairmen who conform much more closely to the traditional pattern of the British elite. Most have been to public school, with Eton standing out as a particularly important school. Today, most large company chairmen have a tertiary educational qualification, with Oxford and Cambridge providing the dominant source. More than half the chairmen in the professionally managed concerns had also served in the armed forces with the army being a far more common background than either of the other services. In addition almost all these individuals were members of the officer corps. The chairmen of nationalised industries had a somewhat similar background. Most went to public school, although a significant number were grammar school pupils, and most went to Oxford or Cambridge with the latter being more important than the former.

The family led concerns are perhaps especially interesting. In sharp contrast to their entrepreneurial antecedents the subsequent generations in family concerns have been provided with almost the classic British elitist upbringing. The majority of the chairmen in these companies attended public school and in particular Eton, the 77 per cent with a university qualification went exclusively to Oxford or Cambridge, with Cambridge predominating, while the remaining 23 per cent had no tertiary qualification at all. While more served in the armed forces than the entrepreneurs, most had no military service. For those that did, however, the army was by far and away the most common service and most of the chairmen were also selected as members of the officer cadre.

One final area of comparison concerns membership of the traditional London clubs. Entrepreneurs, without exception, had virtually no such club membership, those held by chairmen of entrepreneur led concerns being the cases of the traditional elite, non-executive chairmen. By comparison the descendants of entrepreneurs were readily assimilated into the club environment, as indeed were the chairmen of professionally managed companies.

A partial explanation of these differences concerns the ethnic background of the chairmen. The leaders of entrepreneur managed companies were predominantly Jewish. A number of these were refugees from Nazi persecution who came to Britain in the interwar years, but more were British born Jews. While a number of family companies had a similar ethnic background it was much less common, these enterprises tending to date back to the strong protestant ethic of the late nineteenth century. In sharp contrast virtually none of the professional managers had a Jewish background. The results of this analysis have interesting implications. Firstly, they clearly indicate that individual motivation is an important determinant of economic growth, high achievement generally being associated with entrepreneurship and ownership, success in which seems almost positively discouraged by the traditional British system for educating its elite. Secondly, they indicate perhaps that religious and other deep seated value systems which positively encourage an attitude of enterprise should be encouraged rather than that of economic liberalism, if economic growth is to be a desirable objective of society.

Conclusions

The service industries revealed a clear relationship between strategy and structure with a gradual tendency toward both product and geographic diversification over time as the original business of the firm matured. The normal pattern of product diversification was a gradual movement from the single business firm to the development of related diversification. A substantial number of service corporations, however, had developed as conglomerates largely as a result of acquisition programmes. Overseas strategies were largely of two types. Firstly, a number of service firms had traditionally operated overseas, servicing the British Empire via the commodity markets in particular. Secondly, a number of these firms had continued to diversify geographically toward the more developed economies as had more recently emerging multinationals, moving overseas for the first time.

Similarly as diversification proceeds so organisational change takes place with functional forms initially giving way to holding company structures before reorganising to a multidivisional system. This pattern which has been commonly found among manufacturing concerns is modified somewhat among service business companies by the emergence of the critical function structure. This system, although containing profit centre features normally associated with the divisional organisation, incorporates a critical function which is strictly centralised making the creation of fully autonomous profit centres difficult. A variety of divisional structures were observed, which in large measure were a function of the geographic spread of the company concerned.

Significant relationships were shown to exist between the main strategic and structural variables and the financial performance of the firms. In general, related diversification seemed to be given an economic performance superior to either limited or conglomerate diversification. In particular, stable dominant business and passive conglomerate strategies seemed significantly inferior. Interestingly, increased overseas activity did not lead to improved financial performance in general although within specific industries this did seem to be the case.

Growth strategies seemed more appropriately managed using a divisionalised structure although, largely as a result of the businesses concerned, functional and critical function structures entailed the best rates of return on capital. Leadership was also observed to be a significant structural variable. While entrepreneur led firms easily outperformed all others, family managed businesses also succeeded in producing significantly better results than firms managed by professional managements – a fact that may be partially related to the ownership by management of a substantial element of the equity capital of the enterprise.

3. New Strategies in the City

The banking and financial service industries make up an important segment of the service industries.[1] In 1974 the major financial service firms were responsible for the employment of 1.1m. people, and the companies operating in the sector, including insurance, contributed a positive benefit of £630m. to the UK balance of payments. Excluding insurance, which is considered separately below, in the post war period firms engaged in banking and other financial services have exhibited significant growth and substantial changes in both strategy and structure, although much of this change has been relatively recent. As late as 1959 the Radcliffe Committee[2] report on the working of the UK monetary system was able to clearly differentiate the major types of financial institutions by the relatively discrete market segments in which they operated. By the early 1970s the traditional demarcation lines between the major classes of financial institutions had been largely blurred and, while some differentiation was still discernible, in large measure the critical differences were now a function of size, rather than product range.

The majority of the financial service firms are primarily 'banks'. This can be a relatively loose description, however, since in the United Kingdom there is currently no precise definition of a bank, but rather legislation exists which establishes that a particular organisation is engaged in some form of banking business. Under the Exchange Control Act 1947, banks delegated by the Bank of England to deal in foreign exchange were established as authorised banks for this purpose. Secondly, under the Companies Act 1948, a second list of banks was drawn up in conjunction with the Bank of England to cover those organisations which were permitted to maintain hidden reserves when reporting their accounts. These were known as Schedule Eight banks, after the relevant schedule in the Act, and until the early 1970s membership of this list meant that a bank enjoyed the highest standing.

The remaining legal definitions incorporate the rules laid down to cover the conditions under which organisations may advertise for deposits, with certain banks being exempted from those conditions, so creating a group known as Section 127 banks. Finally, in order to clarify differences between

banking and moneylending, under Section 123 of the 1967 Companies
Act, the Board of Trade was given responsibility for deciding which
institutions could be treated as banks. This led to the establishment of a
number of objective criteria which defined a banking business, resulting in
a form of banking status being conferred on any firm technically meeting
these criteria, regardless of its quality or reputation. As a result of these
legal ambiguities a profusion of organisations have therefore traded as
banks in the United Kingdom.

Virtually all of the companies studied were engaged in banking by at
least one of the above definitions. They included the five major clearing
banks and the largest merchant banks which, although much smaller than
the clearers, have traditionally played an important role in the management of the domestic capital market. Also included were leading British
overseas banks,[3] the largest of the secondary banks and a number of major
credit finance organisations which were granted banking status under the
Section 123 or 127 criteria. A list of these firms is shown in table 3.1. The
sample companies were selected prior to the collapse of the secondary
banking sector in 1974. Since that time First National Finance and Slater
Walker Securities have cased to be leading banks or financial institutions, while UDT and part of C. T. Bowring have also needed Bank of
England assistance. Mercantile Credit was also seriously affected by the
secondary bank collapse and was ultimately rescued when acquired by
Barclays in 1975. A number of the companies included in the financial
services sector were part of groups which in the main were engaged in other
activities. Usually these other interests were related, in so far as they were
City of London based activities such as commodity trading. However,
S. Pearson is an industrial group composed mainly of publishing and
industrial manufacturing activities which also includes Lazard Brothers, a
leading merchant bank and member of the Accepting House Committee.

THE TRANSFORMATION OF THE CLEARING BANKS[4]

History and background

The five main clearing banks dominate domestic banking in the United
Kingdom. These banks all operate extensive branch networks throughout
England and Wales dealing mainly with the receipt, transfer and cashing
of deposits repayable on demand. The banks also operate via subsidiary
companies in Scotland where the banks' respective subsidiaries maintain a
quasi-autonomous position, while the Royal Bank of Scotland makes up
the principal company in the National and Commercial Banking Group.
Ranged against the main private banks are the Co-op Bank, which is a
component element in the Cooperative Movement, the state-owned
Trustee Savings Bank Movement and the National Giro subsidiary of the
nationalised Post Office Corporation.

The Service Industries

Table 3.1   Banking and Principal Financial Services Corporations, 1974

	Principal Activities	Assets, 1974 (£m)	Employees 1974
National Westminster Group +	Clearing banking, diversified financial services, limited overseas involvement.	13,586	65,432
Barclays Bank Group +	Clearing banking, diversified financial services & international, commercial & merchant banking	14,198	62,822
Midland Bank Group + (Samuel Montague)*	Clearing banking, diversified financial services, merchant banking, joint venture international operations.	9,940	59,700
Lloyds Bank Group +	Clearing banking, diversified financial services & international commercial banking.	8,955	41,051
National and Commercial Banking Group +	Clearing banking, limited diversified financial services.	3,004	13,842
Hill Samuel*	International merchant banking, insurance and other financial services.	1,005	3,533
Kleinwort Benson*	International merchant banking and other financial services.	882	1,133
Schroders*	International merchant banking and other financial services.	672	792
Mercury Securities (S. G. Warburg)*	International merchant banking and other financial services.	354	1,031
Hambros*	International merchant banking, insurance and other financial services.	1,104	1,682
Morgan Grenfell*	International merchant banking and other financial services.	350	528
Slater Walker Securities	International investment banking, insurance and other financial services.	393	807

Table 3.1 Continued

	Principal Activities	Assets, 1974 (£m)	Employees 1974
Guinness Peat[1] (includes Guinness Mahon)*	Merchant banking and commodity trading.	111	2,981
C. T. Bowring[1] (includes Singer and Friedlander)*	Insurance broking, insurance credit finance and merchant banking, shipping and trading operations	622	6,538
United Dominions Trust	International credit finance and secondary banking.	1,389	7,621
Mercantile Credit	International credit finances and secondary banking	377	3,107
First National Finance Corporation	Secondary banking, credit and property finance.	501	1,000
Tozer Kemsley and Millbourn	Export credit finance, merchant banking & trading operations.	174	3,512
S. Pearson & Son[1]	Banking & financial services, newspapers & publishing, insurance broking, china & glass manufacture & engineering.	283	26,531

Source: Annual Reports

+ Member of the London Clearing House
* Member of the Accepting Houses Committee
1 Assets of the consolidated parent company rather than the banking operation.

By comparison with the clearing banks the Co-op Bank operates a strictly limited branch network. A more aggressive strategy has been adopted recently, however, and the Co-op Bank has expanded by beginning to make use of the 4,000 retail outlets making up the Co-operative movement, as cheque cashing points offering a 6-day service. The Trustee Savings Bank Movement has traditionally been restricted by heavy handed state control yet has built up a deposit base of some £4,000m., and a local branch network totalling some 1,550 branches. Following a government sponsored report in 1973, the regional fragmentation of the movement has been partially consolidated, with the objective of developing the bank into an alternative force to the private enterprise banks. As part of their development strategy therefore, both the Co-op Bank and Trustee Savings Bank joined the Bankers London Clearing

House in 1975. The final rival to the major clearers, the National Giro, was established by the Labour government in 1968 to provide a cheap, quick money transmission service, operating via the nation's 24,000 post offices. By the mid 1970s and after years of losses the Giro was also endeavouring to emerge as a possible competitor to the main commercial banks.

The clearing banks evolved largely as a result of a rapid consolidation of the banking industry in Britain during the latter part of the nineteenth, and early twentieth centuries. Most were major provincial banks which grew by a process of expansion and acquisition, an essential component of which involved the purchase of a London based, joint stock bank. Thus, the Midland Bank was founded in Birmingham, but moved its head office to London in 1891 following the purchase of a London bank; Barclays Bank was formed as the result of a merger between 20 private banks, based mainly in East Anglia, while Lloyds Bank also grew as the result of a merger between several Midland based, private banks. By the beginning of the first world war, the many small local banks, which had originally made up the bulk of the banking industry, had been acquired by the emerging, large banking groups. After 1919, mergers between groups of banks began to occur and by 1924 the number of banks operating in England and Wales whose cheques were cleared via the London Clearing House had been reduced to 26. The leading English banks had also absorbed the main Scottish and Irish banks with the exception of the Royal Bank of Scotland.

Government disquiet at growing concentration led to an essential halt to further amalgamations after the 1920s. From 1936 a pattern was established of the 'Big Five', Barclays, Lloyds, Midland, Westminster and the National Provincial, and the 'Little Six' Coutts, Glyn Mills, William Deacons, National, Martins and the District Bank. This structure remained stable for the next 30 years and the effective end of acquisitions, coupled with an officially sanctioned cartel system of interest rates, essentially ended competition and led to stagnation.

The effect of the interest rate cartel

The interest rate cartel operated by the major banks provided a stability to the monetary system which was traditionally controlled by the Bank of England, via the classical money market. In this, the Bank of England acting on behalf of the Government, sells Treasury bills to the discount market on a weekly basis. The discount houses, which make up the market, have traditionally been obliged to purchase whatever bills the Bank places obtaining most of their funds from the liquid resources held by the clearing banks. In the last resort, however, the discount houses can always borrow funds from the Bank itself. These Treasury bills themselves carry no interest, but are purchased at a discount so effectively creating an interest charge.

By buying or selling Treasury bills, the Bank has therefore traditionally been able to smooth the supply of short term funds and domestic interest rates. By increasing the amount of bills offered, coupled with the fact that the discount houses are obliged to take up whatever is offered, the Bank can force the discount houses to borrow in order to maintain their liquidity. The interest rate charged for these funds thus becomes a weapon in macroeconomic policy and the rates charged on borrowings and offered on deposits on the clearing banks were traditionally directly related to the Bank Rate of interest charged on loans to the discount market.

The interest paid on time deposits placed with the clearing banks was historically 2 per cent below Bank Rate and such deposits made up some 40 per cent of interest and deposit accounts held by the banks in 1958. This rate was relatively unattractive by comparison with other possible interest bearing deposits, although general lack of awareness meant that considerable deposits tended to be maintained. Moreover, the remaining 60 per cent of deposits were largely credit balances on current accounts, on which the banks paid no interest, although to a considerable degree such funds could be lent to bear interest fully attributable to the banks themselves. The banks were also relatively uncompetitive in their lending, prefering self liquidating types of short term loans and offering virtually no competition on interest rates which were usually set at one per cent over Bank rate.

The interest rate cartel was not only condoned, but welcomed by the authorities, especially the Bank of England. Further, although the clearing banks themselves were rarely innovative, moves to increase competition were generally frowned upon. Indeed throughout the 1950s and early 1960s the banks were subjected to numerous Bank of England guidelines which severely restricted the possibilities of a free market. Nevertheless, competition for deposits began to grow from those institutions not restricted by the Bank. The building societies, trustee savings banks, finance houses and especially the merchant and overseas banks began to attract deposits away from the clearers. In reply, the clearing banks made a limited response. Subsidiary companies were formed, which were later to influence organisation restructuring, to enter the growing market for credit finance and also, to some extent, to circumvent interest rate restrictions and so maintain deposits. Credit and cheque guarantee cards were introduced, along with free credit transfers, personal loans and direct debiting services.

The mergers and new competition
A mounting level of criticism developed, however, both from consumers and official bodies. Such criticism focused on the cartel arrangements, possible overbanking and the general lack of competition. This led to demands to end the interest rate cartel and for rationalisation of the branch banking system, including possible further industrial consolidation. In response, in January 1968 the National Provincial and Westminster banks announced their intention to merge to create a new bank, the National

Westminster, with a deposit base exceeding any of the remaining major clearers. To the surprise of the banks, the Bank of England and the Treasury were not opposed to the merger.

This merger was rapidly followed by another between the National Commercial Bank of Scotland, which had already purchased the English and Welsh branches of the National Bank in 1966, and the Royal Bank of Scotland, so forming the National Commercial Banking Group. In 1969, the Groups three small English subsidiaries were welded into the unified Williams and Glyn's Bank. This move was followed by an attempted merger between Barclays, Lloyds and the one remaining small independent Martin's Bank. The ultimate result of such a merger was clearly the probable concentration of the banking industry into essentially a duopoly since the Midland could also be expected to join one of the two leading groups, and therefore the proposition was referred to the Monopolies Commission. The Commission found little to recommend the merger and indeed commented initially on the relative inefficiency of the banks. As a result the merger was rejected, although Barclays was allowed to absorb the smaller, Martin's bank.

The new merger movement, together with increased competition from other British financial institutions, a growing threat from the leading foreign, and specially American, commercial banks and changing market needs led to a new competitive awareness among the clearing banks. These factors, coupled with increased costs and changing technology, especially resulting from computerisation, led to a major strategic transformation commencing in the late 1960s.

Key changes which occurred in traditional clearing bank operations included a strong move to automate such services as cash dispensing, the introduction of on line accounting and the subsequent development of further through the wall mechanical cash card services. These moves, coupled with a limited increase in decision making authority at local level have helped the banks to contain the rapid increase in labour costs and service the substantial growth in demand for banking services. At the same time the banks have begun to compete in areas such as personal account charges.

Domestic business diversification

Most significant, however, has been the rapid diversification of the clearing banks into other financial services. During the early 1960s the banks made limited moves into the credit finance area, commonly by acquiring a significant share stake in one or more leading firms. Thus, in 1958 Barclays purchased a 25 per cent stake in United Dominions Trust and this was rapidly followed by the purchase of North Central Wagon by the National Provincial, the acquisition of Forward Trust by the Midland, and Westminster and Lloyds taking strategic shareholdings in other finance houses.

These early moves were essentially arms-length investments. The banks took little managerial interest and made no attempts to integrate the finance companies into their other activities. From the late 1960s this policy has largely been reversed with all the banks acquiring full ownership of a major finance house except for Lloyds and National Commercial which operate a jointly owned venture, Lloyds and Scottish. Further, the credit finance subsidiaries have become an integral component in a financial services division and have provided the main vehicle for developing new interests in leasing and factoring.

Most diversification has occurred since 1968, however. This period has seen a general trend for the banks to extend into the corporate and wholesale markets by either acquiring or developing internally a full merchant banking capability. Secondly, there has been a general move to enter the market for insurance initially by adding broking services, but more recently by extending into policy writing. The overall activities of the individual banks are reflected in table 3.2 which illustrates the extent of the change since 1968 and shows not only the increased range of activities conducted, but also the move away from investment holdings toward a full managerial role.

The chosen methods of entry into the new areas of activity have mainly been by means of joint ventures, and by acquisition. Thus most moves into factoring and leasing were undertaken initially in partnership with major American commercial banks, although subsequently such joint ventures were often bought out by the British participants. Similarly, in investment management, early moves were often undertaken in conjunction with more experienced partners which were subsequently bought out. Acquisition, although used in a number of important cases has been a generally less used to gain entry into new markets than experienced elsewhere in other service industries. Completely new ventures generated internally were rare as a method of diversifying, although, once established, the financial strength of the clearing banks could be observed on occasion leading to new innovations within a particular market.

International business development

In addition to domestic diversification, the dramatic expansion of the Eurocurrency markets and the growth in demand for international banking services has led the British clearers to respond to market needs and the challenge presented by the emerging US multinational banks. A time span similar to domestic diversification is important with events proceeding more quickly since the end of the 1960s, although some banks had a much earlier history of international operations. Unlike domestic diversification, however, the banks have chosen significantly different strategies with which to achieve their international objectives.

The most developed multinational strategy is that of Barclays which is

Table 3.2 Diversification of Clearing Bank Groups in New Financial Services

	Merchant Banking	Eurocurrency	Unit Trust Management	Factoring	Leasing	Insurance Broking	Insurance Underwriting	Credit Finance	Venture Capital	Computer Bureau	Travel Services	Channel Island Trustees	Credit Card	Personal Tax & Financial Planning
1968														
Barclays	–	W	W	–	–	–	–	A	A¹	–	–	W	W	–
Lloyds	W	W	W	–	A	–	–	J	I¹	–	–	–	W	–
Midland	A	A	–	C	–	A	–	W	J,I¹	–	–	W	–	–
National Westminster	W	W,I,J	J,I	–	W	–	–	W	I¹	W	–	W	A	–
National & Commercial	J,W		–	–	–	–	–	J,A,I	I¹	–	–	W	–	–
1975														
Barclays	W	W	W	W	W	W	W	W²	I	A	–	W	W	W
Lloyds	–	W	W	J	W,C	W	W	J	I	–	–	W	A	W
Midland	W	W	W	W	W	W,C	W	W	I	W	W	W	A	W
National Westminster	W	W	C	W	W,I	W	I	W	I	W,J	–	W	A,A	W
National & Commercial	W	W	–	A	W,W	W	–	J,W	I	–	W³	W	A	W

1. Industrial & Commercial Finance Corporation Ltd owned jointly by the clearers
2. Following the acquisition of Mercantile Credit in 1975
3. Loganair a small feeder airline serving remote parts of Scotland

W = Wholly owned subsidiary
C = Controlling interest
A = Associate Interest   25%   < 50%
I = Equity interest > 25%
J = Joint venture

Source: Adapted from H. Chryssaphes, 'The Evolution of the U.K. Clearing Banks, 1950–72', unpublished MBA dissertation, Manchester Business School, 1973.

the largest of the clearers in terms of the number of overseas branches, their geographic spread and the volume of business done abroad. The bank was the first to move overseas when in the 1920s, it created a new bank, Barclays Bank (Dominion, Colonial and Overseas), by the amalgamation of three overseas banks. This bank, which like other British overseas banks examined, largely operated a branch banking system in former colonial territories of the British Empire, was strong in Southern Africa, Nigeria and the Caribbean. By the late 1960s, however, Barclays still had little or no representation in the world's leading financial centres and, after buying out the remaining outside shareholders in Barclays DCO, the group began an aggressive expansion of geographic coverage. In addition to opening branches in the leading financial centres around the world, Barclays opened a branch banking network in California and began to develop its international corporate and wholesale services to meet the needs of major multinational firms.

In sharp contrast to Barclays, the Midland Bank, until 1973, consciously avoided establishing a direct presence overseas. Initially it preferred to work with correspondent banks, and from the early 1960s, the Midland was an innovator in the development of consortium banks. In 1963 Midland was a partner in the formation of the European Advisory Committee made up of a number of leading European banks which subsequently established a number of specialised consortium banks to operate in leading financial centres including the USA, Asia and Latin America. This joint venture policy has not proved wholly satisfactory however, and following the appointment of a few chairman in 1973, Midland reformed its management structure to create an international division and began to open its own representative offices around the world.

The strategy of the remaining clearers more resembles that of Barclays than the Midland. Lloyds bought out the National Provincial Bank's share of an international joint venture in 1955, and this has served as a nucleus for international operations. This base was substantially increased by a merger with the British Bank of London and South America in 1971. Renamed Lloyds Bank International, this organisation was the international arm for the group. The new bank was relatively well represented in Europe and Latin America, but was again weak in the leading world finance centres. Lloyds had begun to rectify this deficiency and like Barclays had also acquired a branch banking network in California. National Westminster had also initiated an active overseas branch opening programme based on the leading financial centres, although the banks relative international weakness had also led it to seek membership of a number of consortium banks. The National and Commercial Group strategy most resembled that of the Midland, since with its smaller size, the bank's international operations had been limited, greater reliance being placed on consortium membership.

THE STRATEGIC DEVELOPMENT OF MERCHANT BANKS[5]

The Early Years

There is no precise definition of a merchant bank but the leading group among the 100 or so organisations calling themselves merchant bank are the 17 members of the Accepting Houses Committee. Since 1945 only 5 firms have been invited to join this select group while one bank has resigned in 1975, following a series of losses. Founded in 1914, the committee has no formal rules for admission other than that members should have a substantial business in acceptances, and these command the finest discount rate also being eligible for ultimate rediscounting at the Bank of England. In order to retain this priveleged position, these banks are expected to maintain the highest standards of behaviour. The research covered the nine largest Accepting House Committee members and the largest merchant bank outside this group, Slater Walker Securities.[6]

The merchant banks tended to have grown from two principal roots. Firstly many developed as merchant traders before or during the nineteenth century when London was the centre of world trade. In order to facilitate international trade there was a need to provide guarantees for bills of exchange which then made these negotiable into cash and a number of the leading merchants began to provide this service. As a result this bill 'acceptance' business grew in some cases to the extent that it came to supercede merchanting as the firms' principal activity and the firms themselves became banks. The second group were created by the move to London of a number of banking families, many of which were Jewish, to escape the political disturbances of the Napoleonic wars and to exploit the trade and finance opportunities London offered.

The banks' early success was largely founded on acceptance credits and the London bill became a leading financial instrument in world trade. International acceptance and a widespread network of overseas information sources led to the development of other business, especially the finance of overseas government bills. A number of the banks became London bankers to foreign governments, giving them substantial power and influence and leading to much of the mystique surrounding merchant banks. Overseas government finance and acceptances led also to a rise of foreign currency deposits, leading in turn to the development of foreign exchange services in the banks, and in some cases, bullion dealing operations. Further, the banks' international connections resulted in their use by investors, including other financial and banking institutions, to provide investment advice and to act as funds managers.

The decline of Britain as the centre of world trade and the reduced importance of sterling forced the merchant banks for the first time, to turn their attention to domestic business opportunities. In particular, they focussed upon the growing market for corporate finance, and during the 1930s, when government sponsored concentration took place in many

British industries, the banks were called upon to assist in share issuing, capital raising and to provide financial advice. A number of banks also increased their domestic investment management activities.

In the immediate post war period to the end of the 1950s, the merchant banks lost ground, due to the creation of the sterling area which markedly restricted international activities. Overseas banks moved in to finance commodity trade, while a number of corporate accounts were lost to the clearing banks which remained the Bank of England's preferred route for authorised transfers of sterling. Then, in 1958 Britain made the first move toward a return to the free exchange of sterling. Meanwhile, overseas many other industrial economies moved to relax restrictions on international financial and trading activities. The merchant banks began to expand rapidly again both domestically and in international finance, and London began to recapture its prominence as an international finance centre. A number of the banks were also involved in the establishment of the fledgling Eurodollar market based on London.

Apart from the renewed growth of international financial activities, the whole character of merchant banking was transformed by a bitterly contested acquisition struggle in 1957. The great 'aluminium war', whereby the US-owned Reynold Metals, in conjunction with the British Tube Investments Company, bid for the British Aluminium Company, divided the City. On the side of British Aluminium were many of the oldest established merchant banks, led by Hambros and Lazards, while the aggressors were advised by newer banks such as Warburgs and Helbert Wagg, skilled in the area of corporate finance.

The 'aluminium war' was the forerunner of a spate of contested acquisitions and corporate finance skills became an essential ingredient for a successful merchant bank. As a result, a series of mergers took place between the traditional banks, strong in acceptance business and investment management, and the newer concerns which had developed corporate finance skills. These mergers led to the creation of many of the present leading banks including Hill Samuel, Kleinwort Benson Lonsdale, Schroder Wagg and S. G. Warburg.[7]

During the 1960s the banks enjoyed a favourable environment. Foreign currency based deposits expanded rapidly with the growth of the Eurodollar market which was led by the banks. International transactions in credit finance and the growth of international money movements resulted in increased foreign exchange dealings. Domestically, corporate finance skills were extensively used in the increasing number of acquisitions. Finally, the banks moved heavily into the market for savings, expanding their investment management activities with the development of unit and investment trusts.

Diversification at home and abroad
The clear demarcation which had traditionally existed between the

merchant banks and other financial institutions became rapidly blurred from the late 1960s on, as the leading American commercial banks moved to London to enter the Eurodollar market, the clearing banks began to diversify their range of services and the Bank of England moved to increase competition with the introduction of new policies on credit control.

This increase in competition made it more difficult for the merchant banks to maintain their role as the key institutions for providing long term capital and corporate financial advice. The small asset base of the banks also proved an inhibiting factor, although traditional wholesale banking remained the most important single merchant banking function. Competition was also increased as a result of the banks themselves diversifying their range of services offered as shown in table 3.3 Many of the larger banks added leasing and factoring services, and became even more active in insurance broking and in some cases underwriting. The conservative investment policies of the insurance companies also allowed the merchant banks to attack the life assurance market, as a natural adjunct of their investment management activities. Closely associated with the development of life business and also related to investment management, a number of banks entered the market for pension fund consultancy. While some of these new activities came from internal development, in many cases and especially those which were most specialised, were added by the acquisition of specialised firms operating in these sectors. The resulting portfolio of services offered by the merchant banks seems relatively similar to those offered by the clearing banks. The two groups of institutions do, however, differ in one respect. As a result of their relatively small asset base, the merchant banks have increasingly been forced to concentrate on fee generating services rather than lending as their source of additional income. By comparison the much larger asset base of the clearing banks has enabled them to use their lending facilities as a lever for gaining market share in the traditional areas occupied by the merchant banks.

While in the main these new activities were almost identical to those adopted by the clearing banks, direct involvement in property development was undertaken only by the merchant banks and by a number of insurance companies. The rapid post war development of the property sector introduced the banks to the market, firstly as bankers to the developers, but ultimately as developers in their own right. To improve the quality of their lending, some banks began to add their own advisory services and to employ property specialists. Some launched property based investment funds in the later 1960s and early 1970s. The continued boom in property in the early 1970s, however, led a number of banks to become directly involved in development by the purchase or formation of their own property subsidiaries.

In addition to domestic diversification the larger merchant banks were also forced to modify their traditional policy of using a loose network of overseas correspondent banks to service international clients. In the late

Table 3.3 The Sample Merchant Banks: Involvement in Newer Financial Services

At End 1960

	Insurance Broking	Bullion Broking	Shipping Broking	Property Development	Unit Trust Management	Credit Finance
Hambros	C	C				I
Mercury Securities	I					
Schroder Wagg						
Slater Walker	(Incorporated 1965)					
Morgan Grenfell						
Kleinwort Benson				A		
Hill Samuel						
Whitehall Trust (Lazards)						

At End 1973

	Insurance Broking	Metal Trading	Shipping Broking	Property Development	Credit Finance	Leasing	Factoring	Special Credit	Venture Capital	Unit Trust Management	Insurance Underwriting	Life Assurance	Shipowning	Branch Banking	Computer Services	Employee Benefit Consultancy
Hambros	C			C	C	A,I	I	I	W	W,I	C	C		W		
Mercury Securities	A	W	A				I	A	I	I	A	C	A		A	C
Schroder Wagg				W,A	C	W,I	I		W,I	W	W	W			W	W
Slater Walker	W				W									W		
Morgan Grenfell			I	I	C	W,I				W	W				W	A
Kleinwort Benson	I	W		W		W,I	W	W		W,I				W	W	
Hill Samuel	W		W			W	W	C	W	W,I	W,A	W	W	W	W	C
Whitehall Trust (Lazards)	C		A			I			W	W	A	W	A			

KEY: W = Wholly owned operation
C = Controlling equity stake
A = Associate interest < 25% > 50%
I = Interest equity stake > 25%

Source: D. Robinson, The Strategy, Structure & Financial Performance of Some Major Merchant Banking Groups 1958 to 1974. Unpublished, MBSc dissertation, Manchester Business School, 1976, Chapter 4.

66 *The Service Industries*

1960s and early 1970s, therefore, these banks moved aggressively to establish direct branch and representative offices in the world's leading financial centres, as shown in table 3.4. Three main strategies were used to build international representation. Firstly, there was a substantial growth in the number of overseas branches, with new openings being largely concentrated in major financial centres and/or sited to provide an element of geographic concentration. Secondly, former correspondent banking linkages were strengthened and formalised by the acquisition of direct equity stakes in overseas banks, or by the formation of joint ventures specifically to service particular geographic areas. Finally, mainly because of their relatively small size, some banks had relied on consortium associations in which they supplied technical skills, while their partners provided a suitably large deposit base.

For the smaller merchant banks, outside the sample firms, the cost of embarking upon an international strategy proved prohibitive. The smaller banks had also been forced increasingly to adopt a niche strategy even with respect to domestic activities. The large banks included in the sample were also affected by the growing competitive threat from the large diversified British and foreign commercial banks. The development of merchant banking operations by these banks coupled with their much greater size, led the merchant banks to adopt defensive measures. Apart from merging with other financial service companies, such as Guinness Mahon merging with commodity brokers Lewis and Peat and Singer and Friedlander being acquired by C. T. Bowring, many of the remaining independent merchant banks had formed less formal links with other, larger institutions. In particular, a number of banks had formed relationships with insurance companies which had taken strategic, but not controlling, share stakes in them. In this way independence was maintained to counter the threat that had overtaken those banks which were absorbed into other industrial or banking groups.

OTHER FINANCIAL SERVICE STRATEGIES

Excluding the British overseas banks which are discussed in chapter 8 the remaining companies in the sample had all moved from a relatively discrete strategy, based upon a particular service, to becoming increasingly diversified and therefore entering into direct competition with the banking groups. Unfortunately, for most of these non-bankers, entry into the banking arena had proved disastrous.

Mercantile Credit and United Dominions Trust (UDT) are two such examples. Both were formed in the inter war years to provide for the growing market in credit finance. The companies remained almost exclusively within this segment which they dominated, although some diversification into different segments of credit finance to specialised client

Table 3.4 The Sample Merchant Banks: International Banking Activities

At end 1968	EUROPE												N. AMERICA			S. AMERICA			ROW	COMMONWEALTH			
	Ireland	Isle of Man	Channel Isles	France	Holland	Austria	Germany	Belgium	Switzerland	Greece	Italy	Spain	U.S.A.	Canada	Bahamas	Brazil	Mexico	Argentina	Lebnon	S. Africa	Rhodesia	Nigeria	Australia
Lazards				A									A	A									I
Mercurity Securities			W						C				W										
Hill Samuel	W								W				R		I					W	A	I	
Morgan Grenfell	I			A									A	A									I
Hambros			W	R	C		R		W	W	R		C										
Kleinwort Benson	I			R			R		W	R	R	A	W										
Schroders			W					W	C						I	R		R	R				A
Slater Walker																			R	A		I	A

Table 3.4 Continued

At end 1973	EUROPE														N. AMERICA				S. AMERICA				COMMONWEALTH				FAR EAST				ROW		
	Ireland	Isle of Man	Channel Isles	France	Holland	Austria	Germany	Belgium	Switzerland	Greece	Italy	Spain	Denmark	Norway	U.S.A.	Canada	Cayman Is.	Bahamas	Brazil	Mexico	Argentina	Columbia	S. Africa	Rhodesia	Nigeria	Australia	Malaysia	Hong Kong	Singapore	Japan	Thailand	Iran	U.A.E.
Lazards				A	A		A	A	A						A	W																	
Mercury Securities		W		I	I			I	I						A															A			
Hill Samuel	W	W	W	R	R		W		W			I			W				I	R			C	I	I	C		W					
Morgan Grenfell				I	R		W		W		R	R			A	A										W		A	A				
Hambros				I	W				W	W	R	R	R		R	R	A	I	I						A	A		A	A			R	I
Kleinwort Benson		W	W	I	A			W	I						W	I	I	I	I				A			A	W	I	W	I		R	I
Schroders				I		R		W	W						W	W	W	W	C	W	W		A		A	A		A	R	R			
Slater Walker				A		W										A							A			A		A	A				

Key: W = Wholly owned subsidiary, C = Controlling interest (>51%), A = Associate interest (>25%), I = Interest (>5%), R = Representative Office.   ROW = Rest of the World.

Source: D. Robinson, op cit, Chapter 5.

groups did occur, as did .very limited overseas expansion into Southern
Africa. In the post war period growing consumer affluence led to a rapid
expansion in the demand for hire purchase credit. Competition for funds
brought the credit finance companies into conflict with the clearing banks
which also entered the market. As a result of the actions of the clearers, the
two leading finance houses forged close links to one or more clearing
banks, and equity participation by the banks continued for much of the
1960s. Rationalisation of the banks' holdings took place at the end of the
1960s, and as a result UDT was left independent of the clearing banks
while Mercantile Credit remained connected to Barclays, the only bank
not to own its own credit finance activity.

Although remaining largely specialised, during the 1960s the finance
houses pioneered the new services of leasing and factoring in the UK.
These new activities were imported from the USA, often in the form of
joint ventures with American commercial banking partners. UDT in
particular also expanded overseas, firstly in former Empire territories, but
later into Western Europe.

Following the introduction of the Bank of England's new policy of
competition and credit control in 1971 there were significant advantages
for the credit finance companies to obtain banking status. As a result, the
leading firms applied to the Board of Trade and were granted the necessary
banking status as secondary banks. This move, however, was to prove their
downfall. Both UDT and Mercantile Credit, faced with a restricted
market for credit finance in the early 1970s, plunged heavily into property
finance. The finance houses were therefore caught with the collapse of the
property sector in 1973–4 and proved to be the largest passengers in the
Bank of England sponsored lifeboat operation.[8] In the event Mercantile
Credit was ultimately rescued by being fully acquired by Barclays late in
1975 leaving UDT as the sole remaining major independent finance house,
other than the clearing bank connected firms.

Both First National Finance and C. T. Bowring, also had credit finance
operations of significant proportions and both were similarly badly mauled
by the secondary banking collapse in the early 1970s. First National
Finance Corporation grew rapidly from a small reformulated credit
finance company in 1963 to become the largest secondary bank of all.
Concentrating its activities in the parallel money markets which expanded
in the late 1960s and early 1970s alongside the Eurocurrency markets, First
National made the classic banking mistake of borrowing short and lending
long.

The secondary banks obtained the bulk of their deposits through the
wholesale parallel interbank market, in particular making use of the
relatively newly introduced certificate of deposit (CD). Although these
instruments were generally short term, it was possible to purchase forward
CD's and so theoretically create medium or long term financial instruments. Moreover, the secondary banks were always willing to pay

marginally more for their deposits, hence a significant flow of funds took place from deposits placed with primary banks to the secondary sector. Most of these funds were then used to finance property development where, because of the rapid rise in capital values, developers were prepared to pay extremely high rates of interest for funds.

First National expanded dramatically through the 1960s diversifying from credit finance into merchant banking, property development and other financial services. The bulk of the deposit base was, however, lent for property speculation, much of it on the company's own account. This formula was apparently successful and First National expanded rapidly. The company was actively supported by a number of first quality financial institutions including Hambros and Phoenix Assurance both of which acquired significant share stakes, as did the Crown Agents. Courtship of the Bank of England also brought full banking status in 1972. Indeed, First National was chosen to head the City rescue mission to London and County Securities, the first of the secondary banks to collapse. With the total collapse of the property sector, however, First National became a victim itself and massive write offs were made to the company's loan book. Only the fact that First National had become accepted by the Bank of England ensured its survival, as part of the price paid to maintain confidence in the overall banking sector.

C. T. Bowring[9] by contrast, had proved the most successful of the new banking groups. Traditionally managed by the Bowring family the company developed from an early strategy of trading with Nova Scotia. These trading activities had persisted with the company being concerned with distribution in Nova Scotia, shipping and, most importantly, insurance. The disproportionate growth of insurance broking interests, however, led Bowring to become one of the largest insurance broking concerns in the world. In the early 1960's, the company finally went public and began to diversify by acquisition into other areas of financial services. In particular it purchased interests in insurance writing, in credit finance by the acquisition of Bowmaker, and finally in merchant banking with the purchase of Accepting House Committee member, Singer and Friedlander. Like other credit finance companies, Bowring's Bowmaker subsidiary fell a victim to the secondary bank crash, but the Group's continued success in its traditional insurance broking business, together with firm managerial action, led to an early recovery for the finance house subsidiary.

S. Pearson and Son,[10] a vehicle which incorporated the main investment interests of the Cowdray family, was somewhat similar to Bowring. Both had traditionally been family dominated and had only recently become public companies. Both were highly diversified although the interests of the Pearson Group were split between industrial and financial service activities. The company, perhaps, provided the closest parallel to the continental model of an investment bank.

Originally the group was a holding company of diverse and unrelated investments. This had, since 1969, been rationalised into four divisions covering banking and financial services, industrial and commercial interests, newspapers and publishing and North American interests. The banking interests were essentially Lazards, a long established merchant bank linked with banks of the same name in Paris and New York. In addition Pearson had a substantial interest in insurance broking. Outside of banking the group had built its disparate interests into a series of industry leaders in specialised sectors. Thus in newspapers and publishing, the merger and subsequent purchase of minority interests in the Penguin Publishing Company in 1969 and 1971 when added to the group's existing ownership of the Pearson Longman publishing house created one of the largest publishing organisations in the U.K. This was later followed by the further purchase of Willis and Hepworth in 1971 and the acquisition of certain provincial newspapers to add to those of the Westminster Press, Pearson's wholly owned newspaper group.

The acquisition of the Spearshaft Industrial Group in 1967, brought the company into a new range of industries, including engineering. These interests were regrouped in 1970, following the purchase of J. H. Peck, while the group's glass interests were rationalised around Allied Merchants. In 1971, the Doulton pottery group was purchased to supplement Allied English Potteries, so creating the largest tableware group in the U.K. This company then became the overall holding company for all the group's industrial interests.

The traditional strategy of Tozer Kemsley Millbourn (TKM) was that of a confirming house. Formed in 1899, the company provided international credit to bridge the gap between the time goods left a manufacturer until the time they were purchased by a final consumer. The company offered overseas importers a wide range of credit facilities to assist them to carry stocks and granted credit to dealers, while the exporter was paid immediately. During the early part of the twentieth century, TKM became established as a leading confirming house, acting primarily for importers in the former Empire territories of Australia, New Zealand and South Africa, and also to the United States.

The company made only limited strategic changes during the 1950s. Some modest expansion took place by the purchase of companies with similar interests in Central and Southern Africa and the introduction of operations in Germany. During the 1960s the group entered the factoring market and substantially increased its chain of international offices around the world. During the 1970s diversification from traditional activities started when the company expanded its investment interests in the UK by acquisitions which took it into automobile distribution, plant hire, road haulage, shipping and forwarding, and wholesale distribution. The close relationship with the clearing banks for TKM's traditional business, however, was confirmed in 1975 when a major shareholding in the company was acquired by Barclays.

STRUCTURAL CHANGE IN FINANCIAL SERVICES

The common strategic development of increased domestic diversification and the expansion of international operations had led to the largely predictable move of widespread adoption of some form of divisional organisation. Since diversification did not take place to any marked degree in most of the banks and other financial institutions until the late 1960s, little structural change took place until this time.

Among the clearing banks the long period of limited competition led not only to strategic stagnation, but to bureaucracy in their organisations. The traditional structure of the major banks comprised a largely non-executive board, with decision making heavily centralised in the hands of a limited number of general managers, who were usually not members of the main board. The non-executive board members tended to be drawn from traditional banking families, members of the peerage, senior directors of other industrial corporations, former politicians and civil servants. Barclays, perhaps had the strongest tradition of executive main board directors, although many were descendants of the family banks which had originally amalgamated on the formation of the clearing bank. It has been argued that the common practice by the main financial institutions to make heavy use of non-executive boards in part represents the presence of a powerful, closely interconnected elite which is responsible for the allocation of many of the resources within the economy[11]. There certainly are close ties between many of the City companies by kinship, education, background and societal memberships in addition to cross directorships which at least partially support this view. The clearing banks do differ from one another in this respect, however, as is illustrated in table 3.5 which shows the common directorship links between each of the banks and other organisations.

There is no direct overlapping of the boards of the major banks although there are certainly a significant number of links at board level between the main clearers and other banking firms, principally located overseas. With the exception of the Midland, however, the remaining major banks tend to have common directorships with one or more of the UK merchant banks. The main area of overlap between the banks themselves however, is via cross directorships with a number of the insurance companies. It was quite common to find shared directors of several of the clearing banks on the boards of a few major corporate insurance groups, the most notable of these being Sun Alliance and Commercial Union. One further notable difference between the banks concerned their cross holdings with industrial companies, where the Midland & National Westminster were particularly strong, while Barclays did not form many such linkages, emphasising perhaps the more executive nature of the Barclays board.

Table 3.5 Cross Directorships of Leading Clearing and Overseas Banks, 1974-75

Bank	Other banks	Insurance companies	Other leading service industry firms	Public sector corporations and organisations	Leading manufacturing industry firms
Barclays Bank Ltd	Banque de la Societe Financiere Europeene Bank of New South Wales Yorkshire Bank Robert Fleming Holdings Lazard Bros & Co Australia & N Z Bank Societe Financiere Europeenne Bank of Scotland	Commercial Union Assurance Co Sun Alliance & London Assurance Norwich Union Royal Insurance Co Friends Provident Life Office	Booker McConnell Save & Prosper Ocean Transport & Trading Gillett Bros Discount ICFC	Finance for industry	English China Clays Burmah Oil GKN Ltd Pilkingtons Smiths Industries
Lloyds Bank Ltd	Yorkshire Bank Grindlays Bank Citicorp Brandts Ltd Dao Heng Bank (Hong Kong) Hill Samuel Group National Bank of N.Z. National & Commercial Banking Group Royal Bank of, Scotland	Sun Alliance & London Assurance Eagle Star Phoenix Assurance	Ocean Transport & Trading Furness Withy Abbey National Building Soc W H Smith	National Nuclear Corporation Port of London Authority British Steel Corporation National Research Development Corporation	Vickers Birmingham Post & Mail Hldgs Massey Furguson (Canada) GEC Baker Perkins Holdings Consolidated Gold Fields Lead Industries Grp Simon Engineering Renold Chains British Aircraft Corporation Unigate Imperial Metal Industries Whitbread Investment Co B P Redland Delta Metal Davy International Hawker-Siddeley Group ICI Powell Duffryn United Biscuits Fisons Lucas Industries

Table 3.5 Continued

Bank	Other banks	Insurance companies	Other leading service industry firms	Public sector corporations and organisations	Leading manufacturing industry firms	
National and Commercial Banking Group	Lloyds Bank Yorkshire Bank	Prudential Assurance Co Standard Life Assurance Co Legal and General Assurance Society Scottish Widows Fund & Life Assurance Society	Lloyds & Scottish Finance Co Gillett Bros Discount Jardine Matheson	Manchester Ship Canal Co Harland & Wolff	United Biscuits Gallaher Ciba Geigy (UK)	Honeywell U.K. Distillers
Grindlays Bank	Citicorp Dao Heng Bank (Hong Kong) Arbuthnot Latham Holdings	Sun Alliance & London Insurance Ltd UK Temperance & General Provident Institution Royal Insurance Co		Nuclear Power Co National Nuclear Corpn Port of London Authority	GEC Shell Transport & Trading Barrow Hepburn Group	
Standard & Charte...	Antony Gibbs National Westminster Midland Bank	Guardian Royal Exchange Assurance	Inchcape Booker McConnell P & O		Thomas Tilling Consolidated Gold Fields Consolidated Tin Smelters Shell Transport & Trading	Chartered Consolidated B P Ultramar London Tin Corpn Mitchell Cotts

Table 3.5 Continued

Bank	Other banks	Insurance companies	Other leading service industry firms	Public sector corporations and organisations	Leading manufacturing industry firms
National Westminster Bank	Arbuthnot Latham Holdings; Hong Kong & Shanghai Banking Corporation; Orion Bank; Robert Fleming Holdings; Leopold Joseph & Sons	UK Provident; University Life Assurance Soc; Allied Insurance; Sun Alliance & London Assurance; Commercial Union Assurance Co; Guardian Royal Exchange; General Accident Fire & Life Assurance; Equity & Law Life Assurance Co; Legal & General Assurance Soc; Friends Provident Life Office	Alexanders Discount; Halifax Building Society	Electricity Council	Associated Portland Cement; British Portland Cement; Birmid Qualcast; John Brown & Co; Sheepbridge Engineering; Gallaher; Compair; Imperial Group; Delta Metal; Glaxo Holdings; Turner & Newall; BTR; Tube Investments; Redland; English China Clays; N.C.R.; Mather & Platt; IBM (UK); BAT Co; Dunlop Holdings; Tunnel Cement; BLMC

Table 3.5 Continued

Bank	Other banks	Insurance companies	Other leading service industry firms	Public sector corporations and organisations	Leading manufacturing industry firms	
Midland Bank	Bank of Bermuda Canadian Imperial Bank of Commerce Banque Europeenne de Credit European-American Banking Corpn European Arab Bank European Asian Bank Standard & Chartered Banking Group Grindlays Bank Banque Blege	Canada Life Assurance Co General Accident Fire & Life Assurance Corpn Commercial Union Assurance Scottish Amicable Life Assurance Soc Eagle Star Insurance Guardian Royal Exchange Assurance	ICFC United Dominions Trust Metropolitan Estates Property Co	National Nuclear Corpn British Airways Board	Dunlop Holdings Spillers BICC Shell Transport & Trading Rowntree Mackintosh Imperial Metal Industries Imperial Group Swan Hunter Group Allied Breweries Rothmans International Rolls Royce	BLMC Burton Group Glaxo Holdings ICI Pirelli Consolidated Goldfields Rank Organisation Stone Platt Industries Cussons Group Delta Metal Bass Charrington

Sources: Annual Reports; Directory of Directors.

By the late 1960s it had become commonplace for the clearing banks to supplement their centralised domestic banking management with a system of regional boards of management. This move in most cases signified a modest attempt at decentralisation in order to improve local image and increase the normally slow speed of decision making. Like the main board these regional boards were largely composed of non executive senior businessmen. In addition the growing complexity of banking operations led to the expansion of the central senior executive group as illustrated in figure 3.1 which traces the structural evolution of the Midland Bank.

1950	2 Chief General Managers 5 Joint General Managers 1 General Manager (Research & Statistics)

1962	1 Chief General Manager
	1 Assistant Chief General Manager
	5 Joint General Managers
	3 General Managers
	  (Administration)
	  (Overseas)
	  (Executive & Trustee)
	11 Assistant General Managers
	7 Regional Managers

1970	1 Chief General Manager
	1 Deputy Chief General Manager
	1 Assistant Chief General Manager
	6 Joint General Managers
	5 General Managers
	  (Administration)
	  (Agriculture)
	  (Overseas)
	  (Staff)
	  (Executor & Trustee Co)
	9 Assistant General Managers
	  (Business Department)
	  (Administration)
	  (Agriculture)
	  (Staff)
	  (Executor & Trustee) 3
	  plus 2 unspecified
	21 Regional Directors

Source: H. Chryssaphes, op. cit. p. 74.

Figure 3.1   Evolution of the Midland Bank's Top Administrative Structure 1950–70

Following the moves to increased competition in the late 1960s, the diversification of domestic services and the spread of overseas activities led to the widespread use of consultants to help with the introduction of divisional structures. Such a structure is illustrated in figure 3.2 which outlines the subdivision of the National Westminster Bank into three divisions covering UK banking, international banking, and related banking services. The other clearing banks operating a divisional system had a similar, three division structure. The introduction of a divisional structure has also led to the increased use of senior managers as executive main board directors. Following divisionalisation the introduction of modern budgetary control procedures was also commoh, although formal long range planning systems and clearly allocated profit responsibility were still rare. Moreover, although the UK banking division remained largely centralised, the international and financial services divisions in these structures, tended to be managed largely on a mother-daughter or holding company basis, with loose central office control. The banks too, were slow to integrate their new services into their conventional banking activities and make use of their extensive, and expensive, branch networks as a marketing system for these services. Despite the nominal acceptance of a divisional organisation therefore, the banks still did not operate with many of the expected characteristics of such a structure. By comparison with their major American competitors they remained over bureaucratised, conservative, short of marketing skills and without well established planning systems and profit controls.

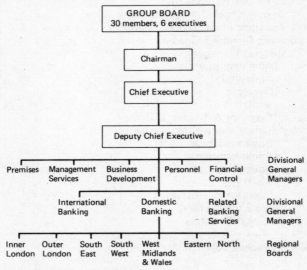

Source: D. F. Channon, *British Banking Strategy*, p. 57

Figure 3.2   Structure of National Westminister Bank Limited, 1975

In a similar manner, diversification of product range and by geography resulted in structural strain for the major merchant banks. Nevertheless strong family relationships still dominated the structure of many of the banks. Moreover, there were significant kinship relationships between many of the leading banking families, as illustrated in table 3.6 which shows connections between leading financial institutions because their directors were relatively close members of the same family. While the banks were small and limited in their diversity, they were often managed with a partnership structure with all key decisions tending to be

Table 3.6 Connections Between 27 Large Financial Institutions Through Kinship Relations among Directors

	Bank of England	Alexanders	Barclays	Cater, Ryder	Clive	Flemings	Hambros	Hill, Samuel	Kleinworts	Lloyds	Midland	Minster	Montagu	Nat. West	Rothschilds	Schroders	Slater, Walker	Union	Mercury	Commercial U.	Eagle Star	Gen. Accident	Guardian R.E.	Phoenix	Prudential	Royal	Sun Alliance
Bank of England		I						I		I			I	I	I				I					I		I	I
Alexanders										I				I							I		I	I		I	
Barclays				I	I					I				I				I	I	I	I	I	I	I		I	I
Cater, Ryder										I				I			I	I									
Clive										I							I	I	I		I	I	I				
Flemings											I		I	I	I											I	I
Hambros								I													I		I	I			I
Hill, Samuel									I					I					I		I		I	I			I
Kleinworts																					I	I					
Lloyds											I			I				I	I	I	I	I	I	I			I
Midland													I	I					I		I	I					
Minster																											
Montagu																					I						I
Nat. West																		I	I	I	I	I	I	I	I	I	I
Rothschilds																					I		I				I
Schroders																		I	I		I	I					
Slater, Walker																											
Union																			I		I		I	I		I	
Mercury																					I	I	I				I
Commercial U.																											
Eagle Star																						I	I	I		I	I
Gen. Accident																							I				
Guardian R.E																								I			I
Phoenix																											I
Prudential																											
Royal																											
Sun Alliance																											

Integration Score = 0.91
Firm not in Network: Minster Assets
Proportion in Network = 26/27 = 96%

Source: R. Whitely, op cit.

taken by a few executive directors, most of whom were members of the
founding family. Since the range of operations was limited, any necessary
information regarding overall activity could be communicated between
the directors by means of daily meetings. It was also common for directors
to be involved in all aspects of the bank since there was little need for
specialised skills.

Diversification resulted in changes to the partnership structure. Firstly,
the range of activities increased and led to the need for specialists in
particular areas. Many of these had been drawn from outside the main
families, resulting in a decreased dominance by family directors in many of
the banks. Secondly, usually with the aid of external consultants, the
merchant banks began to change their organisations during the late 1960s
and early 1970s, toward a divisional form. Traces of the old partnership
structure were often retained, however, since this structure offered
advantages in speed of decision making and flexibility of response to
change, although it added to the difficulties of establishing clearly defined
and measurable profit centres.

The revised working structures of many banks, while adopting some
features of a divisional system, also retained elements of their traditional
structure and they tended to make extensive use of overlapping committees
for both communication and policy formulation. A typical programme of
such meetings is shown in figure 3.3 which sets out the system in one of the
major divisionalised banks. A number of the leading merchant banks had,
however, been slow to change their structure to meet strategic needs. These
concerns usually operated as loose holding companies with little or no
central coordination or integration between activities. Moreover, most of
the banks had been slow to adopt modern management methods, thus few
had established planning and forecasting systems while in some cases, even
budgetary control systems had only recently been established.

The merchant banks, by comparison with many other financial
institutions made less extensive use of non executive directors, although
many did operate with multiple internal directorships resulting in
especially large boards. Individual banks differed on their attitude toward
outside directorships with some banks encouraging the practice, while
others adopted the opposite view. Generally those banks with especially
large boards such as Hill Samuel, had directors with board appointments
in other institutions. The cross directorships of the merchant banks are
shown in table 3.7, which demonstrates the extensive interfirm connections
of Hill Samuel, compared with very limited external involvement of
newcomers Slater Walker Securities. As with the clearing banks there was
generally no direct contact between the banks via cross directorships, but
again a similar set of intermediate companies appeared as common
meeting places for directors of a number of the banks. In general, however,
despite interconnections it cannot be taken that the banks had operated a
formal cartel. Indeed on many occasions and despite an unwritten code of
accepted practice, the banks actively competed with one another.

Level	Committee	Meeting Frequency	Committee Composition	Purpose
Group	Group Management Committee	Fortnightly	Group Chairman, Finance Director, Senior Subsidiary Chairman	To make policy and strategic decisions which affect the Group as a whole. Progress review of operating problems which may also affect the Group
	Chairmans Committee	Monthly	Chairman & Chief Executives of operating divisions	To review progress on planning decisions already made as well as monitor some operational decisions
Subsidiary	Director Committee	Weekly	Each available director on a country wide basis	To update each director across the range of the bank's activities for the country concerned
	Operations Committee	Daily	Subsidiary Executives and Directors	Functions as the traditional morning executive meeting
Division	Specialists Committee	Weekly	Executives & Directors within the division	To discuss the specialist problems particular to fund management corporate finance and investment management

Source: Adapted from D. Robinson, op cit, p 184.

Figure 3.3 Divisionalised Merchant Bank–Principal Operating Committee Structure

Table 3.7 Cross Directorships of Major Merchant Banks, 1974–75

Bank	Other Banks	Insurance Companies	Other Leading Service Industry Firms	Leading Manufacturing Firms
Mercurity Securities	Banque De Paris et de Pays Bas Bank of England		Times Newspapers	Bunzl Pulp & Paper Chrysler UK Merck Sharpe & Dohmme (USA)
Slater Walker Securities			Solicitors Law Stationary Society	British Leyland Rockware Group Allied Polymers
Schroders	Lloyds Bank Royal Trust Co (Canada)	Commercial Union General Accident	Los Angeles Times-Mirror (USA)	British Petroleum Boots IBM Corporation Scottish and Newcastle Breweries Burton Group British Gas Corpn Guthrie Corpn

Table 3.7 Continued

Bank	Other Banks	Insurance Companies	Other Leading Service Industry Firms	Leading Manufacturing Firms
Morgan Grenfell	Bank of New Zealand Nat Bank of Australia Banque de Suez et Union Des Mines Commercial Bank of Australia	Equity and Law Life Assurance Canada Life Assurance Guardian Royal Exchange Assurance National Mutual Fire Assurance Soc Cornhill Insurance Co	Yule Catto Union Discount Willis Faber Dumas Alexanders Discount	Charter Consolidated (SA) Rank Hovis McDougall GEC Fisons GKN International Computers (Holdings) Ltd Baker Perkins Holdings BICC Ultramar United Biscuits Sidlaw Industries Coalite & Chemical Products Harris Lebus Brent Walker
Hambros	Bank of Montreal Bank of England	Sun Alliance Phoenix Assurance Guardian Royal Exchange	Hutchinson Intl (Hong Kong) Taylor Woodrow Furness Withy Guardian & Manchester Evening News	Charter Consolidated (SA) Union Corpn (SA) Consolidated Tin Smelters International Harvester The Laird Group David Brown Corporation Thorn Electrical Industries Wilkinson Match SKF (UK) Norsk Hydro (UK) Atlas Copco A. B (Sweden)

Table 3-7 Continued

Bank	Other Banks	Insurance Companies	Other Leading Service Industry Firms	Leading Manufacturing Firms
Guiness Peat	Banque Belge	Sun Life Assurance Provident Mutual Life Assurance		Sheepbridge Engineering Courtaulds Rugby Portland Cement Pirelli Ltd Ransome Hoffman Pollard Morgan Crucible
Kleinwort Benson	Bank of America Intl Toronto Dominion Bank Australia & NZ Bank Royal Trust of Canada	Commercial Union Assurance Sun Alliance Assurance Equitable Life Assurance London & Manchester Assurance Provident Mutual Life Assurance	British Home Stores Inchcape & Co Trafalgar House Investments Mercantile Credit National Westminster Unit Trust Managers Ltd	RTZ National Cash Register Tunnel Cement Cadbury Schweppes Chubb & Son B.P. Associated Biscuit Manufacturers ICI

Table 3.7 Continued

Bank	Other Banks	Insurance Companies	Other Leading Service Industry Firms	Leading Manufacturing Firms
Hill Samuel	Chemical Bank	Eagle Star Insurance	Times Newspapers	Beechams
	Lloyds Bank	Royal Insurance	Fitch Lovell	Rolls Royce (1971)
	Royal Bank of Canada	Clerical Medical & General	Trust Houses Forte	Norcros
		Life Assurance		Hickson & Welch Holdings
				Imperial Metal Industries
				IBM (USA)
				National Distillers &
				Chemical Corporation
				British Airways
				Molins
				ICI
				Averys
				Tube Investments
				British Printing Corporation
				Courtaulds
				CEGB
				UKAEB
				Staveley Industries
				Stone-Platt Industries
				Whessoe
				Wilkinson Match
				Sandoz Products
				Alusuisse UK

Sources: Annual Reports, Directory of Directors.

Conclusion

The major financial service companies demonstrate a strong apparent relationship between strategy and structure. Environmental factors and especially increasing competitive pressures, have resulted in a clear trend to diversification within the UK and, concurrently, an extension of overseas activities. Moreover, while the overall market for financial services could once be clearly subdivided into discrete segments associated with particular types of institution, diversification has led to the various institutions entering one anothers traditional markets. The chosen route for such new market entries was heavily weighted to acquisition, with joint ventures with an experienced partner taking second place. The internal development of new activities was uncommon, except in straightforward banking operations, where for example, the establishment of international wholesale banking offices was usually the result of direct actions.

As diversification proceeded this led to the introduction of divisional structures based on the key activities of domestic banking, international banking and other services in the case of the clearing banks, while merchant banks tended to subdivide into divisions concerned with wholesale and other money market transactions, corporate and investment banking and funds management, with international activities occasionally being a further subdivision, dependent upon their size and scale.

These divisional structures are not wholly autonomous however, with banking operations in particular being highly centralised. Opportunities for interdivisional integration also tend to be poorly exploited. More commonly, newer non banking activities were usually managed in a quasi-autonomous fashion, all such services being placed in a catch all division, irrespective of how closely they were related to one another or to the domestic and international banking operations. In general, however, the basic strategy-structure model appears to work well among the financial service companies. The extensive use of non executive directors and the extensive cross directorships were, however, an unusual feature, not experienced in manufacturing industry, or even in most other parts of the service industries outside the City.

Only limited analysis of financial performance was attempted in view of the difficulties in establishing a true picture due to the bank's legal right not to declare their true profitability. Reactions were therefore somewhat impressionistic, although in terms of growth rate in net assets those firms which had expanded overseas and adopted a divisional structure first tended to show the most progress. In part this could be attributed to the effect of a declining value of sterling, but speed of reaction and degree of aggression certainly appeared to be greater among the divisional companies.

4. The Slowly Changing World of Insurance

London is the world's foremost international centre for insurance and the leading British institutions have established for themselves an enviable reputation taking some 10 per cent of world premium income in 1972.[1] Insurance was also the principal City contributor to invisible earnings earning £244m. for the UK balance of payments in 1974. Over 40 per cent of the premium income of the member companies of the British Insurance Association and 75 per cent of that of Lloyds is derived from overseas policies. Excluding whole life policies, this percentage rises to an average of over 60 per cent of which the USA, the most important market, accounted for £705m. in 1973. Increased penetration in Western Europe during the early 1970s has led to premium income from within the Community rising to £369m. by 1973, with the rest of the world accounting for £1194m.[2]

Early history
The foundation of the British insurance industry dates originally from the introduction of marine insurance in the sixteenth century. Then, early insurers of British merchant activities and their shipowning clients began to congregate at a common location – the London meeting house of Edward Lloyd. During the eighteenth century, the informal gatherings at Lloyds began to take on a more established character. A committee of the patrons was established and soon after moved to rooms at the Royal Exchange, leading to the formal association of underwriters which has become Lloyds. Concurrent with this development the first companies writing marine insurance were established and organisations providing cover against fire were also created. In 1706, the first life company, the Amicable, was formed as a mutual benefaction society in which premiums contributed by the members were to be shared among the relatives of those who died, the total sum available depending upon the actual number of deaths per annum.

The Amicable and other similar early life assurance schemes were rudimentary, having no scientific foundation. Precision was provided by the mathematician, James Dodson, who used the concepts of probability theory to derive the idea of actuarial insurance. Dodson's ideas were the inspiration behind the formation of the Equitable Assurance Society in 1762, the forerunner of the modern life assurance corporation.

The nature of the insurance market

There is an enormous range of risks for which insurance is nowadays written and classification presents some problems. The simplest classification scheme would divide insurance into two broad categories: long term and general. The first of these is concerned with risks spread over time and is made up principally of life assurance[3] and premiums against the contract are usually paid over a period of years. In general insurance, cover is usually provided on an annual basis and premiums are paid accordingly, with both the insurer and the insured having the right to cease, modify or renew the contract at the end of that time.

The main forms of life assurance contracts are firstly, 'whole life' policies under the terms of which premiums are paid throughout the life of the insured in return for an agreed sum to be paid by the insurer on the death of the insured. Endowment assurance makes up the second major class of life policies, under which the insurer pays the insured a given sum after some specified time or at death. There are also pure endowment policies which are essentially methods of saving, providing no death benefit. A further type of policy provides a guaranteed annuity in return for a given lump sum payment. Over the years, and especially from the mid-1960s, an increasing number of variants of these basic contracts have been offered to meet the needs of particular market segments. For example, many life assurance companies have developed endowment mortgage policies for house purchase, whereby an endowment policy is used in association with a building society which supplies an advance which is ultimately repaid upon maturity of the policy.

One further distinction must be drawn, namely that between ordinary life policies and industrial life policies. These latter policies and the companies issuing them were allowed by law to provide for the funeral expenses of one's relatives and industrial life policies therefore, were originally associated with poorer working familes, premiums usually being collected by door to door agents on a weekly basis. By contrast ordinary life policies were associated with salary earners and higher income groups with premiums usually being paid monthly by banker's order.

Since 1931 a further important class of life assurance to emerge has been group life assurance which provides death benefits or pensions for the members of such schemes out of the premiums paid. Insurance based pension funds have expanded rapidly in the post-war period and employment pensions are now statutory, either as independent schemes or state managed.

There are six statutory classes of general insurance business, namely:

Marine, aviation and transport
Motor vehicle
Pecuniary loss

Personal accident
Property including fire and theft
Liability insurance

The last four of these classes are usually grouped under the common heading of 'fire and accident (non-motor)'. General insurance covers a vast array of risks, although motor vehicle insurance makes up the largest single class, accounting for 34.4 per cent of the £3332m.[4] accident premium income of the members of the British Insurance Association in 1973. Marine, aviation and transport accounted for 8.7 per cent, with the balance coming from the remaining four classes. Some 65.2 per cent of this general premium income was derived from overseas in 1973 of which the USA (21.1 per cent) and EEC countries (9.2 per cent) represented the most important areas. In the post-war period, inflation and rising costs have led to increasing difficulties in general insurance as these have risen faster than premium incomes, leaving frequent years of underwriting losses.

Reinsurance forms a further significant component of the non life market, with London being the leading international centre. This market arises from the fact that each insurance company internally sets a limit on the amount it is prepared to risk in any one situation. When the liability is in excess of this limit the 'leading' company in effect takes out insurance with another 'reinsurance' company for the excess. As a result, particularly large risks may be spread amongst insurers either on a percentage or non-proportional basis.

There were some 625 companies incorporated in Britain and over 160 foreign companies in the British insurance market at the end of 1973. The majority of insurance business was held by the joint stock or mutual companies comprising the 290 members of the British Insurance Association which transacted nearly 95 per cent of all British insurance in 1973. There are two distinctive corporate forms operating in the market. Firstly, there are the proprietary companies, which are owned by shareholders. Many of the largest insurance companies are of this type. Secondly, there are mutual companies, which have no shareholders but are owned by the policy holders. These receive all the profits but are also technically liable for any losses, although this liability is usually limited by guarantee. Many mutual companies are only engaged in life assurance where, theoretically, they offer a distinct advantage in that no profits need be shared with outside shareholders.

The main competition to the insurance companies comes from the Corporation of Lloyds whose 6000 underwriting members are organised into marine and non-marine syndicates. This unique Corporation, which grew from the informal coffee house gatherings, was legally established as an incorporated society of private insurers by Act of Parliament in 1871. The Corporation is administered through a committee elected from among the active underwriting members. This committee is responsible for the election of new members and is concerned with the financial stability of those doing business at Lloyds. The committee does not, however, have any corporate responsibility for the underwriting liabilities of members, although it takes on a supervisory role which includes a strict annual audit of underwriting accounts and the holding of members' deposits held in trust.

The members of Lloyds are private individuals who must meet the stringent financial requirements of the committee prior to acceptance. These requirements include assets of at least £75,000 and a deposit of some £15,000 must be lodged with the Corporation as security for underwriting liabilities. These individuals are organised into syndicates each led by a specialist full time underwriter, who writes policies committing his syndicate members to specific proportions of risk, each member bearing unlimited liability. Currently there are some 270 syndicates of varying sizes, some with up to several hundred names.

Lloyds traditional business has been in the Marine market where the Corporation provides the most comprehensive shipping intelligence service in the world. Much of this intelligence is gathered by a world wide system of some 1500 agents and sub-agents who are principally responsible for collecting shipping movement information but who also may be used to investigate damage or to deal with claims. While marine business is still important, in the past 80 years or so however, there has been a great expansion in non-marine business. Lloyds has been especially aggressive in the aviation and motor markets and is the leading centre for disaster insurance. In 1971, premium income amounted to over £817m. One important area where Lloyds does not operate is the long term market. Since the members of Lloyds change relatively frequently and liability is on an individual basis, the syndicates can only take on comparatively short term contracts. Only seven of the 270 syndicates write short term life assurance which provides for payments in the event of the assured's dying within a year.

Business at Lloyds is conducted entirely through intermediate brokers of whom there are some 250 accredited concerns. This practice is necessary due to the mechanics of operations in the Lloyds underwriting room. In addition, the broker is a key figure in the Lloyds market, being the sole channel between the underwriters and their clients. The close relationship between the brokers and the Lloyds underwriters actually provides an important competitive influence in the overall market, for while barriers to entry from new companies can be substantial, the problems of creating a new Lloyds syndicate are less serious. For while it is necessary to gain the approval of the committee, once established any such syndicate would immediately gain the overall mantle of credibility given to Lloyds as a whole. The Lloyds brokers are frequently involved either directly or indirectly in the formation of such syndicates and a number of market segments have been developed as a result of the creation of syndicates to service particular, specialised client needs.

THE PATTERNS OF INSURANCE COMPANY STRATEGY

The research focussed on 23 of the leading insurance companies which control the majority of the market.[5] The companies could be subdivided both by the markets they served and by their legal form. Firstly, there were specialised firms which handled just one type of insurance. The specialised mutual life companies were the primary example of this kind of firm. Secondly, there were the general companies which wrote only non life business. Finally, there were the large composite concerns which handled both life and general business. The degree of product market specialisation and premium income level for the insurance companies investigated are shown in table 4.1. The companies are also categorised by legal structure. The table illustrates how the strategies of the firms have evolved over the period from 1950. In general there has been only limited change in the overall premium income source of many firms and especially the mutual firms which have remained mostly single business area firms. There has usually been some modification and extension of the product range offered by the mutual life companies, although this has not always increased diversification. For example the concentration of the Clerical and Medical on pension fund policies, has actually led to a relative narrowing of the company's product market scope.

The large proprietary companies were the earliest concerns to diversify from over concentration on a specific sector, although there remained many examples where some firms had developed a dominant position within a particular market segment. Thus, General Accident which was located in Scotland was especially strong in motor insurance which accounted for 60 per cent of its premium income; Sun Alliance was strong in the market for household insurance; the Commercial Union and the Royal were both especially concerned with the North American market which accounted for around 50 per cent of premium income for each company in 1972; the Prudential, largest of all the insurance firms was the biggest industrial life company and was built up by its door-to-door selling in the nineteenth century.

Diversification, where it had occurred tended to be gradual, unless generated as the result of a merger or acquisition. In the main it occurred as a result of penetration into market segments held by competitors and by the discovery of entirely new segments. In addition a number of firms embarked on expansion overseas. A few firms endeavoured to pursue all these policies but in general the pace of change was relatively slow for much of the period for most of the companies.

Table 4.1   Insurance Companies Analysis of Premium Income 1950 – 72

Company		1950 O	I	F	A	M	1955 O	I	F	A	M
Britannic	%	31	64	5		–	32	63	6		–
	£M	3.3	6.7	0.5		–	4.1	8.2	7	0.7	–
Clerical	%	100	–	–		–	88	(Pensions 12)		–	–
	£M	2.3	–	–		–	3.0	0.1	–		–
Commercial Union	%	11	–	43	42	4	10	–	38	48	4
	£M	4.5	–	18.8	18.3	1.8	6.5	–	23.0	29.3	2.5
Eagle Star	%	43	–	15	33	9	48	–	15	30	7
	£M	6.4	–	2.3	4.9	1.4	12.3	–	3.8	7.8	1.7
Equity and Law	%	100	–	–	–	–	100	–	–	–	–
	£M	3.6	–	–	–	–	5.7	–	–	–	–
Friends Provident	%	49	–	29	12	11	59	–	–	40	–
	£M	4.1	–	2.4	1.0	0.9	8.0	–	–	5.5	–
General Accident	%	4	–	9	84	3	4	–	9	85	1
	£M	1.2	–	2.7	25.7	1.0	2.2	–	4.4	41.1	0.5
Guardian & R. E.	%			n.a.					n.a.		
	£M										
Legal and General	%	89	–	7	4	1	90	–	5	4	1
	£M	22.9	–	1.8	0.9	0.3	40.3	–	2.2	1.7	0.7
Norwich Union	%	100	–	–	–	–	100	–	–	–	–
	£M	10.6	–	–	–	–	19.4	–	–	–	–
Pearl Assurance	%	29	51	15	5	–	30	48	12	10	–
	£M	8.2	14.5	4.1	1.4	–	11.0	17.3	4.4	3.5	–
Phoenix	%	7	–	35	49	9	7	–	32	54	6
	£M	1.9	–	9.2	12.7	2.3	2.4	–	11.2	18.8	2.2
Prudential	%	40	50	5	5	–	44	44	4	7	–
	£M	32.6	40.1	3.7	4.1	0.3	47.9	47.5	4.3	7.6	0.4
Refuge (General business wholly reinsured pre 1972)	%	42	57	–	–	–	43	56	1		–
	£M	6.5	8.7	–	–	–	7.7	10.0	0.1		–
Royal	%	8	–	43	40	8	9	–	37	49	5
	£M	3.2	–	16.9	15.5	3.3	7.7	–	32.2	42.1	4.7
Royal London (General business reinsured)	%	28	68	–	4	–	28	68	–	4	–
	£M	3.4	8.3	–	0.5	–	4.0	9.6	–	0.7	–
Scottish Amicable	%	100	–	–	–	–	100	–	–	–	–
	£M	2.7	–	–	–	–	6.4	–	–	–	–
Scottish Provident	%	100	–	–	–	–	100	–	–	–	–
	£M	n.a.	–	–	–	–	3.9	–	–	–	–
Scottish Widows	%	100	–	–	–	–	100	–	–	–	–
	£M	n.a.	–	–	–	–	n.a.	–	–	–	–
Standard Life	%	100	–	–	–	–	100	–	–	–	–
	£M	13.7	–	–	–	–	22.9	–	–	–	–
Sun Alliance	%			n.a.					n.a.		
	£M										
Sun Life	%	100	–	–	–	–	100	–	–	–	–
	£M	10.1	–	–	–	–	16.2	–	–	–	–
U.K. Provident	%	89	–	–	11	–	100	–	–	–	–
	£M	2.4	–	–	0.3	–	3.4	–	–	–	–

Table 4.1 Continued

Company		1960 O	I	F	A	M	1965 O	I	F	A	M
Britannic	%	30	62	⌐7¬		–	30	63	⌐7¬		–
	£M	5.1	10.3	1.2		–	6.4	13.4	1.6		–
Clerical	%	76 (Pensions 23) –		–	–	–	73 (Pensions 27) –		–	–	–
	£M	3.9	1.2	–	–	–	6.6	2.4	–	–	–
Commercial Union	%	15	–	36	45	4	18	–	31	48	4
	£M	20.5	–	47.7	59.7	5.3	29.5	–	51.0	78.9	6.4
Eagle Star	%	40	–	14	40	6	33	–	13	48	6
	£M	18.5	–	6.2	18.4	2.6	25.9	–	10.2	37.4	4.3
Equity and Law	%	100	–	–	–	–	100	–	–	–	–
	£M	14.6	–	–	–	–	16.2	–	–	–	–
Friends Provident	%	68	–	–	{ 32	–	69	–	–	31	–
	£M	13.9	–	–	{ 6.4	–	21.2	–	–	9.3	–
General Accident	%	7	–	10	82	1	9	–	15	75	1
	£M	6.0	–	7.7	66.6	0.7	11.7	–	18.9	94.0	1.2
Guardian & R.E.	%			n.a.					n.a.		
	£M										
Legal and General	%	89	–	5	5	1	87	–	5	6	2
	£M	57.0	–	3.0	3.3	0.7	87.9	–	5.4	5.6	1.7
Norwich Union	%	51	–	20	24	5	57	–	13	23	4
	£M	34.9	–	14.1	16.6	3.4	51.7	–	12.1	22.8	3.6
Pearl Assurance	%	33	49	7	11	–	37	48	4	11	–
	£M	15.4	22.4	3.2	5.1	–	22.6	29.0	2.7	6.6	0.1
Phoenix	%	10	–	29	55	6	13	–	27	52	8
	£M	4.6	–	13.0	24.7	2.9	8.6	–	17.7	33.4	4.9
Prudential	%	48	39	4	9	–	51	34	4	10	–
	£M	70.9	58.2	5.7	12.6	0.5	105.4	70.7	7.6	20.8	0.6
Refuge (General business wholly reinsured pre 1972)	%	43	55	⌐2¬		–	43	54	⌐3¬		–
	£M	9.3	11.7	0.5		–	11.4	14.2	0.9		–
Royal	%	8	–	37	51	4	8	–	33	55	4
	£M	11.8	–	58.2	79.1	6.9	22.5	–	90.2	152.1	11.4
Royal London (General business reinsured)	%	28	66	–	6	–	27	65	–	8	–
	£M	4.8	11.5	–	1.1	–	5.8	13.9	–	1.6	–
Scottish Amicable	%	100	–	–	–	–	100	–	–	–	–
	£M	12.2	–	–	–	–	17.3	–	–	–	–
Scottish Provident	%	100	–	–	–	–	100	–	–	–	–
	£M	6.5	–	–	–	–	9.7	–	–	–	–
Scottish Widows	%	100	–	–	–	–	100	–	–	–	–
	£M	14.8	–	–	–	–	22.4	–	–	–	–
Standard Life	%	100	–	–	–	–	100	–	–	–	–
	£M	40.1	–	–	–	–	60.5	–	–	–	–
Sun Alliance	%	10	–	38	45	7	13	–	31	46	10
	£M	50	–	19.3	22.6	3.6	15.5	–	38.4	56.0	12.4
Sun Life	%	100	–	–	–	–	100	–	–	–	–
	£M	23.9	–	–	–	–	39.6	–	–	–	–
U.K. Provident	%	100	–	–	–	–	100	–	–	–	–
	£M	5.0	–	–	–	–	8.2	–	–	–	–

The Service Industries

Table 4.1 Continued

Company		1970 O	I	F/A	M	1972 O	I	F/A	M
Britannic	%	27	65	7	–	27	65	8	–
	£M	7.8	18.6	2.0	–	9.0	22.0	2.6	–
Clerical	%	63 (Pensions 36)		–	–	61 (Pensions 38)		–	–
	£M	11.6	6.6	–	–	12.8	8.0	–	–
Commercial Union	%	16	–	77	7	15	–	78	6
	£M	74.5	–	355.7	33.8	101.4	–	524.3	42.9
Eagle Star	%	38	–	54	8	49	–	46	6
	£M	56.1	–	78.9	11.2	119.0	–	111.9	13.5
Equity and Law	%	100	–	–	–	100	–	–	–
	£M	25.8	–	–	–	37.4	–	–	–
Friends Provident	%	62	–	33	6	61	–	33	6
	£M	31.1	–	16.5	2.8	41.9	–	22.8	3.9
General Accident	%	16	–	81	3	14	–	83	3
	£M	39.8	–	195.7	7.7	46.9	–	279.6	9.1
Guardian & R. E	%	31		60	8	26		63	9
	£M	54.3		169.2	25.9	78.2		243.4	35.6
Legal and General	%	86	–	12	2	82	–	16	2
	£M	123.1	–	17.0	2.5	149.9	–	29.1	2.9
Norwich Union	%	52	–	43	5	49	–	47	4
	£M	77.1	–	63.4	6.9	98.9	–	95.0	8.7
Pearl Assurance	%	39	44	16	1	39	43	16	1
	£M	33.4	37.4	13.4	0.7	39.9	43.8	16.5	0.8
Phoenix	%	14	–	74	11	21	–	69	10
	£M	17.0	–	87.8	13.1	36.3	–	118.6	18.1
Prudential	%	53	29	18		50	21	28	
	£M	161.9	88.2	54.4		228.3	97.7	129.3	
Refuge (General business wholly reinsured pre 1972)	%	41	55	4		41	53	6	
	£M	12.6	17.2	1.3		14.6	18.9	2.0	
Royal	%	8	–	87	6	10	–	85	5
	£M	33.7	–	380.6	24.8	55.7	–	474.9	28.7
Royal London (General business reinsured)	%	30	62	8		33	57	9	
	£M	7.6	15.4	2.0		9.5	16.5	2.7	
Scottish Amicable	%	100	–	–	–	100	–	–	–
	£M	22.9	–	–	–	32.4	–	–	–
Scottish Provident	%	100	–	–	–	100	–	–	–
	£M	14.6	–	–	–	22.8	–	–	–
Scottish Widows	%	100	–	–	–	100	–	–	–
	£M	37.4	–	–	–	51.8	–	–	–
Standard Life	%	100	–	–	–	100	–	–	–
	£M	90.8	–	–	–	129.8	–	–	–
Sun Alliance	%	12	–	72	15	14	–	74	12
	£M	22.3	–	131.1	28.1	34.2	–	187.8	30.6
Sun Life	%	99	–	1	–	100	–	–	–
	£M	57.1	–	0.7	–	68.8	–	–	–
U.K. Provident	%	100	–	–	–	100	–	–	–
	£M	11.3	–	–	–	16.5	–	–	–

Sources: Annual Reports
Key: O = Ordinary life; I = Industrial life; F = Fire;
A = Accident; M = Marine (includes Aviation)

Table 4.2 shows the changing nature of the life assurance market in greater detail indicating the annual premium income received by each of the companies and their percentage share of the total market. Most analyses of life assurance tend to concentrate on the value of the total assurance in force rather than annual premium income. While this is probably a more significant value of overall corporate size in the life market, table 4.2 reveals trends in the ability of individual companies to maintain their market share over time. Table 4.3 extends the data on market share to examine the relative concentration held by the major companies in the life assurance market over the post war period.

During the post war period there has been a substantial and relatively steady decrease in concentration in the life assurance market. The market leader has consistently been the Prudential but the most significant single feature of the market has been the dramatic decline in the Prudential's market share, which has been almost halved. Legal and General has consistently remained in second place, with Standard Life holding third place since the early 1950s. The most aggressive composite companies have tended to increase their share with Commercial Union, Eagle Star and the Royal improving their relative position, although not necessarily their market share. A number of the less aggressive composites have suffered significant share declines with the Pearl, the Refuge and the Brittanic performing notably badly.

There are several reasons for these changing patterns. The overall decline in concentration, while largely attributable to the Prudential has also occurred as a result of increased competition from other savings media and especially equity linked schemes introduced by the merchant banks and other banks and financial institutions. It was noticeable that all the companies with a substantial decline were significantly involved in industrial life policies which were a low growth segment in the overall market. A number of the other proprietary companies have however registered gains in share. After a relatively poor performance in the 1950s when the mutual companies capitalised on their inherent advantage of sharing all profits among policy holders, these proprietary companies began to stage a comeback from the mid 1960s by more aggressive marketing policies with some modest success. Overall however, the leading mutual life companies have tended to hold their share relatively more successfully than the proprietary firms and the overall share taken by the mutual firms has remained quite stable.

Premium income is a more appropriate measure of size for non life business and by contrast with the life market there has been a dramatic increase in concentration in the post war period. This is illustrated in tables 4.4 and 4.5. The first of these illustrates the market position of the individual leading non life firms since 1950 while the second examines the trends in industry concentration. In 1955 the seven largest sample companies accounted for 38.4 per cent of net non life premium income

Table 4.2 Life Insurance Premium Income Growth and Market Share (£million)

	1950 £m	1950 %	1960 £m	1960 %	1965 £m	1965 %	1970 £m	1970 %	1972 £m	1972 %
Mutual Companies										
Clerical	2.3	0.8	5.1	0.7	9.0	0.8	18.2	1.1	20.8	0.8
Friends Provident	4.1	1.4	13.9	1.9	21.2	2.0	31.1	1.9	41.9	1.6
Norwich Union	10.6	3.5	34.9	4.8	51.7	4.8	77.1	4.8	98.9	3.8
Royal London	11.7	3.9	16.3	2.2	19.7	1.8	23.0	1.4	25.0	1.0
Scottish Amicable	2.7	0.9	12.2	1.7	17.3	1.6	22.9	1.4	32.4	1.3
Scottish Provident	n.a.		6.5	0.9	9.7	0.9	14.6	0.9	22.8	0.9
Scottish Widows	n.a.		14.8	2.0	22.4	2.1	37.4	2.3	51.8	2.0
Standard Life	13.7	4.6	40.1	5.5	60.5	5.6	90.8	5.6	129.8	5.0
U.K. Provident	2.4	0.8	5.0	0.7	8.2	0.8	11.3	0.7	16.5	0.6
Total Mutual Cos.	47.5	15.9	148.8	20.3	219.7	20.5	326.4	20.2	439.9	17.1
Proprietary Companies										
Britannic	10.5	3.5	15.4	2.1	18.8	1.8	26.2	1.6	31.0	1.2
Commercial Union	4.5	1.5	20.5	2.8	29.5	2.7	74.5	4.6	101.4	3.9
Eagle Star	6.4	2.1	18.5	2.5	25.9	2.4	56.1	3.5	119.0	4.6
Equity & Law	3.6	1.2	16.2	2.2	25.8	2.4	25.8	1.6	37.4	1.4
General Accident	1.2	0.4	6.0	0.8	11.7	1.1	39.8	2.5	46.9	1.8
Legal & General	22.9	7.7	57.0	7.8	87.9	8.2	123.1	7.6	149.9	5.8
Pearl	22.7	7.6	37.8	5.1	22.6	2.1	33.4	2.1	83.7	3.2
Phoenix	1.9	0.6	4.6	0.6	8.6	0.8	17.0	1.1	36.3	1.4
Prudential	72.7	24.3	129.1	17.6	176.1	16.4	250.4	15.5	326.0	12.6
Refuge	15.2	5.1	21.0	2.9	25.6	2.4	29.8	1.8	23.5	0.9
Royal	3.2	1.1	11.8	1.6	22.5	2.1	33.7	2.1	55.7	2.2
Sun Alliance	n.a.	n.a.	5.0	0.7	15.5	1.4	22.3	1.4	34.2	1.3
Sun Life	10.1	3.4	23.9	3.3	39.6	3.7	57.1	3.5	68.8	2.7
Total Proprietary Cos.	174.9	58.5	365.2	49.8	500.5	46.6	788.9	48.8	1113.8	43.2
Overall Total	222.4	74.4	514.0	70.0	720.2	67.0	1115.3	68.9	1553.7	60.2
Industry Total	299	100	734	100	1074	100	1618	100	2580	100

Source: Annual Reports, British Insurance Association.

Table 4.3   Concentration of market share of premium income for life assurance among companies (%)

	1950	1960	1965	1970	1972
Largest Company	24.3	17.6	16.4	15.5	12.6
Largest 2	32.0	25.4	24.6	23.1	18.4
Largest 3	39.6	30.9	30.2	28.7	23.4
Largest 5	49.3	40.8	38.7	38.1	31.8
Largest 10	65.7	54.5	50.7	52.0	45.8

Sources: Annual Reports, British Insurance Association

written by members of the British Insurance Association. By 1960, this had risen to 58.6 per cent, while the largest three non life companies, Commercial Union, Royal Insurance and the newly created Sun Alliance had taken their share to 37.4 per cent. During the 1960s the trend toward increased concentration continued and even accelerated, especially for the largest firms. By 1970, the same largest three firms had expanded to take nearly 50 per cent of the market, with the Commercial Union in particular gaining ground on the traditional non life market leader, Royal. Both, however, increased their lead over their rivals and held roughly equal shares of around 19 per cent each by 1970, with Commercial Union seizing the lead by 1972. The creation of Guardian Royal Exchange added a new, strong contender, and by 1972, the top 10 sample companies accounted for over 83 per cent of the non life market. This trend to increased concentration has been the result of a number of factors. Firstly, toward the end of the 1950s a number of mergers and acquisitions took place which tended to increase concentration, and led to the formation of Sun Alliance and the entry of Norwich Union, one of the major mutual companies, into the non life market. Secondly, especially from the mid 1960s, there has been a significant increase in the level of competition which, accelerated by mergers, has resulted in a substantial growth in market share by the largest companies. Thirdly, those companies such as Commercial Union and Royal, with substantial overseas interests have seen their premiums incomes rise sharply as the result of the declining international exchange rate for sterling.

International activity is also largely concentrated among the major composite insurers. This is shown in table 4.6 which shows the geographic distribution of premium income by company for recent years. Few of the mutual firms have found it necessary to enter the market for general insurance or expand overseas, although a few have built a substantial non life and international business. Norwich Union perhaps provides the prime example of a diversified mutual company. The Norwich structure is interesting in that the non life business is a separate entity which is wholly owned by the Life Society. For most mutual firms, however, competition

Table 4.4 Non Life Insurance Market Share and Growth 1955–72

Company	1955		1960		1965		1970		1972	
	Premium Income (£m)	Market Share(%)	Premium Income (£m)	Market Share(%)	Premium Income (£m)	Market Share(%)	Premium Income (£m)	Market Share(%)	Premium Income (£m)	Market Share(%)
Commercial Union	54.8	7.7	112.7	12.3	136.3	10.6	389.5	18.6	567.2	19.8
Royal	112.2	15.5	144.2	15.6	253.7	19.7	405.4	19.5	503.6	17.6
General Accident	46.0	6.5	75.0	8.1	114.1	8.8	203.4	9.8	288.7	10.1
Guardian Royal Exchange	–	–	–	–	–	–	199.7	9.6	279.0	9.7
Sun Alliance	32.2	4.5	87.4	9.5	106.4	8.3	159.2	7.6	218.4	7.6
Phoenix	12.3	1.7	40.6	4.4	56.0	4.3	100.9	4.9	136.7	4.8
Prudential	13.3	1.8	18.8	2.0	30.0	2.3	54.4	2.6	129.3	4.5
Eagle Star	–	–	27.2	3.0	51.9	4.0	90.1	4.3	125.4	4.4
Norwich Union	4.6	0.7	34.1	3.7	38.5	3.0	70.3	3.3	103.7	3.7
Legal & General			7.0	0.8	12.7	1.0	19.5	1.0	32.0	1.1
Total Non-Life Premium Income	715	100	921	100	1,289	100	2,084	100	2,862	100

Sources: BIA, Annual Reports

Table 4.5   Concentration of market share of premium income for non life insurance among largest companies (%)

	1955	1960	1965	1970	1972
Largest Company	15.5	15.6	19.7	19.5	19.8
Largest 2	23.2	27.9	30.3	38.1	37.4
Largest 3	29.7	37.4	39.1	47.9	47.5
Largest 5	36.0	49.9	51.7	65.1	64.8
Largest 10	–	–	–	81.2	83.3

Sources: Annual Reports, British Insurance Association

has been strictly limited, and perhaps as a result they have not felt it useful or necessary to extend their operations overseas even for life business.

While the USA is the largest single overseas market for British insurance companies relatively few of the major firms actually operate there. Five companies are strong with the Royal, Commercial Union and General Accident being especially important. Many more of the companies were active in the smaller White Commonwealth markets of Canada, Australia and New Zealand where similarities in the legal structure meant that life business was also written. Most recently the more aggressive insurers have been extending into western Europe. Interestingly, perhaps this movement has not been led by those firms strong in the US market but by such firms as Guardian Royal Exchange, Norwich Union, Legal and General and Sun Alliance none of which have significant American interests. As with banking, therefore, international expansion strategy is strongly directed toward the developed countries with less developed nations offering little or no significant growth opportunities that the firms have been ready to exploit.

THE PROCESS OF STRATEGIC CHANGE

Acquisitions and rationalisation

In the immediate post war period profitability in the insurance industry was initially high. Increased selling expenses and commission rates, coupled with the effect of inflation on claims resulted in pressure on profits due to rising expense ratios. Further, changes in technology led to the introduction of new risks which were on a substantially enhanced scale, such as increasing hull sizes in marine insurance, larger civil aircraft with more passengers and the like. The administration of insurance companies also involves substantial elements of bureaucracy where the introduction of computerisation offered the prospect of reduced processing costs for a suitable scale of operation.

Table 4.6　International Sources of Premium Income (% Distribution) 1968–72

		U.K. & Ireland					U.S.A.					Canada					Australia & N. Zealand					Western Europe					Rest of the World				
		68	69	70	71	72	68	69	70	71	72	68	69	70	71	72	68	69	70	71	72	68	69	70	71	72	68	69	70	71	72
Britannic		100 →→→→→→→																													
Clerical, Med. & Gen.		100 →→→→→→→																													
Commercial Union	L	n/a	82	82	77	→	n/a	–	–	4	n/a						9	9	9	9	9	–	–	–	9	10	n/a	5	6	6	6
	N-L	24	23	24	24	23	45	44	43	46	45	8	16	16	16	6	7	7	7	6	7	9	9	9	10	11	8	9	9	8	8
Eagle Star		N.A.																													
Equity & Law	All Ins.	100	100	100	99	97																									
Friends' Provident	L	n/a	89	90	90	90						n/a	4	3	4	3	5	5	5	5	6	–	neg	neg	1	3	n/a	2	2	1	1
	N-L	n/a	54	60	66	65						16	16	16	16	14	7	8	8	8	10						n/a	23	16	10	11
General Accident	All Ins.	43	41	40	42	43	39	40	41	39	36	5	6	5	6	6	3	3	3	3	3	4	4	4	5	5	5	6	6	5	6
Guardian Royal Ex.	L	51	51	52	53							10	12	10	9	8	7	2	2	2	8	11	13	13	15	17	21	15	17	15	15
	N-L	67	64	78	78												17	17	18	13	14	23	25	24	2	2	8	8	12	10	10
Legal & Gen.	L	56	58	68	67																	12	13	12	9	2	9	14	12	10	10
	N-L	n/a	76	79	76																						14	13	10	8	8
Norwich Union	L	n/a	n/a	76	55	60	n/a	n/a	4	3	4	n/a	n/a	4	3	4	n/a	n/a	6	7	8	n/a	n/a	4	4	5	n/a	n/a	9	8	8
	N-L	n/a	n/a	97	96	97	n/a	n/a	9	7	7	n/a	n/a	9	7	7	n/a	n/a	10	9	9	n/a	n/a	14	12	13	n/a	13	13	13	12
Pearl	L	n/a	97																								3	3	4	3	
	N-L	43	42	45	49		24	25	25	26		9	9	9	8	9		9	8	8							15	16	14	16	
Phoenix	L	76	71	65	74	n/a	32	34	31	29	n/a	–	9	10	9							–	–	–	1	–	24	29	35	26	n/a
	N-L	25	29	26	29							7	7	7	7												33	28	33	33	
Prudential	L	80	80	80	78		–	–	–	1	8	7	7	7	7	8						–	–	–	–	6	8	6	6	6	6
	N-L	61	57	55	56	44	–	–	–	2	17	20	23	23	19	8						–	–	–	–	17	14	16	16	15	10
Refuge	L	100 →→→→→→→																													
Royal Ins.	N-L	18	18	18	18	20	53	52	53	52	48	10	11	12	12	6	6	6	6	6	6						13	13	12	12	14
Royal London		100 →→→→→→→																													
Scottish Amicable		95	93	92	91	91						5	7	8	9	9															
Scottish Provident		100 →→→→→→→																													
Scottish Widows		100 →→→→→→→																													
Standard Life		100 →→→→→→→																													
Sun Alliance	L	90	88	81	82	86	2	2	2	2	1	5	6	6	5	6	–	–	–	–	–	3	4	11	11	7					
	N-L	40	40	41	39	39	16	17	18	18	19	10	9	10	9	9	10	10	10	10	11	24	24	21	24	22					
Sun Life		100 →→→→→→→																													
U.K. Provident		100 →→→→→→→																													

Some business in Canada, Australia & N.Z. Beginning in U.S.

Key:　L – Life　N-L – General　Sources: Annual Reports

As a result of cost pressures, therefore, the composite companies in particular, embarked upon a wave of amalgamations commencing in the late 1950s. These are illustrated in table 4.7 which lists the major mergers between British insurance companies since 1956. This process of amalgamation began in 1956 when the Guardian acquired Licences and General which was followed by the further purchase of the Caledonian the following year. In 1958, Eagle Star acquired Threadneedle but the next years brought a major series of moves. In 1959, Sun Alliance was formed by the merger between the Sun and the Alliance, Norwich Union acquired Scottish Union, Commercial Union purchased North British and Mercantile and Royal Exchange absorbed Atlas. A further rush of mergers took place over the next two years which included the creation of the Royal London by the merger between the Royal and the London & Lancashire.

In the main the majority of mergers took place between the composite companies which were especially under competitive pressure in general insurance. These companies were, therefore, anxious to reduce their expense ratios by increasing market share, by the diversification of their insurance product range and extending geographic coverage. By contrast, the mutual companies which were primarily concerned with the life market, were less affected by competitive pressures and were invulnerable to take over threats as a result of their constitution. The trend to increased geographic coverage and expanding the product range continued during the 1960s with firms which had previously been largely domestic in their operations opening new overseas branches or acquiring foreign subsidiaries. Towards the end of the 1960s and in the early 1970s, this pattern of overseas expansion shifted from the former Empire territories and North America into Western Europe. By the early 1970s most of the leading composite groups were broadly diversified both by product and by geography, although the remnants of former areas of specialisation often remained.

Changing methods of marketing

The life market

The two main insurance markets are very different. In particular the bulk of life business is conducted with individuals whereas much of the general market is written with industrial and public corporations which often employ their own insurance experts. As a result purchasers of life assurance are often poorly informed about the range of options open to them. This situation has become increasingly confused as a result of a profusion of products being offered by the insurance companies during the 1960s, in attempts to identify and service specialised market segments. Partially as a result of this lack of awareness, the available terms and benefits for similar policies from different companies have been shown to vary markedly.[7]

Over the post war period there has been a marked decline in the relative

Table 4.7 Major insurance company mergers and acquisitions, 1956–72

Company	1956–59 Horizontal	1956–59 Geographic Diversfcn. WC	USA	WE	ROW	1956–59 Product Diversification Other / I	P	Misc.	1960–67 Horizontal	1960–67 Geographic Diversfcn. WC	USA	WE	ROW	1960–67 Product Diversification Other / I	P	Misc.	1968–72 Horizontal	1968–72 Geographic Diversfcn. WC	USA	WE	ROW	1968–72 Product Diversification Other / I	P	Misc.	Total
Britannic																									0
Clerical																									0
Equity & Law		W								C												I			3
Friends Provident		W															C								2
Legal & General									W																2
Norwich Union	W								W																1
Refuge	W																								0
Royal London																									1
Scottish Amicable	W																								0
Scottish Provident																									0
Scottish Widows	n.a.	n.a.						n.a.						I						I					3
Standard Life														I								W			2
Sun Life																									0
UK Provident	W								W(4) I			W								I		W			10
Commercial Union	W								W			W					W(2)	W		W		W		I(2)	9
Eagle Star									W					W				C							2
General Accident												W								I					1
Pearl Assurance									W(2)											W			I		8
Phoenix Assurance									W								W		I(2) W			W			2
Prudential									W											I		W W			6
Royal									W								W	W		W		W(3) I			6
Guardian & R.E. (formed 1968)																		W		W					
Sun Alliance (formed 1959)	W								W																2
Total	6	2	–	–	–	–	–	–	11	5	–	1	2	1	–	1	6	3	4	1	–	2	8	4	60

Key: WC=White Commonwealth, USA=United States, WE=Western Europe, ROW=Rest of the World, Other I=Other Insurance Activities, P=Property Development, Misc=Miscellaneous, =Wholly Owned, C=Controlling Interest, I=Investment Interest
Sources: Annual Reports

importance of industrial life policies and by 1967, ordinary life policies comprised nearly two thirds of all life and annuity business. Endowment and endowment assurance have been the most popular policy types, although the insurance market has lost share in the overall savings market, with the building societies, in particular, increasing in importance. Newer forms of insurance have, however, experienced high growth, with annuities growing rapidly during the late 1960s. Equity linked life schemes have also grown in importance, largely as a result of the marketing efforts of the merchant banks and a number of newer insurance companies, especially Berkely-Hambro.

Increased competition, both from outside the traditional insurance companies and between the companies themselves, has led to significant marketing changes. The major marketing channels used by the companies are:

Direct: using own sales outlets; a direct sales force and/or new business inspectors; the use of full time agents; direct mail and coupon advertising selling.

Captive or semi-captive intermediaries: the use of part time agents representing one or more insurance companies including solicitors, accountants, building societies, estate agents, brokers, garages etc.,

Independent Intermediaries: the use of independent brokers.

The majority of life assurance has traditionally been sold on a direct basis, through company agents or representatives. There has been some significant growth in coupon advertising selling, especially to higher income groups where brokers have also achieved some penetration. Marketing support activities have been substantially expanded and consumer advertising in particular has shown significant growth of both institutional and product specific types, press being the most widely used of the media.

The general market

In addition to the life assurance market, private motor insurance and household building and contents insurance are two major sectors of the non life market sold to the individual, making up over 40 per cent of the total non marine general market. Private motor insurance is the largest single segment in the personal insurance sector, accounting for over 25 per cent of all personal and commercial non marine general business.

The motor insurance market in particular was largely covered by a collective cartel from the early twentieth century, in order to prevent excessive price competition and insurance company failures. This cartel was administered by the Accident Officers Association and was the dominant pricing method for the industry for many years. In the early 1950s these 'tariff companies' controlled around two thirds of the market, while Lloyds syndicates which were not involved in the tariff arrangements held around 15 per cent. During the 1960s, the tariff companies lost market share consistently to more aggressive, non tariff concerns which priced their policies up to 10 per cent below the cartel, and also offered larger discounts to specialised segments creamed off from the tariff companies. By using the tariff companies as market leaders and relying on them to calculate from accident statistics the appropriate premium rates, the non tariff concerns enjoyed lower overheads. Marketing was also aggressive with high commissions being given to agents and brokers. As a result, by 1968 the market share of the tariff companies had fallen to 30 per cent.

Concern about the motor insurance industry led the British Insurance Association to commission a study of the market by McKinsey & Company in 1965. The consultants' highly critical report concluded that fundamental reforms were essential, including improvements in underwriting methods, management efficiency and broker remuneration. This report, coupled with a continued decline in competititive position, led ten of the largest tariff companies to request the abandonment of the common rate in 1968.

The collapse of the tariff system led to a new wave of competition in the motor insurance market as the more aggressive tariff concerns moved to innovate new policies aimed at recapturing the prime business lost to the non tariff firms prior to 1968. These new policies offered price discounts and improved benefits for good risk drivers. Their position was also improved by the collapse of a number of the non tariff companies which had taken on higher risk business. Further there was an increasing use of direct sales forces rather than the former reliance on brokers.

The second major personal non life segment, home insurance, can be differentiated between building and contents insurance. In both cases, the direct sales forces of the industrial life companies have been used to ensure that these firms held a consistently high share of both market segments. In particular, however, the industrial life firms have been especially strong in the number of contents policies written for lower income groups, accounting for some two thirds of the number of policies, while brokers, other agents and direct sales forces deal more with higher income and lower age group families.

Owner occupation is more concentrated among higher income groups and as a result the strength of the industrial life companies has been less significant. The primary channel for home building insurance has been developed through the building societies. Individual insurance companies have established special relationships with particular societies which make the granting of a house purchase loan conditional upon the adoption of a satisfactory building policy on which the society obtains commission. Solicitors are a second, although declining, intermediary for building insurance with brokers being relatively little used.

The commercial insurance market, while competitive in most areas, also contains cartel or tariff operations which have remained relatively stable, especially in the market for fire insurance. Like the Accident Officers Association, the Fire Offices Committee fixes minimum premium rates from a complex set of risk clauses. In addition the committee aims to standardise policy conditions, commission rates, and coordinates relations between the tariff and non tariff companies. Competition has been less intensive in this market sector although by the late 1960s there were signs that the near monopoly market share held by the tariff companies was under increasing attack.

Although overall results for most insurance companies must be considered poor, individual firms have established results superior to their rivals in some segments. Nevertheless, the lack of knowledge by many of the purchasers of insurance, especially in the life market, means that substantial imperfections are common. This lack of knowledge is also aggravated by the distribution system where, despite a theoretical independence, brokers are paid by the insurance companies they represent and can hardly be expected to remain wholly objective in their representations to potential clients. It is therefore, perhaps, not surprising that a number of those firms with the most competitive prices do not pay commissions while others pay a smaller commission than average.[8]

The increased importance of investment

Underwriting performance in the general insurance market has tended to be relatively poor in the post war period. After an initially successful period in the early 1950s increased competition and a relative failure to keep expense ratios down has led to severe losses in many years. After the mid 1950s, for the majority of the major companies, underwriting was unprofitable and even in the few cases of profitable performance, returns as a percentage of premium income were extremely low. Investment performance has therefore substantially increased in importance for most companies.

The main competition to the insurance companies for investment funds has come from outside the industry. The merchant banks in particular have proved a substantial force in increasing investor awareness and emphasising performance. As a result, the insurance companies have been forced to respond and take a more active role in the management of their portfolios. In the early 1950s it was common to find that many insurance companies had no established investment function and in some cases funds were invested, either directly by or on the advice of, outside advisers, notably the merchant banks. Since the early 1960s, this practice has been transformed, with the introduction of a specialised investment management function in most of the companies.

The change in policy is also illustrated by the transformation of the make-up of the investment profile of insurance company funds. This is shown in table 4.8, which indicates the value and percentage distribution

Table 4.8 Investment Pattern of Insurance Companies (£m Net Book Value)

	Long-Term Funds												Other Funds[1]										
	1947	%	1955	%	1960	%	1964	%	1970	%	1973	%	1947	1955	1960	%	1964	%	1970	%	1973	%
British Govt. Authority Securities	1,004	39.2	1,242	28.0	1,138	21.0	1,506	19.0	2,058	15.8	4,156	22.9	Included in Long-Term		194	16.4	187	12.6	203	8.2	351	12.1
Foreign & Commonwealth Govt., Provincial & Municipal Stocks	247	9.6	419	9.4	188	3.5	243	3.1	442	3.4	449	2.5			324	20.0	382	25.9	457	18.6	80	2.7
Debentures, Loan Stocks, Preference & Guaranteed Stocks & shares	521	20.4	939	21.2	1,103	20.3	1,668	21.0	2,420	18.5	2,775	15.3	Included in Long-Term		255	21.5	281	19.0	529	21.9	267	9.1
Ordinary Stocks & Shares	272	10.6	680	15.4	1,187	21.9	1,782	22.5	3,597	27.5	4,597	25.4			230	19.4	353	23.8	847	34.4	867	29.6
Mortgages	158	6.2	532	12.0	870	16.0	1,375	17.3	2,227	17.0	2,685	14.8			57	4.8	76	5.2	127	5.2	145	4.9
Real Property & Ground Rents	149	5.8	357	8.1	549	10.1	829	10.4	1,775	13.4	2,636	14.5			66	5.6	110	7.4	178	7.2	296	10.1
Other Assets	211	8.2	261	5.9	392	7.2	531	6.7	571	4.4	507	2.8			56	4.8	91	6.1	112	4.5	365	12.4
Totals	2,561	100	4,430	100	5,428	100	7,934	100	13,070	100	18,125	100			1,182	100	1,480	100	2,463	100	2,933	100

[1]Since 1969 funds have been called Long Term funds (instead of Life funds and General funds) and Other funds (instead of Life funds and General funds) and Permanent funds have been tranferred to Long Term funds. The Tables apply to balance sheet values of invested assets, only current assets are omitted.
Source: British Insurance Association

by major asset types for insurance industry investment funds over the post war period. For much of the time there was a marked decline in the companies' holdings in government securities and a corresponding increase in investments in equities and real property. The early post war dominance of government securities in investment portfolios was in large part a result of agreement between the government and the insurance industry to channel new money toward the public sector. The return to a more competitive economy, coupled with a realisation of the dangers of inflation, caused an increased interest in equities and a sharp move away from government stocks. In addition, first at the end of the 1950s and again toward the end of the 1960s, booming property values have led to a substantial increase in property investment. Initially, this was often achieved by providing direct finance to developers, but more recently a number of the companies have entered into developments on their own account via internally created or acquired property firms.

The 1970s have brought something of a revival in the holdings of government securities. The return of a socialist administration in 1964 led to a sharp increase in the percentage of GDP taken by the public sector and a sharp decline in the relative profitability of equity investments. Higher interest rates to combat inflation and fund the public sector debt requirement have, therefore, resulted in a growing scepticism in the value of equities as a long term inflation hedge. High interest rates and relative security have also favoured government debt issues.

The trend to increased diversification
A number of the proprietary companies in particular, together with one or two large mutual concerns, have begun to diversify, generally outside the insurance industry, since the late 1960s. The first such move which has become relatively common has been the build up of a direct stake in property development. In the main this was a natural evolution from the practice of particular insurance companies lending finance or forming close relationships with particular developers. While these early moves enabled the insurance companies to expand their property portfolios, and by additional equity participations, enjoy some of the benefits of growth achieved by the developers, the substantial capital profits made from the property boom largely eluded them. As a result in the early 1970s, a significant number of insurance companies, having already added property and project evaluation skills to their investment departments, made the ultimate move of becoming prime developers in their own right. This was usually achieved by the purchase of a property company which could then be expanded.

In addition to diversification into property a number of the companies, again primarily proprietary firms, have begun to develop interests in other financial service sectors. Substantial stakes were acquired in a number of leading secondary merchant banks, partially as a mechanism for develop-

ing property interests but also some insurance companies considered a
move into certain areas of banking was not inconsistent with their long
term objectives. By 1975 however only Norwich Union had actually
purchased an authorised bank, Anglo Portugese, and a Bank of England
investigation was initiated to examine future policy regarding likely
expansion moves by the insurance industry. It was, however, certainly true
that a number of the leading proprietary firms, faced with a strategic
attack on their markets by the banks, saw their own future as financial
service conglomerates, operating in a number of financial service areas
including banking.

THE STRUCTURAL EVOLUTION OF INSURANCE

The slow development of increased product and geographic diversification
together with the increased importance of investment management and
moves into property and other services, has resulted in structural change.
In general, this change has been gradual and reflects closely the
developments in strategy. The structural forms noted, although similar,
were not strictly the same as those found in manufacturing industry. Thus,
in the simplest of structures, a functional form of organisation could be
identified such as that shown in figure 4.1. This form of organisation was
found in a number of the life companies during the 1950s and in a few
cases, lasted until the early 1960s. Key decisions were highly centralised,
with actual policies being prepared centrally under a general manager
who might also be responsible for investment management and be in
charge of control systems and administration. The sales function was
normally handled by a second general manager who might also be
responsible for policy administration. The precise nature of the sales
function varied according to the distribution policy adopted but in general

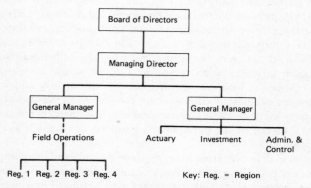

Figure 4.1   Early Functional Insurance Company Structure

such insurance companies operated through a series of regional branches which might or might not provide a base for an internal sales force.

As business expanded this simple structure tended to be further subdivided as in figure 4.2, showing the growing importance of specialised activities, especially investment management. This structure was commonly found in most mutual life companies which had not diversified into other areas of insurance or expanded overseas. One modification to this structure, which became more common in later years, was the subdivision of the investment management function by the addition of a specialised property department.

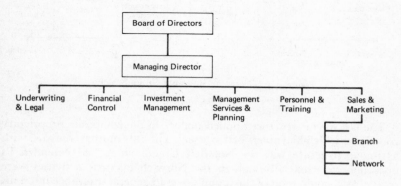

Figure 4.2   Modern Functional Insurance Company Structure

By contrast the composite insurance companies naturally divide their life and non life business, resulting in the formation of a semi divisional structure such as that shown in figure 4.3. The actuarial function in such an organisation tends to be broken into life and non life components, under separate general managers who are also responsible for sales in the respective product areas. Some life offices are further subdivided to provide a specialised coverage of pension business, with a separate actuarial function and occasionally another sales and marketing function. This subdivision is also found in some mutual life companies, thus providing them with a limited version of a divisional structure.

The division of activities may not always be as precise as that indicated since some companies have effectively organised on the basis of client type rather than by product. Thus some general insurance, especially home and vehicle, is written for individuals and, while different personnel may be involved, these operations usually share the regional sales organisation which may be operated by the life office or vice versa for those concerns where general insurance dominates. Marine and aviation especially, tend to be treated centrally, as are other key commercial accounts. As with the functional companies, a further variant of this structure involves the extension of the investment management function by the addition of property management.

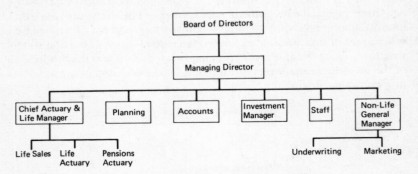

Figure 4.3   Composite Insurance Group Structure

The last major structure applied mainly to the composite proprietary companies which had diversified overseas. The only mutual company with a similar structure was the Norwich Union which had extended its operations overseas although in the Norwich overseas activities were treated as a subdivision of the group's overall general insurance interests. In these firms the activities are subdivided either by geography or by a combination of product and geographic divisions according to the product mix. Those firms operating a large life business tended to prefer the latter variant while those most widely diversified by geography usually treated the UK in a similar way to other areas. This structure is illustrated in figure 4.4, and most of the large composite firms had adopted a variant of this by 1974.

The clear lines of responsibility shown in the above diagrams were not always found and very commonly senior general managers took on divided areas of responsibility. Partially as a result, from the late 1960s a number of firms had used management consultants, especially McKinsey, to tidy up their organisation. These reorganisations had tended to result in the introduction of a number of management techniques including new control and planning systems, improved marketing and a revision of investment management practices. More importantly, however, re-organisation moved the firms further toward a divisional form, with each of the product or geographic divisions being treated as far as possible as profit centres, instead of cost centres. A move to full profit responsibility was, however, somewhat artificial since overall group profitability was essentially determined in part by investment performance. All premium income was invested centrally, although this operation could be subdivided into specialised investment areas. As a result, therefore, investment management became a 'critical function' in the structure of an insurance company.

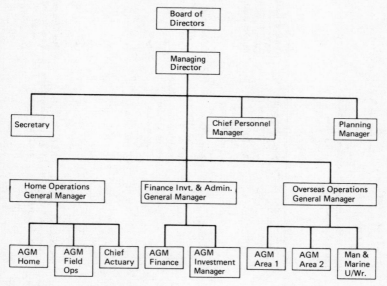

Figure 4.4   International Composite Insurance Group Structure

The board structures of insurance companies, like those of the banks, were historically mainly composed of non-executive members. Until the consultant led reorganisations, many companies had no executive members on the board. Like the banks, again, these non executive board members tended to be drawn from a City elite. Multiple cross directorships were found as shown in table 4.9., with a few of the leading composite firms being especially prominent. The board members of Sun Alliance, Guardian Royal Exchange, Commercial Union and Equity and Law Life held a particularly large number of other directorships and notably provided a link between many of the clearing and merchant banks. Cross holdings with other service industry firms were limited although the same group of insurance firms were also represented on the boards of a number of leading industrial firms.

Table 4.9 Cross Directorships of Leading Insurance Companies, 1974–5

Insurance Co	Banks	Other Service Industry Firms	Public Sector Corporations and Organisations	Leading Manufacturing Firms
Friends Provident	Lazard Bros Barclays Bank National Westminster	Phoenix Assurance Scottish Television Associated Fisheries Gillett Bros Discount Halifax Building Society	Forestry Commission British Railways	Associated Biscuits C & J Clark Lesney Products
General Accident	Schroders Midland Bank National Westminster			Shell Transport & Trading BICC BLMC Burton Group Glaxo Holdings Imperial Group BAT Delta Metal Dunlop Holdings
Commercial Union	Kleinwort Benson Barclays Bank Schroders Baring Bros Antony Gibbs First National Bank of Boston National Westminster Bank of America International Toronto Dominion Bank Lazard Bros Australia & NZ Bank	American Airlines P & O Finance for Industry Trafalgar House Investments British Home Stores	British Steel Corporation Electricity Council ICFC	Burton Group Foseco Minsep RTZ Amerada Hess (USA) British Enkalon Corning Glass N.C.R. Tunnel Cement Debenhams George Cohen 600 Group Tube Investments ICI BP Boots
Eagle Star Insurance	N. M. Rothschild Australia & NZ Banking Group Lloyds Bank National Bank of N.Z. Midland Bank Royal Bank of Scotland	Jessel Toynbee Great Portland Estates Bristol & West Building Society Beaverbrook Newspapers British Caledonian Airways	British Rail (Regional Board) British Nuclear Fuels	RTZ Whitbread Investment Co Hall Thermotank Bass Charrington Consolidated Gold Fields Delta Metal

Table 4.9 Continued

Insurance Co	Banks	Other Service Industry Firms	Public Sector Corporations and Organisations	Leading Manufacturing Firms
Sun Alliance	Grindlays National Westminster Hambros Arbuthnot Latham Kleinwort Benson Barclays Bank Hill Samuel Lloyds Bank (Regional Board) Ionian Bank Lazard Bros Yorkshire Bank N. M. Rothschild Manufacturers Hanover Citicorp	Times Newspapers British & Commonwealth Shipping Associated Television Corpn Jardine Matheson Beaverbrook Newspapers London Weekend T.V.	British Transport Docks Board Port of London Authority Nuclear Power Co National Nuclear Corpn	British Enkalon Gulf Oil (UK) Swedish Match Wilkinson Match Vickers IBM (UK) Allied Breweries David Brown Corpn Atlas Copco (Sweden) English China Clays John Brown Sheepbridge Engineering Cadbury Schweppes Chubb and Son Thorn Electrical SKF (UK) GEC
Norwich Union	Lloyds Bank (Regional Board) Barclays Bank Bank of Scotland		British Railways (S.E. Board)	SKF (UK) Stone Platt Industries Imperial Group
Legal & General	National & Commercial Banking Group Lazards Lloyds Bank (Regional Board) National Westminster	Abbey National Building Society Alexanders Discount		IBM (UK) Turner & Newall London Brick Dicknson Robinson

Table 4.9 Continued

Insurance Co	Banks	Other Service Industry Firms	Public Sector Corporations and Organisations	Leading Manufacturing Firms	
Guardian Royal Exchange	Morgan Grenfell Hambros Barclays Bank (Regional Board) Standard & Chartered Australia & N Z Bank Brown Shipley Holdings National Westminster Midland Williams & Glyns Bank National Bank of Australia	Taylor Woodrow Metropolitan Estates	Port of London Authority	Allied Breweries Nairn & Williamson Rank Hovis McDougall Charter Consolidated B.P. Burmah Oil P & O English China Clays Sheepbridge Engineering Rank Organisation	Cussons Group Rothmans International
Phoenix Assurance	National Westminster (Regional Board) Lloyds Bank Hambros S.G. Warburg Banque Belge Royal Bank of Canada Lazard Bros	First National Finance Corpn Woolwich Equitable Building Society Orion Insurance Provident Life Assurance Friends Provident		Charter Consolidated Hawker Siddeley Group ICI	
Prudential Assurance	National & Commercial Banking Group National Westminster Barclays Bank			Chrysler UK Rugby Portland Cement Rank Organisation Unilever Standard Telephones & Cables	Consolidated Gold Fields Gallaher Honeywell (UK)

Table 4.9 Continued

Insurance Co	Banks	Other Service Industry Firms	Public Sector Corporations and Organisations	Leading Manufacturing Firms
Royal Insurance	Baring Bros Hill Samuel National & Grindlays Barclays Bank	Mercantile Credit Richard Costain S. Pearson Tozer Kemsley & Millbourn (Holdings) Alexanders Discount Ocean Transport & Trading	Bank of England Midlands Electricity Board	Donald McPherson Group Tarmac Tricentrol Rolls Royce (1971) Tube Investments United Biscuits ICI Averys
Sun Life	Lazard Bros Robert Fleming Arbuthnot Latham Guinness Peat Banque Belge	Halifax Building Society Save & Prosper Group		Metal Box London Tin Corporation De La Rue SKF (UK) Courtaulds
UK Provident	Grindlays National Westminster Lloyds (Regional Board)			Boots Coates Bros. Lucas Industries
Clerical Medical & General	Warburgs Robert Fleming Hill Samuel	British United Provident Assocn	BBC	BP BAT Hawker Siddeley Group Wilkinson Match Welcome Foundation BPB Industries
Equity & Law Life	Morgan Grenfell Bank of New Zealand Lloyds Bank (Regional Board) National Westminster Bank of Scotland British Bank of the Middle East Barclays Bank UK Management	W.H. Smith		Smiths Industries Thomas Tilling Fisons GKN International Computers British Oxygen Tarmac Glaxo Tunnel Cement

Table 4.9 Continued

Insurance Co	Banks	Other Service Industry Firms	Public Sector Corporations and Organisations	Leading Manufacturing Firms
Scottish Widdows	Bank of Scotland Royal Bank of Scotland	Save and Prosper Group Jardine Matheson (Hong Kong)		Scottish & Newcastle Breweries Burmah Oil London Tin Corporation
Standard Life	Bank of Scotland Bank of Montreal Kleinwort Benson National & Commercial Banking Group Clydesdale Bank	Canadian Pacific Railway Owen Owen		Ronson Products
Scottish Provident	Royal Bank of Scotland Barclays Bank Bank of Scotland			Burmah Oil Weir Group William Baird & Co
Scottish Amicable	Clydesdale Bank			
Refuge	National Westminster (Regional Board)			
Brittanic Assurance				
Royal London Mutual		Percy Bilton		
Pearl Assurance		Provident Financial Group		

Sources: Annual Reports, Directory of Directors

The practice of widespread cross directorships, however, was far from universal. Many of the mutual insurance firms had few board linkages with other major firms and a number of the large proprietary groups, such as the Prudential, also had relatively few. It was noticeable, that in particular those companies with headquarters located away from the City, such as General Accident, Norwich Union and the Scottish mutual companies, had very few boardroom connections with other companies, reinforcing the importance of a City location in the establishment of a closely knit managerial elite.

Conclusions

The insurance companies have been subject to only gradual change. Competition from within the industry and without has led to most of the change that has taken place. Cartels have tended to be broken in general insurance, where there has also been a marked increase in concentration in favour of the large composite groups. In the life market, concentration has actually been reduced, due in part to increased competition fron new entrants to the market such as the merchant banks, and also to a changing pattern away from industrial life policies, which has adversely affected some market leaders. Competition has also led to limited rationalisation in the industry by a series of acquisitions which began toward the end of the 1950s. Nevertheless, lack of information by purchasers has resulted in a high level of imperfection in the insurance market, thus allowing relatively poor performers to maintain their position. However, the overall financial performance of the major insurance companies whether in terms of investment returns, expense ratio, or market share of the savings market has been poor to modest.

There has been a slow trend toward increased diversification, both into new areas of insurance and, more recently, into property and other financial service activities. In addition, overseas diversification has increased, principally in the non life markets. These moves have resulted in turn, in structural change in a direction away from a functional structure and toward a form of multi-divisional organisation. Two forms of the latter were experienced, primarily among the proprietary composite groups, based upon insurance type and/or geography. These structures, which have become increasingly profit centre based, suffer however, from measurement difficulties brought about by the critical function nature of investment management.

5. Strategies for the End of an Empire

The post war period has seen the almost total dissolution of one of the greatest colonial empires ever created. While the dominance of Britain has been in decline since the beginning of the present century it was not until the end of the second world war that local nationalist pressures led to the transfer of power from the Empire's colonial rulers. Even among those territories largely settled by the British such as Australia, New Zealand, Canada and South Africa, the post war period has brought a weakening of traditional ties and the growth of independence and nationhood.

The decline of the British Empire has brought profound change to a significant group of companies whose very existence was largely a result of the growth of the Empire. These were the concerns which thrived on trading both with and within particular countries or world regions. They were the plantation and agricultural produce managers of the Empire, and had usually developed from family concerns created by early pioneers who had carved out a personal empire, from what had previously been a wilderness. Most were also involved with the development of the City of London, where they had concentrated on the purchase and distribution of specific commodities drawn from the colonies, while others had developed by providing the essential merchant fleet and other key services required for international trade.

With but one exception, all these companies had a history dating back at least to the nineteenth century. Most had strong connections with a particular family or group of families, and all were predominantly located outside of the United Kingdom at the beginning of the post war period. Moreover, many of the companies were dominant in the respective territories in which they operated, so finding themselves prime targets for nationalisation or at least severe restriction upon the transfer from colonial rule. Their managements were composed mainly of family members and long serving executives, schooled in the traditional territory of the Empire where there was little competition in their specific markets. In many ways therefore, this group of companies was particularly ill prepared to adjust to a new world where imperial power was no longer dominant, where local governments might well be hostile and where competition in world markets was the norm.

There were 13 companies in the sample which could be grouped as colonial based concerns and these are shown in table 5.1. These were the survivors which have evolved a strategy enabling them to sustain the change brought about by decolonisation. Many other colonial companies had not survived, often being absorbed by one of the survivors. There were also a few other successful adaptors which, due usually to the circumstance of finding themselves in an economic environment more attractive than the UK, moved their central offices to the scene of operations. Such firms include the trading house of Jardine Mathieson and the Hong Kong and Shanghai Banking Corporation, both of which had located in the Crown Colony of Hong Kong. The companies themselves divide into four basic groups namely, the overseas trading companies, the UK commodity traders, the shipping concerns and the British overseas banks. Some of the companies had become involved with more than one of these activities and a few were engaged in all these areas. More usually, however, one activity had expanded disproportionately to the rest, as in the case of C. T. Bowring, so as to alter the balanced nature of the company toward a strategy of specialisation.

THE OVERSEAS TRADING COMPANIES

The major overseas trading companies were mostly created in the late nineteenth century, initially often concentrating on a specific territory and/or agricultural commodity. Thus Booker McConnell dates back to the early nineteenth century when Josias Booker, having been connected with a firm of Liverpool sugar merchants, set off to seek his fortune in the colony of 'Demerary', as Guyana was then known. He later acquired sugar estates and formed the firm of George Booker and Company, which in 1900 merged with John McConnell and Co. Likewise Inchcape was founded by an expatriate Scot, later to become the first Lord Inchcape, who started as a clerk in the offices of Mackinnon Mackenzie and Company in India, rising to become its chairman, from which base the Inchape family interests eventually emerged. Similarly, Dalgety was founded on the wool trade with Australasia, Harrisons and Crossfield on rubber from Malaysia and Borneo, and Mitchell Cotts on pyrethrum and other commodities from Southern and East Africa. Often from an initial trading base such companies have become involved in a diversified, yet related, chain of activities required to service this trade. Thus commonly it has been a practice to integrate forward into agricultural estate management, into retailing and merchandising to supply the needs of the agricultural estates, into ship broking to deal with commodity and goods transportation between the colony and the UK, occasionally into ship owning, into shipping insurance and broking which then leads to more general insurance activities, and into finance and commodity trading.

Table 5.1   The Empire Traders, 1974

Company	Principal Activities	Group Assets (£m)	Turnover (£m)	No. of employees (worldwide) UK only
Booker McConnell	Food wholesaling and retailing, food manufacturers, overseas retailing, agricultural production, alcohol production, shipping, engineering, artists' services. Overseas activities in Guyana, West Indies, East Africa.	145	285	(34,200) 11,238
Mitchell Cotts	Construction & civil engineering, mechanical engineering, engineering distribution, agricultural estate operations, shipping and forwarding, road transport, vehicle distribution, and commodity trading. Overseas activities in Southern Africa, East Africa, Australia, Latin America and Canada.	55	213	(11,700) 1,730
Inchcape	Import-export merchants, commodity broking, travel agents, insurance broking, motor vehicle distribution, general merchants, construction, timber and builders merchants, shipping, port operators. Activities in many countries in Europe, the Arabian Gulf, East Indies, Australia, US, Caribbean and elsewhere in the Pacific Basin.	123	534	(25,759) 5,935
Dalgety	Pastoral trading, wool broking, commodity trading, wholesaling & retailing, shipping & travel agents, insurance agents, wharf operations, food & medical manufacturers, livestock & land agents. Overseas activities principally in Australia, New Zealand, Canada and the USA.	160	470	(n.a.) 4,674
Lonrho	Mining, sugar & tea plantations, textiles, wines, shipping, motor vehicle distribution, finance & general trading. Overseas activities principally in Africa & Sri Lanka.	202	321	(n.a.) 3,000

Table 5.1 Continued

Company	Principal Activities	Group Assets (£m)	Turnover (£m)	No. of employees (worldwide) UK only
Harrisons & Crossfield	General merchants, importers & exporters, insurance brokers, shipping, industrial & timber agents, manufacturers & processors of industrial raw materials, chemicals & rubber & engineering products. Overseas activities principally in Australia, New Zealand, Papua New Guinea, Canada, Hong Kong, Malaysia & Singapore.	45	342	(n.a.) 4,712
S & W Berisford	Sugar traders & packers, manufacturing, food packaging & distributors, commodity traders, meat trading, finance, and insurance.	27	533	(2,800) 2,265
Gill & Duffus Group	Commodity traders, manufacturers of cocoa products, insurance broking. Overseas commodity trading in many countries.	16	376	(n.a.) 788
Peninsular & Oriental Navigation	Passenger & cargo shipping, air transport, wharves, road transport, construction, property development. Overseas operations principally in Australia, New Zealand, the Pacific Basin & Western Europe.	636	487	(n.a.) 21,594
Ocean Transport & Trading	Passenger & cargo shipping, shipping services, fuel distribution.	373	285	(n.a.) (12,975)
British & Commonwealth Shipping Company	Passenger & cargo shipping, air transport, insurance, hotels, investment holdings.	175	148	(n.a.) (7,688)
Standard & Chartered Banking Group	Operates 1450 banking branches around the world but concentrated in South and South West Africa, Ghana, Nigeria & the Pacific Basin, banking & financial services in the UK & some limited manufacturing, bullion dealing.	268	1191[1]	(n.a.) 1,898

Table 5.1 Continued

Company	Principal Activities	Group Assets (£m)	Turnover (£m)	No. of employees (worldwide) UK only
National & Grindlays Holdings	Majority shareholder of Grindlays Bank, operates banking & financial services around the world but especially in the Indian sub continent & East Africa, and the Middle East. Some limited industrial hire purchase, insurance, light engineering & manufacturing.	70	73[1]	(n.a.) 2,705

Note: [1]non banking turnover only. There is no suitable turnover measure for banking activities.

Source: Annual Reports.

The lynchpin of this traditional strategy remained the trade base of a particular commodity or territory and often both. Decolonisation therefore threatened a firm's control over this critical ingredient in its strategy and as this threat developed, so strategic change necessarily took place. Two broad policies emerged commonly among the trading companies, with some pursuing both concurrently. Firstly, there was an effort to diversify by product into other commodities, or by developing one or more of the steps in the existing chain of activities, such as retailing or insurance broking. Secondly, there was a move to diversify into territories which appeared to offer less political risk, although these too, were often developing countries. Most notably, however, there was a tendency for these firms to withdraw their assets and regroup them in the United Kingdom by acquiring interests there. This latter trend was heightened by changes in the system of UK taxation, which tended to penalise overseas earnings which were unmatched with an adequate UK earnings base.

The strategic development of Booker McConnell[1] illustrates these trends. The company's founder, Josias Booker, focussed his trading activities on the colony of British Guiana (later Guyana), and became involved in sugar growing after purchasing the sugar business of the Liverpool merchant with which he had earlier been associated. In 1900 the firm merged with John McConnell and Company, a similar company also developed by its founder in Guyana. Then in 1939, Booker Bros. McConnell merged with Curtis Campbell, which had been engaged in the sugar trade between Guyana and London since the end of the eighteenth century. Growth brought the need to develop shipping capacity and the company added its own shipping line. Rum production also followed as a natural vertical integration from sugar production, while the company's original trading activities expanded into retailing and wholesaling interests, operating a variety of general and specialised outlets, largely in Guyana and East Africa. In addition Bookers developed local printing and drug manufacturing interests and operated wharf and lighterage facilities in Guyana. In 1927 the company went public and by the second world war was the dominant enterprise in the Guyanan economy, so much so that the colony was sometimes referred to as Booker's Guiana rather than British Guiana. The main links in the integrated chain of Booker McConnell's activities are illustrated in figure 5.1.

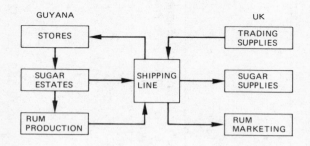

Figure 5.1   Booker McConnell Integrated Trading Strategy

In 1952, Jock Campbell (later Lord Campbell of Eskan) succeeded to the chairmanship of the company. Campbell's attitudes were in many ways in advance of the time and largely by his efforts and inspiration the company was able to undertake an orderly shift in strategy, while still maintaining a respected and politically acceptable position in Guyana. Campbell pursued an enlightened policy of cooperating with, actively developing, and taking a serious interest in the people of Guyana. The company aided the construction of good housing, trained local technicians and managers, and took an active part in developing local skills and resources. At the same time Campbell gradually with drew from Guyana and dispersed the company's assets in less sensitive political areas.

This change is illustrated in figure 5.2 which shows the percentage of Booker's capital employed by product area and by geography over the period 1950–73. In 1950 the company was heavily dependent upon its sugar operations in Guyana. By 1966 the year Lord Campbell gave up the chairmanship, investments in Guyana had been reduced as a percentage of the total from 60 per cent to 48.6 per cent, while dependence on sugar had been reduced even further from 41 per cent to 27.8 per cent. This change took place largely by a process of acquisition. Bookers first moved into engineering, initially by purchasing a leading UK based sugar machinery

1950	Sugar	Stores	Shipping	Rum	Other	% Capital Employed
UK	*					
British Guiana	*		*	*		26
Trinidad		*	*	*	*	60
Barbados		*				
Central Africa		*				14
% Capital Employed	41	27	13	9	10	£6m

1960	Tropical Agricultural (mainly sugar)	Retail & Wholesale	Shipping	Rum & Other Spirits	Engineering & Printing	Other	% Capital Employed
UK	*	*	*	*	*	*	35.8
Guyana	*	*	*	*	*	*	48.6
Jamaica	*			*			
Trinidad		*		*	*		
Barbados				*	*		
Central Africa	*	*			*		6.8
Other	*				*		7.8
							1.0
% Capital Employed	27.8	30.6	8.1	16.3	12.0	5.2	£36m

Figure 5.2 Strategic Evolution of Booker McConnell

1973	Tropical Agriculture (mainly sugar)	UK Food Dist.	Overseas Shop-keeping & Mnftg.	Rum & Spirits	Shipping	Engineering	Other	% Capital Employed
UK	*	*	*			*		52.4
Guyana	*		*	*	*		*	33.8
Other Caribbean	*		*	*	*		*	6.3
Africa	*	*	*	*		*		6.8
Other								0.7
% Capital Employed	24.0	20.6	17.7	9.0	5.6	14.9	0.8	£83m

Figure 5.2 continued

Source: Annual Reports

producer, and later extended into other engineering products. The
company extended its liquor operations by purchasing the manufacturers
of the Jamaican liqueur, Tia Maria. Retailing was developed by
acquisitions elsewhere in the Caribbean and most importantly in the UK.
In Canada, the company bought into automobile component wholesale
distribution while in the UK, the group's shipping interests were extended
by the purchase of coastal shipping operations.

Not all these moves were successful, some such as the Canadian
wholesaling venture were clear failures. In large measure this was due to
the company's lack of management skills outside of traditional, colonial
trading operations. Nevertheless, Campbell went some way toward the
introduction of a partial divisional system in 1952. This move served to
ultimately provide some opportunities for management development, but
in large measure leadership subsequently came from outside after
Campbell retired. After 1966, and in keeping with the accelerating pace of
political events in Guyana, Bookers continued to pursue the strategy
evolved by Campbell. In particular, the company concentrated on the
development of food retailing in the UK. Structurally, Bookers moved
gradually to a full divisional organisation which also brought an increasing
trend toward financial performance objectives.

Mitchell Cotts[2], originally established in 1895, specialised in agricultural activities over a wider area than Booker McConnell, concentrating in
the main on Southern and Eastern Africa. While the company was
strongly represented in the British colonial territories, its sphere of
influence widened to include Ethiopia, the French territory of the Afars
and Issas and Mozambique, in a belt of territory stretching from the Red
Sea to the Cape of Good Hope. In addition Mitchell Cotts operated a
variety of agricultural interests, specialising in cotton, tea, coffee grains,
dairy farming, ranching and pyrethrum.

Like Bookers, Mitchell Cotts developed merchanting and broking
interests for the commodities produced, especially tea and other food
products, and interests in shipping, warehousing, travel agency operations
and insurance. The company had been less involved in retailing, but in
South Africa expanded into civil engineering and construction and a
variety of mechanical engineering products including industrial switch-
gear, pumps, mining equipment, vehicle components, and boilers and
pressure vessels. The company had also become involved in the specialised
distribution of mining and metallurgical equipment in South Africa,
together with a range of engineering products.

A number of Mitchell Cotts' traditional interests had been nationalised
and it was forced to withdraw from a number of African markets. Like
Bookers, as the threat of local nationalisation or intervention grew,
Mitchell Cotts moved to expand its interests in more politically stable
areas. Investments in the UK were increased and, by acquisition, the
company developed substantial interests in road transport, engineering

and automobile distribution. Similarly, activities in Canada, South Africa, Australia and to a lesser extent the USA were increased, by comparison with the position in the non-white governed former colonies.

Dalgety[3], although not faced with the same degree of political risk, had also found it necessary to reduce its dependence upon its traditional business and had largely achieved this by a similar process of differential product and geographic diversification. Similarly created toward the end of the nineteenth century, Dalgety was originally concerned with the provision of services to farmers and pastoralists in Australia and later, New Zealand. Dalgety supplied their equipment and seed, ran retail stores, sold the farm produce, especially wool, where the company became the primary auctioneers, and arranged for the shipping and finance of crops pending sale. The company was also a major agent for freight and passenger traffic between the UK and Australasia and operated a number of local agency activities.

The company began to adjust its traditional strategy in the 1960s, largely by a process of acquisition. In 1961 the company merged with a similar business, the New Zealand Loan and Merchantile Agency Company, and in 1966 acquired the San Francisco based wholesale lumber merchants and commodity traders, Balfour Guthrie. In addition to integrating forward into the direct ownership and operation of farming in Australia, Dalgety acquired agricultural production facilities in Britain in livestock, eggs and animal feedstocks. Further moves into manufacturing in the 1970s, especially in Britain, added the production of agricultural and industrial chemicals and electrical appliances, and malt and fine chemicals. The company also expanded its lumber operations in North America.

Rubber was the foundation upon which Harrisons and Crossfield developed. Centred upon Malaysia, the company extended its activities throughout the Pacific Basin, sometimes by acquisition of other agency businesses but also by opening other branches. In addition, operations were established in Australia, India and the Western Hemisphere. The company did not however, develop the chain of vertical activities commonly found in other colonial traders. Harrisons and Crossfield thus concentrated its activities on plantation agencies and trading in the rubber growing areas of the Pacific Basin. Some integration into processed rubber products took place in the UK and this was later extended to other areas of industrial chemical production and distribution in both Britain and elsewhere. Some diversification into timber and tea trading also took place and in the post war period the trend toward diversification has increased together with a greater concentration of assets in the UK and other developed economies.

Inchcape and Company[4] was founded upon trade with India. The Mackay family built up a wide range of interests in the subcontinent and in London both by developing internally and by acquisition. The many companies and interests accumulated were mainly operated under a group of three holding companies which in 1958 were consolidated into a new public company, Inchcape, in order to reduce the risks from death duties. The first of the three holding company subsidiaries, Gray Dawes and Company, was based in London and had developed activities in insurance broking, ship management and as travel agents. In addition, the company operated a small merchant bank and was responsible for purchasing merchandise to be sold by its trading subsidiaries operating in East Africa, the Arabian Gulf and the Far East. One of the largest of these, Binney and Company (Madras) and its associates, was a major mercantile group in the Indian subcontinent, which had integrated back into textiles and metal castings. Other major subsidiaries were engaged in merchanting and shipping in East Africa and the Arabian Gulf. The group's second major subsidiary, Duncan MacNeill and Company, managed a larger group of tea companies in North Eastern India and also ran a major inland waterway fleet in India and Pakistan. The final direct subsidiary, St. Mary Axe Securities, acted as an investment trust, operating a portfolio of quoted securities.

After independence and mainly by acquisition, Inchcape diversified from India, which by 1974 accounted for only 2 per cent of net assets. The major move in this transformation took place in 1967 when the company merged with a similar colonial trading concern, the Borneo Company, which operated in the more attractive Pacific Basin countries. The Borneo Company also had important interests in automobile assembly and distribution which provided a growth activity for the future. Inchcape also expanded its activities in East Africa, by the purchase of Dalgety's operations in the area, and built upon its interests in the Arabian Gulf, as economic growth in the area accelerated.

The final concern classified as a colonial merchant company, Lonrho[5], has emerged with a uniquely different strategy. Unlike the other colonial traders, Lonrho is a very recent creation in its present form being generated from the shell of a small Rhodesia based mining company, by its present Chief Executive Mr. 'Tiny' Rowland. In 1961 when Rowland joined the Board, Lonrho was still a small concern, operating almost entirely within Rhodesia, although it had been formed in 1909.

At this time when decolonisation in Africa was proceeding, Rowland adopted a strategy contrary to that being practiced by other white owned companies and individuals. These concerns, fearful of the treatment they might expect from the new black governments of emerging African states, were anxious to sell up their assets and retreat to more politically stable countries. Rowland adopted the attitude that the new states would welcome western capital investment and during the early 1960s proved a willing buyer for many such colonial ventures. Moreover, these purchases were often made at a significant discount on net asset value and the newly purchased assets were used as collateral for debt finance for making further purchases. Rowland also employed many local black managers in his own organisation and established close political and economic linkages between Lonrho and the governments of the countries in which the company operated. After an initial strategy which saw the growth of Lonrho's mining activities in Rhodesia and South Africa, the company spread geographically after the declaration of UDI in Rhodesia. Initially it moved into the neighbouring territories of Zambia and Malawi, but later went north of the Zambesi to a variety of East, Central and West African states. In addition the company's product interests grew to incorporate a wide variety of activities including newspapers, sugar and tea plantations, ranching and a number of manufactured products.

In the early 1970s, Lonrho continued its policy of operating in decolonised countries but increasingly acted in partnership with local governments. The company did, however, increase its asset base in Europe, while asset investment in the developing countries was limited by undertaking management contracts on projects using local government funds, with Lonrho providing know how rather than placing its own funds at risk. Lonrho's strategy, therefore, used political connections as a key element, due largely to the personality of Mr. Rowland, a factor which enabled the company to adopt a strategy almost exactly contrary to that pursued by the traditional colonial trading concerns.

Historically the colonial trading companies have usually been administered as holding companies, although of late there was a tendency towards divisionalisation, as family influences diminished and new business activities superceded traditional ones. Mitchell Cotts, Harrisons and Crossfield, Lonrho and Inchcape still operated as holding companies, although the pattern at Lonrho was somewhat different, due to the personality of Mr. Rowland. Booker McConnell and Dalgety reorganised to a divisional form, although elements of the traditional structure tended to remain.

The trading companies were not wholly uncoordinated, however, and argued that a high level of local autonomy had to be granted, since considerable entrepreneurial skill was required within the specific trading environments in which the firm operated. In the early days of its existence, pressure for expansion and the pursuit of business opportunities would have been generated by the founding entrepreneur. As these men have given way to subsequent generations of family or to professional managers, this early stimulation was replaced by a search for opportunities by local general managers, supported by a small UK based, central office. Historically the need for strong local management willing to take advantage of opportunities in remote markets clearly sprang from a lack of adequate fast communication systems and the development of specialised products and services for local markets. Today with improved communications and the development of global products and services the need for high levels of local autonomy may well be reduced. However, the historical development of such autonomy may well make it difficult for the colonial merchants to achieve greater central control. Lonrho, interestingly, still worked largely with the entrepreneurial model, Rowland being the prime initiator of most of the group's major moves, so much so that a major board room split occurred in 1973, largely because many of the directors did not know much about the company's activities.

In Inchcape, family interest was still strong with the Mackay family and its descendants still holding a substantial equity interest in the group and also providing a significant number of the executive members of the board. Inchcape perhaps typifies the style of the overseas traders. Apart from the finance director, chairman and deputy chairman, each of the remaining executive directors looked after a number of specific regional or product groups, when these latter are deemed of sufficient importance to justify specific segmentation. The central directorate then provided the essential, and almost only control link, with the overseas operating companies. The only central service department was the accounts function, which conducted formal investment appraisals for the overseas operating companies, and also consolidated the group's financial position.

Management style was highly personalised, each of the executive directors reaching their ultimate central positions only after many years experience in the field, working with key overseas subsidiaries such as those in India and East Africa. Regular weekly meetings between the executive directors decided matters of policy, key projects, finance and discussed the major events taking place in the operating companies, in a way reminiscent of the partnership style of management still found in some of the merchant banks. All the overseas company directors had usually spent many years in the territories they administered, and were similarly inculcated into the personalised traditions and culture of the company.

So far the trading companies appeared to have managed to maintain this strong internal cohesion and loyalty even though in many countries they had been progressively forced to rely more on local nationals. To date, however, relatively few top overseas management positions had been given to locals and the continuation of this traditional pattern was expected to become increasingly difficult. Interestingly, Lonrho has increasingly employed black nationals in senior positions in many African countries. While this has been done, at least partially for political patronage reasons, the company has also extended this policy to include the appointment of black executives to senior central office positions in the United Kingdom. Again, therefore, Lonrho was different from the norm, but in this case could well be setting a pattern which others will need to follow if they wish to maintain their positions in the developing countries.

Booker and Dalgety have both moved to a divisional form of organisation. In the case of Booker, the transition was gradual and was initiated shortly after Lord Campbell became chairman in the early 1950s. The holding company structure gradually gave way to a divisional system as central office controls increased and the 'family' culture of the old colonial trading house gave way to a professional management orientation as the company diversified and the historic interdependencies between activities became diluted.

The different strategies adopted by the two companies are reflected in the form of divisional structure each adopted, as shown in figure 5.3.

1. **BOOKER McCONNELL PRODUCT DIVISIONAL STRUCTURE**

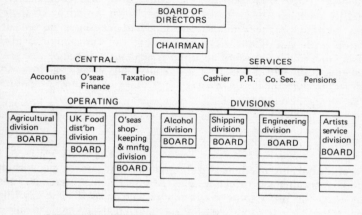

OPERATING COMPANIES UK & OVERSEAS

2. **DALGETY GEOGRAPHIC DIVISIONAL STRUCTURE**

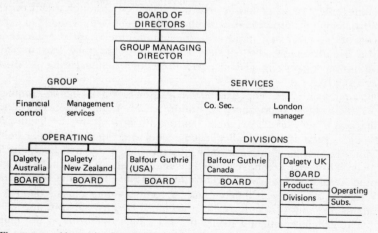

Figure 5.3   Alternative International Trading Company Divisional Structures[1]

[1]These diagrams illustrate only the main features of the organisations concerned
Source: Company Reports

Bookers strategy was built upon its traditional skills, but with each being developed in an independent manner, so reducing the interrelationships between operations. In addition, the company had aimed to progressively reduce its dependence upon the former colony in which it principally operated, with assets being concentrated in the UK. As a result Booker has largely become a UK based conglomerate and the divisional structure used was predominantly focussed on product lines. By contrast Dalgety had not withdrawn from Australasia, although it has progressively increased its asset base in both the UK and North America. In these countries, the activities the company has added had not only no significant relationship with traditional areas of activity, but the activities also differed in each major region. The Dalgety structure therefore was one based on geography with a series of regional divisions being created, each of which was responsible for the management of the operating companies within its sphere of influence.

THE COMMODITY TRADERS

In terms of capital employed the two companies in the sample specialising in commodity trading were much smaller than the colonial merchants but in many ways the two groups of companies were similar. The key difference was that the commodity traders have stayed closely to the dealing side of the agricultural commodities in which they traded, thus Gill and Duffus specialised in cocoa, while S and W Berisford had expanded from a base in sugar trading. These concerns had not expanded into plantation management or other labour intensive activities, although their businesses were heavily international, with the bulk of profitability being generated outside the UK. By comparison, the colonial merchant companies were also usually commodity dealers and traders, but they had significant additional assets engaged in agricultural or manufacturing production and the like.

London and New York are the two leading world centres for commodity trading in natural products. In London, trading takes place in two main markets, the Corn Exchange, dealing in agricultural or "soft" commodities such as sugar, coffee, cocoa, wool and the like, and the London Metal Exchange, dealing in major metals such as copper, lead, zinc and silver. These markets have existed for many years and originated from the time when London was the centre for auctions of physical commodities. While such auctions still take place for some commodities such as tea and furs, in the main these have been replaced by forward trading.

The development of a future market allows operators in the market, such as manufacturers and traders, to hedge against losses incurred as a result of falling prices for a commodity in which stocks are held. Hedging is achieved by either buying or selling a quantity of the commodity for delivery at a future date. Actual physical delivery of the commodity to a buyer is, however, rare since the future market caters primarily as an insurance mechanism against price changes. As a result therefore, the original deals are usually "closed out" by a reverse transaction in the opposite direction. Trading in physical commodities does actually take place, but mainly from the offices of merchants and brokers when ultimate uncleared future contracts mature at a specific date and price.

Gill and Duffus[6], (G & D), was founded in 1907 by F. G. Gill and A. S. Duffus as a private partnership to operate as general produce merchants, mainly in nuts and oils. The company began dealing in cocoa in 1927. It expanded rapidly and in 1949 the company went public. After the second world war G & D integrated backward into the production of cocoa products. In the UK a joint venture was formed with British Cocoa Mills, (BCM), while overseas processing facilities were established in Brazil and Ghana. This latter plant was the largest in Africa while Ghana itself has traditionally been the key world production centre for cocoa.

The company acquired BCM in 1951 and expanded its dealing operations to the Toronto and New York exchanges. In 1962, G & D diversified via the acquisition of Plantation and Colonial Products (Pacol), a private company trading in cocoa, rubber, spices and coffee from London, Paris and Toronto, while a separate subsidiary was established in Ghana. In 1967 the private partnership of Landauer and Company was acquired, which increased G & D's market share in a number of 'soft' markets and, via a subsidiary, took the company into the processing and packing of fruit. G & D also entered the insurance market with the purchase of Lloyds brokers, Leonard Puckle and Company.

In the later 1960s and early 1970s, expansion continued, principally by increasing overseas coverage. In 1968 the New York based Brazilian cocoa traders, Truebner and Company were purchased, while in 1970, Pacol opened two new subsidiaries to operate in the Pacific Basin. Pacol also gained membership of the London Sugar exchange in 1972, while G & D followed shortly thereafter and the first diversification into hard commodities came with the purchase of London metal traders, Vavasseur Kirk, members of the London Metal Exchange. New soft trading activities were established in Germany while in 1973 the Parisian metal dealers, Rene Wiel, were acquired, a move which also gave G & D representation in Geneva. Finally, in 1974 G & D formed a joint venture with international merchant and commodity traders Jardine Matheson, to launch a new Hong Kong based company to cover the two groups' previous interests throughout the Pacific Basin. The strategy of G & D has therefore been one of product diversification into other areas of commodity trading but not outside this activity and of geographic expansion to each of the world's main commodity market centres. Despite these changes the organisation of G & D has remained that of a holding company, each of the main trading units acting largely independently of the others. The holding

company board comprised former managing directors of the main
subsidiaries while the group deputy chairman, a member of the Gill
family, was also chief executive of G & D Limited, the group's main
trading company.

S. & W. Berisford[7] has roots dating back to 1850 and was incorporated in
1910. The company was managed by members of the Berisford family until
the beginning of the 1970s, when they were superceded by executives
largely drawn from companies acquired during the 1960s. Berisford had
traditionally specialised in sugar importing and merchanting, and were
responsible for handling nearly 50 per cent of the UK physical sugar
market from refiners to industry and retailers. In addition, largely by a
number of significant acquisitions, the company had diversified its
commodity interests in the UK, Continental Europe and North America
to include cocoa, coffee and other soft markets, together with some metal
trading. Unlike G & D, Berisford had also developed substantial interests
in food processing, being a major processor, packer and distributor of
canned foods, especially meat and fish, as well as being involved in a
number of smaller food product areas.

Berisford, more diversified than G & D and with a substantial turnover
generated outside the UK, had changed its structure from that of a holding
company to a divisional system. In the main, non-commodity trading
interests were concentrated in the UK and the divisional structure had
thus been organised by product line. Beneath each product division level,
remnants of the former holding company structure prevailed, each
division being made up of a series of subsidiary operating companies,
although in a number of cases overlapping activities had been rationalised
and consolidated.

Strategically the commodity traders have not been subject to the same
political pressures as the colonial merchants. The need for change has
come more from a desire to participate in new commodity markets both for
products and geographically. The businesses have been able to remain
small in terms of capital investment needed, and hence perhaps have also
been able to maintain family managements much later than some other
businesses. The greatest threat to the commodity traders probably comes
from outside acquirers who might perceive in them an attractive high cash
positive business opportunity. At present the business can, therefore,
remain personalised and pressure for a more formal administration system
to manage the individual subsidiaries seems relatively weak. This may not
always be so, however, as the market becomes increasingly mechanised
and less personalised the pressure for a more centralised, bureaucratic
organisation structure may well intensify.

THE COLONIAL SHIPPING LINES

The British merchant fleet was largely built upon the trade routes to the
Empire. Close links were therefore often established with the colonial
trading companies in a particular area such as those between Inchcape
and P & O (The Peninsular and Oriental Steam Navigation Company)[8].
The first Lord Inchcape, James Mackay, started as a clerk in Mackinnon
Mackenzie and Company, which formed the British India Steam
Navigation Company as an adjunct to its trading activities. In 1911, by
which time Mackay was Chairman of Mackinnon Mackenzie, he merged
the company with P & O and became Chairman of the joint organisation.
The Indian company remained as managing agents for British India until
1956 when that company, too, was acquired by P & O. It was then a long
established tradition that P & O's Chairman should be reared in the offices
of Mackinnon Mackenzie. Moreover, the present Lord Inchcape has been
a director of P & O since 1951 and played a major role in the dramatic
transformation of the company in 1971.

P & O was established in 1840 by Royal Charter, being granted the
right to trade with the Indian sub continent, and further charters were
granted to the company through to 1966. At the height of the Empire, P &
O was one of the world's major shipping lines in its own right, but in
addition over the years, it also acquired other shipping companies. Thus
by the early 1950s, P & O consisted of a group of cargo liner fleets and one
major passenger line, the Peninsular and Oriental Company itself. In the
early post war period therefore, the strategic problem for P & O, as for
other shipping companies, was the rebuilding of its fleets which had been
largely destroyed by wartime actions.

During the 1950s adequate finance was available since the worldwide
shortage of shipping and the growth of world trade meant that the
shipowning companies enjoyed a good rate of return. Further, market
rates were largely stabilised by shipping 'conferences' which established
the freight rates prevailing in members' ships in areas and on routes
covered by particular conferences.

By the late 1950s, however, competition was increasing. In particular a
number of governments began to establish their own national shipping
lines and to join the shipping conferences. Unlike the traditional European
shipping companies, however, the objective of the newcomers was less to
provide a high quality service and more to gain a share of the market, and
so make a contribution to their balance of payments. As a result, the
newcomers applied pressure to keep rates down, while at the same time
lowering shipping load factors. Moreover the shipping companies were
slow to observe the changing market trends toward the growing need for
specialised vessels such as oil tankers. P & O for example, did not order its
first tanker until the mid 1950s.

As a result P & O was particularly hit by the changing market for shipping. Its business had largely been built upon cargo liners which called regularly at certain ports and its heavy investment in ships made this pattern difficult to change. Further, its major involvement with the relatively unattractive trade to India and other developing countries in the Pacific Basin also helped to reduce returns, while trade with Australasia came under severe competition from Italian shipping lines and the increased use of air transport. By the early 1960s P & O's financial performance was abysmal and so it remained throughout the rest of the decade.

The company did, however, gradually see the need for change. During the 1960s the company's liner fleet was largely converted to cruising or rundown, the tanker fleet was built up and a new group of bulk carriers developed. In conjunction with Ocean Steam Ship, British and Commonwealth Shipping and Furness Withy, P & O also moved into containerisation with the formation of a joint venture, Overseas Containers Limited. Nevertheless, apart from improved central financial control, the company remained largely a series of almost independent fleets centred upon the companies originally consolidated by the first Lord Inchcape.

In 1968 the shipping world was shaken by the dramatic take over by Trafalgar House Investments of the Cunard Steamship Company, the doyen of the British merchant fleet. This purchase gave Trafalgar House access to Cunards' valuable unused tax losses and to its accumulated depreciation allowances, which were especially valuable to a company with property assets. Following this takeover, other shipping companies became aware of their vulnerability and P & O was no exception. Its poor financial performance was reflected in a low market capitalisation and in 1972 the anticipated bid was forthcoming. The bidder, Bovis, was a building, construction and property developing concern which had also diversified into secondary banking. It was led by an aggressive entrepreneur who had expanded the company rapidly by acquisition.

The Board of P & O were divided on the terms offered by Bovis. While the P & O Chairman and a group of directors were in favour of the bid, a rebel group believed that the shipping company, with its net assets of £1300m, would fall under the control of an upstart company with agressive management but assets of only £20 million and the bid terms therefore did not reflect at all, the true value of P & O. The boardroom rebels were backed by Lord Inchcape who commanded a substantial element of City support, apart from his historic position as chairman of Inchcape. The dissidents therefore favoured the rejection of the Bovis bid and recommended instead, implementation proposals for the P & O's strategic future, drawn up the previous year by McKinsey and Company. These plans called for a full reorganisation of the company and were supported by many of its key operating managers but they were not endorsed by the leading members of the P & O board. In the event the bid from Bovis was finally defeated, and as a result seven P & O directors, including the chairman, resigned. A new board was then constituted and Lord Inchcape was appointed as the company's new chairman.

After the bid battle, the McKinsey reorganisation was implemented and a divisional organisation structure introduced, as shown in figure 5.4. The new structure merged the 50 or so operating companies constituting P & O, into five operating divisions covering bulk shipping, general cargo, passenger, European and air transport and a catch all, general holding group. A further energy division was subsequently established to manage P & O's growing interests in oil and gas exploration and offshore servicing, especially in the North Sea. Ironically too, in 1974 the sharp recovery in P & O's performance following the reorganisation, led the company to bid for, and win, Bovis which had fallen into financial difficulties as a result of the collapse of its secondary banking activities.

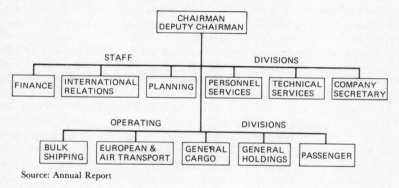

Source: Annual Report

Figure 5.4   Classical Product Divisional Structure of P & O, 1971

Ocean Transport and Trading[9] was formed by Alfred and Phillip Holt in the mid-nineteenth century as the Ocean Steam Ship Company, whose Blue Funnel line ran early steamships in the China trade. For almost a hundred years, to the mid-1960s, the company remained essentially a cargo liner operator from Liverpool to the Far East and Australia. Due to the simplicity of its activities the company was managed in a tightly centralised manner from its Liverpool headquarters, with, for example, the directors and department heads meeting each day at noon to check the movements of the fleet. In addition over the years Ocean's management acquired a reputation for self confidence and intellectual arrogance, key management recruitment being via a deliberately elitist system of carefully selecting bright graduates from Oxford and Cambridge, who were groomed for future senior positions.

In 1965, it was decided that to stave off possible competition on the UK-Australia trade, Ocean should seriously consider the adoption of containerisation. Rather than embark on such a venture alone, Ocean management made approaches to P & O, Furness Withy and British and Commonwealth in an effort to reach joint agreement. As a result the shipping companies agreed to the establishment of a new joint venture, Overseas Containers Limited, to provide a container service from Britain to Australia and the Far East.

Recognising that this move would make many of its traditional ships redundant, Ocean also set out to diversify. Firstly, it acquired Liner Holdings in which it had long held a 38 per cent stake. Liner Holdings was the parent company of the Elder Dempster Line, another major cargo liner company specialising in the trade between Britain and West Africa. During 1969–72, further moves were made to reduce dependence on the company's conventional trade. Ocean moved into bulk carriers, large crude carriers, offshore oil services in conjunction with Inchcape, and, via a joint venture with P & O, into oil and chemicals transport. Non marine ventures were commenced in air freight forwarding, container and trailer repair in the UK, leisure activities in the Caribbean, warehousing, road haulage, and property development in the Far East. Then in 1972, Ocean made its most significant move, with the acquisition of William Cory and Sons, a long established UK group involved in fuel distribution, and with interests in lighterage, towage and tugs.

The strategy to diversify the group had been largely the work of Sir Lindsay Alexander who became chairman in 1971. Following his appointment a major reorganisation was introduced with help from Boston Consulting Group. This resulted in increased decentralisation within a divisional structure where each division was responsible for the operation and planning of the business units under its control. The role of central management was redefined as being responsible for strategic planning, resource allocation, performance monitoring and management development. Under the new organisation the main day-to-day central responsibilities were vested in an executive committee of three, drawn from the members of the main board. The revised structure is illustrated in figure 5.5.

The final shipping company, British and Commonwealth[10], was still dominated by the Cayzer family. It was formed in 1955 to effect the merger between Clanline and Union Castle, both cargo liner companies mainly sailing between Southampton and South Africa. The Cayzer family had earlier placed most of their direct holding in an investment company, Caledonia Investments, which still held almost 50 per cent of British and Commonwealth.

Under the direction of Sir Nicholas Cayzer, the company had diversified sharply from its traditional shipping business. Diversification began before the purchase of Union Castle, with investments in aircraft dating back to 1951. Later a variety of other manufacturing and service industry ventures were added, including insurance broking, hotels, vehicle component

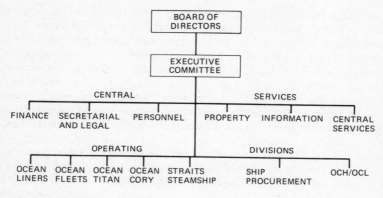

Source: *Financial Times*

Figure 5.5 Divisional Organisation of Ocean Transport and Trading, 1974

manufacture and the like. Moreover, the company's aircraft interests were ultimately built up to form British United Airways, which, in 1970, was sold to Caledonian Airways to form British Caledonian, the main British independent airline. Meanwhile British and Commonwealth retained its interests in helicopter services and a number of other small air transport activities. As a result of these strategic moves therefore British and Commonwealth had increasingly become an investment operation. The individual activities could be largely bought and sold according to their financial performance, and there was little or no central office involvement in the affairs of operating companies. Not surprisingly therefore, British and Commonwealth operated a holding company structure.

The shipping companies have been forced to undertake major strategic reappraisals as a result of the decline of the Empire. Former trade routes have substantially diminished in importance, and this, coupled with changing technology for handling both passengers and freight has led to fundamental change for the great shipping concerns. For the most part they have endeavoured to adapt their traditional business to changing circumstances. In addition, however, they have been forced to make defensive acquisitions in order to diversify and reduce their exposure to corporate raiders. Today, making use of their fiscal and asset base positions, the shipping companies that have survived are reemerging as at least partial conglomerates. One result of this move has been a sharp decline in family management and traditional operating methods in favour of a divisional form of organisation, and a portfolio approach to corporate strategy.

THE BRITISH OVERSEAS BANKS[11]

With the expansion of British business interests abroad, to finance trade between Britain and the Empire markets and to service the needs of local communities, a series of banking corporations grew up in many of the colonies. These banks usually specialised in servicing a particular area, operating a branch banking network similar to that of the domestic clearing banks. The post war trend to independence in the colonial territories tended to pose a particular threat to these British overseas banks, since control over the domestic banking system was usually a priority for emerging nation governments. In many cases, the interests of the banks were completely nationalised while in others major shareholdings were passed to local interests. In addition, the banks were usually required to rapidly increase the number of local nationals engaged in senior management positions. The banks also had difficulties in developing new business which was less vulnerable to political intervention, since their assets were largely located in the developing countries and these countries were relatively unimportant in terms of international trade. The problem was further compounded by the gradual decline of the Commonwealth as a trading entity, the dismemberment of the sterling area and the weakness of sterling itself, and the widespread introduction of exchange control barriers in the former scheduled territories.

Not surprisingly perhaps, many of the banks failed to survive these changes in their environment or alternatively dramatically changed their role. Barclays Bank DCO, Lloyds Bank (Europe) and the British Bank of London and South America were all acquired by the clearing banks with which they were associated. The main alternative strategy, and that adopted by both the overseas banks in the sample, was to diversify geographically in order to reduce exposure to political risk within any one particular territory. Thus in 1969, the Standard Bank merged with the Chartered Bank to form the Standard and Chartered Banking Group. This combined the former's extensive network of some 1200 branches, mainly concentrated in South and West Africa, with the Chartered Banks interests in the Indian subcontinent and the Pacific Basin which had been extended to the Middle East and Eastern Mediterranean by the acquisition of the Eastern Bank and the Cyprus branches of the Ionian Bank. Similarly, Grindlays Bank had been historically concentrated in the Indian subcontinent and had extended to Southern and East Africa.

These moves, however, had not proved sufficient to provide the banks with a viable future. Despite the large size of their overseas branch networks, the overseas banks had been largely engaged in domestic retail banking, rather than international wholesale and corporate banking. This latter activity had been the principal growth area in banking and was centred on the world's leading financial centres. Therefore from the mid-1960s the leading British overseas banks found it necessary to shift their centre of operations back to London, in order to gain access to the Eurocurrency markets. Thus, in 1965, control of Brandts, a family dominated merchant bank and member of the Accepting Houses Committee was acquired by National and Grindlays Bank. Similarly, Standard and Chartered had extended its Euromarket activities, diversified into metal trading and, by the purchase of the Julian Hodge financial group in 1974, extended into secondary banking, property finance, and certain areas of industrial manufacturing.

Despite these moves, however, the long term future of the overseas banks seemed limited. The two biggest were both largely owned by the British clearing banks, with the Midland holding a large share of Standard and Chartered, while Lloyds Bank held a 41 per cent share in National and Grindlays Holdings, the holding company which controlled Grindlays Bank. Structurally, the two major overseas banks had been managed as holding companies. There had been little real integration between the geographically centred branch networks, while new activities had been grafted on and left to run in a quasiautonomous fashion. This was somewhat surprising in that the major American commercial banks, Chase Manhattan and First National City Bank had held significant shareholdings in Standard and Chartered and Grindlays, respectively. These American concerns had developed closely coordinated structures to manage their international operations, but apparently, had not introduced these systems into their British associates.

Conclusions

The end of an Empire has brought dramatic change to those enterprises whose strategies for success were originally based upon the opportunities offered by the colonial territories. For many concerns in trading, shipping, and banking, the trend toward local nationalism, the loss of imperial power and the changing pattern of world trade has brought about their demise. Those that have survived and prevailed have diversified both by geography and by product. This has been achieved in virtually all cases by acquisition and this group of companies represents a good example of how strategies can be transformed by purchasing other companies.

In many cases the acquisitions made were of similar firms operating in related product or geographic markets, few were contested and, perhaps as a result, the normal structure adopted after such moves involved little change in terms of coordination, consolidation or rationalisation. These processes have often been introduced later as a part of a system of reorganisation, usually to a divisional form. In all cases where divisional systems were noted, their introduction followed an initial change of chairman. The holding company structures found among these firms however, were not wholly uncoordinated operations. There was, traditionally, a strong 'family' connection in the underlying companies making up groups such as these, management by familiarity being practiced. Thus extensive personal involvement by the main executive board members in the operations of key overseas subsidiaries was a normal prior requisite before appointment to the top management positions in the parent head office in Britain.

This group of companies was also strongly connected to other City based institutions, reflecting the merchant origin of both the financial and trading and shipping concerns. Family management remained a strong feature, although in most cases shareholding control had long been diluted. The original entrepreneurs, certainly in the case of trading companies, tended to be expatriate Scots and their success had often resulted in appointments to the peerage, so providing the foundation for a subsequent family dynasty. This assimilation by the aristocratic elite of the descendants of the founding entrepreneurs and the consequential close relationships with other City firms via directorships and the like, was in sharp contrast to the latter day entrepreneurs or even the retailing families, neither of which had developed such City connections.

6. The Rise of Property and Leisure[1]

Property development has been one of the most rapid growth industries in the post war period. The construction companies have been closely associated with property development, and in many cases have been active participants. Also closely associated with property development have been the retailing and leisure industries. The first of these has been dealt with more extensively elsewhere. The leisure industries however, have not only participated in property development via hotel building and the like but have also experienced dramatic growth in other areas as a result of rising consumer affluence. For leisure industry firms which were not initially involved in property such as Lex Service Industries and Ladbrokes, investment into hotels and other property has come later as a result of diversification. In these three industry segments property, construction and leisure, there were a total of 15 companies, details of which are shown in table 6.1

THE PROPERTY DEVELOPERS

The explosive growth of property

The explosive growth of the property development industry has been one of the most remarkable phenomena in post war British industry. It has been estimated that over 100 men and women have made personal fortunes exceeding a million pounds out of property.[2] Many of todays largest property companies were formed by individual entrepreneurs during the late 1940s and early 1950s and are still run by their founders. In 1957 the industry had so advanced that it was given its own section on the Stock Exchange.

Growth has not always been regular and sustained however. In particular the industry is noted for periodic politically inspired legal constraints, aimed at curbing high profits generated by speculation. Ironically these interventions have often had the opposite effect to that proposed and it has tended to be the avoidance of the expected results of legislation which has proved a key factor for success. The industry has also been seen as one of the few possible inflation hedges, although in the 1970s fiscal and legal harrying by socialist administrations, incensed at what

Table 6.1 *Property, construction and leisure industry Firms, 1974*

Company	Principal Activities	Turnover 1974 £m	Net Capital Employed 1974 £m	Avg. No. of UK Employees 1974
Hammerson Property * Investment Trust	Property development	22	212	137
Land Securities Trust *	Property development	52	1105	737
MEPC *	Property development	39	672	781
English Property *	Property development	52	707	404
London & Northern Securities	Building & contracting, building products manufacture, haulage, property dealing & development	150	57	12,486
Richard Costain	International building & construction, dredging, mining, concrete product manufacture, property development	193	59	7,067
Taylor Woodrow	International building and construction, open cast mining, property development	229	131	10,926
John Laing & Son	Building and construction, manufacturers of building materials, property development	246	61	45,000
George Wimpey	International building & construction, quarrying, oil industry servicing	358	142	26,000

Table 6.1 Continued

Company	Principal Activities	Turnover 1974 £m	Net Capital Employed 1974 £m	Avg. No. of UK Employees 1974
Trafalgar House Investments	Building & construction, building material manufacture, passenger & cargo shipping, oil rig servicing, hotels, property development	281	269	14,831
Wood Hall Trust	Building & construction, property development, materials handling, plant hire, general engineering, coal mining, wool trading, international trading	259	45	2,416
Ladbroke Group	Credit & cash betting, casinos, hotels, holiday centres, property development	255	58	12,236
Lex Service Industries	Automobile, commercial vehicle & plant distribution, hotels & travel, haulage, vehicle leasing, personnel services, freight handling	165	81	8,055
Grand Metropolitan	International hotels, entertainment & catering, processing & distribution of milk and milk products, production & sale of wines & spirits; brewing & beer distribution, betting & gambling	970	897	88,969
Trust Houses Forte	International hotel operator, industrial catering, confectionery manufacture, restaurants & catering, theatres, amusement parks, holiday centres and airport services	303	270	35,511

* Turnover is not strictly a relevant figure for a property company. The figures quoted for the pure property companies are of gross rental income which is indicative of their size.
Sources: Annual Reports

were perceived as immoral profits, has caused serious damage to many firms in the industry.

In large measure, the post war property entrepreneurs were either estate agents or solicitors who were, by the nature of their work, in an early position to observe opportunities especially in the rebuilding of office accommodation in post war London. After the war the incoming Labour administration introduced the Town and Country Planning Act, aimed at increasing government control over development. Planning permission was required for all new building and a 100 per cent tax was levied on the increased value of the property due to development. Any incentive to the developer, therefore rested on the discovery and exploitation of loopholes in the new law.

The penal 100 per cent betterment charge was abolished by the new Conservative government in 1953. The following year building licences were abandoned and land prices increased dramatically. Developers were now only constrained by the need to obtain planning permission or by the ability of their architects to discover loopholes. Probably the most important such loophole was contained in Schedule 3 of the 1947 Act which remained unamended until 1963. Under the Act the size of a building which could be erected on a site was governed by the 'plot ratio', – the ratio of the floor space of the building to the site area. Within the constraint of a plot ratio of say 4:1 an architect would be able to erect a four storey building covering all the site, or an eight storey building covering half the site and so on. The third schedule, however, allowed a building to be enlarged by up to 10 per cent of its cubic content in order to allow minor improvements to be made to existing buildings without payment of a development charge. Since buildings were thus rated on cubic capacity it was possible for a redevelopment to dramatically increase the floor area with lower ceilings and the like.

A number of architects specialised in placing the maximum amount of building on a plot and despite intense competition in the London office market, a large amount of the work was concentrated into 10 principal firms. From these, one in particular stood out, Richard Seifert and Partners. Seifert was exceptionally adroit at finding loopholes in the law so much so that the LCC town planners were on occasion forced to add new "Seifert Clauses" to the legislation in order to block the deficiencies exposed. Notwithstanding this legislative ability, Seifert was also an architect of some note and in later years produced a number of impressive buildings in London.[3]

The absence of a capital gains tax until 1965 was particularly significant in the property industry, due to rising property values. Not only could capital gains be made from the sale of property as values increased, but unrealised rising capital values went untaxed. The increased value of their portfolios provided the property companies with collateral for increasing their gearing thus providing the funds for further development. The different tax treatment of income and capital gains also led to the most visible abuse operated in the property industry – leaving office blocks deliberately empty. By not letting a property a rental income was not established and as rents in general increased so the potential rental from an empty block would also rise. Since the value of a property is directly related to the rental income achievable large potential capital gains could thus be generated, which upon realisation even after 1965, suffered a much lower tax rate than that on income. The sight of a substantial number of prestige office blocks deliberately left empty was a constant source of political pressure which led ultimately to punitive legislation being directed against the property sector.

After the second world war, therefore, the nature of the property industry changed sharply. Until this time rental income was the primary motive for investment. In the post war period development profits which came principally from increased capital values became the primary measure of success. It is, therefore, perhaps, not surprising to observe a different character between the prewar and post war concerns. Thus of the four pure property firms examined, only MEPC was a traditional concern. The remainder, Land Securities, English Properties and Hammerson have all been established since the war.

In 1944 Land Securities owned three houses, two of which were empty, when it was acquired by Harold Samuel (later Lord Samuel) an estate agent. In 1946 the company put up 50 per cent of the capital in Ravensfield, a company formed by Louis Freedman, and another estate agent, Fred Maynard. Following this move, the company's name changed to Ravenseft. In 1955 Land Securities acquired the balance of the Ravenseft shares and the three founders still operated the company in 1974. In the combined corporation the original companies each maintained a distinctive position. Land Securities specialised in the development of London office blocks while Ravenseft concentrated on working with local authorities in redeveloping the centres of major provincial cities and towns, destroyed by the war. Following the purchase of City and London Real Property in 1969, from its small beginnings Land Securities had built a property portfolio valued at over £1,300m by the early 1970s.[4]

English Properties was only formed in 1959 as Star (Greater London) Holdings, by Sion Potel and his son Robert, as a vehicle for the Potel family property portfolio. A public issue of 27 per cent of the shares was made in 1960 and the company was managed by Robert Potel until he resigned in 1971, following a disagreement with his board who wished to slow the company's rate of expansion. Hammerson emerged following the acquisition of a public investment dealing company, Associated City Investment Trust, by Lewis Hammerson. The company's name was changed to Hammerson Property and Investment Trust and its activity became concentrated on development. Hammerson died in 1958 and was replaced by Sydney Mason, a managing director since 1953.[5]

The process of property development

The essential characteristics of property development are relatively
simple. The developer adopts a classic middleman strategy orchestrating a
series of inputs in order to achieve the final result, as illustrated in figure
6.1. The essential raw material needed for development was sites which
were supplied by estate agents with whom the developers worked closely,
which explains why so many estate agents moved into development on
their own account. For the agents themselves there was often a conflict of
interest in that they could perceive the development value of a site, yet
were nominally expected to work for the seller.

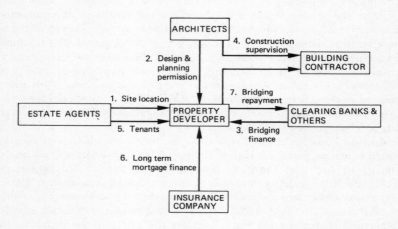

Figure 6.1   The Process of Property Development

After the estate agent came the architect. Few developers, certainly in
London, were concerned with the aesthetics of building. Rather the service
they required of their architects was to design functional buildings to a
certain price, usually the lowest possible, that the estimate should not be
exceeded at the end of the day, and that the architect should organise the
builders so that the development was finished on the specified date.[6]

After planning permission had been obtained by the architect, the
developer would organise finance and building. The role of the banker
might have begun earlier dependent upon whether the developer had
purchased the site or not. Nevertheless, a bank would thereafter be
expected to provide bridging finance, usually a clearing bank overdraft, to
cover site cost and the cost of construction. The main clearing banks were
keen to lend money to the developers because, throughout the 1960s,
property seemed a good investment and in an emergency the bank could
fall back on the security of a charge on the property.

Apart from the clearing banks a number of merchant banks provided bridging finance for the developers in the early years. The continued boom, however, led to the emergence of a new group of secondary bankers from the end of the 1960s. These concerns, borrowing mainly through the certificate of deposit market, grew rapidly by lending on to the developers. By 1974 it is estimated that over £6,000m of short term money was on loan from one source or another to the property market.[7] The serious dangers inherent in this policy only became clear when interest rates were forced up, so causing a collapse in the market which, in turn, proved disastrous to the secondary banking sector and even threatened the clearing banks themselves.

The other major source of interim financing was the building contractor. Traditionally many of the major contractors had always been close to speculative development, although before the war this was largely in residential developments. In this way Richard Costain and John Laing both became significant property owners, while others such as McAlpine's acquired the ownership of property through the default of their clients.[8] Seeing the substantial profits made by the developers, therefore, many contractors were prepared to provide interim finance in return for a share of the development profits. During the 1960s, Laing and Taylor Woodrow began to undertake major developments in their own right, while George Wimpey worked through a major shareholding in Oldham Estates, the property development company, led by Harry Hyams, which acquired an infamous reputation for leaving office blocks empty in order to maximise capital gains.

After completion the developments were let and again the estate agents played a significant role in finding and channelling suitable tenants. While industrial companies were the preferred tenants for prestige office blocks, ironically the largest and most voracious client was central government, referred to as the 'developers friend'.[9] Despite the potentially attractive savings that could have been made by the Government planning its space needs and undertaking its own development, it made extensive use of the commercial developers who on the other hand, it often roundly condemned for making obscene profits.

The final link in the development chain came with the mortgaging of the completed property to an insurance company at a fixed rate of interest, the developer placing a debenture with the insurance company and securing this on a particular completed and let property. A developer would often form links with one or more insurance companies such as those between Land Securities and Legal and General, or between Hammersons and Royal London Mutual and Standard Life. In return, the insurance companies might agree to provide large sums of money over a period of say, five years, and might expect a seat on the board of the property company.

The use of fixed interest financing was especially advantageous to the developers since they obtained the full benefit of increasing property values. Realising that they were not gaining a share of this benefit, from the end of the 1950s the insurance companies began to demand an equity stake in developers as part of the cost of finance. In addition, during the 1960s, the institutions began to tie the interest rates on their loans to the income a property was producing. Thus, for example, an institution might take the first part of the rental income at a fixed rate and divide the residue on an agreed percentage basis with the developer.

A further important financing variable emerged during the credit squeeze at the end of the 1950s. This was the sale and lease back method which involved the sale of a property to an insurance company and subsequent lease back to the developer on a long lease basis. This method was much riskier for the developer, since he could find himself paying more than he took in rent and he no longer had the important advantage of the increasing capital value of the property. In general, however, although the involvement of the insurance companies became progressively more direct, and in recent years a number had integrated forward to acquire development firms, during the boom period of the 1950s and 1960s they missed out on the dramatic gains made by the developers.

Domestic concentration and overseas expansion

The huge success of property development and the relatively simple nature of the management task meant that many developers had not attempted to diversify into other activities. There had however, been rationalisation within the industry, largely by increased concentration resulting from acquisitions. Three of the four large developers examined had grown substantially as a result of acquisition. Initially, most of these moves were small acquisitions, usually uncontested, and could be considered principally as moves to add to a property portfolio. From 1968 onwards however, a spate of large contested bids took place.

MEPC began to accelerate its growth from 1964 following the appointment of Sir Charles Hardie as chairman and in 1968 Metropolitan Railway Surplus Lands Company was purchased for £7m. The same year saw Land Securities purchase City Centre Properties, the property company created by Sir Charles Clore, who also built up Sears Holdings, and Jack Cotton the Birmingham developer. In December 1968, also came the bid battle for City of London Real Property between Land Securities, MEPC and Trafalgar House, which was finally won by the first of these with a bid of £161m.

Between July 1968 and March 1970 English Properties acquired six other property companies. The resulting strain of assimilating this growth led to the removal of Robert Potel, when the remainder of the Board supported a move by Eagle Star Insurance, a major shareholder, for a period of consolidation.

In 1970 MEPC acquired London County Freehold and, in July, made an agreed bid for Hill Samuel the merchant bank. By this deal it was claimed MEPC would obtain the bank's financial expertise and access to funds. This move, however, generated substantial opposition in the City and among key MEPC institutional investors. In addition, it triggered a counterbid for MEPC alone by Trafalgar House, in conjunction with Commercial Union Insurance. In the event neither bid succeeded and MEPC remained independent, but these proposed bids provide another example of the close interrelationships between the financial institutions.

In addition to domestic expansion the property developers turned their attention to prospects overseas. The first country chosen for penetration was Canada, with many firms commencing local operations in the 1950s. Some of these firms moved on from Canada to the United States, and a number of major developments were undertaken by British firms in leading US cities. During the late 1950s several companies began to expand in Australia, while in the mid-1960s British property firms embarked on an invasion of the leading financial centres of western Europe.

In property development the most successful route for overseas operations appeared to be via joint ventures or, at least, a close reliance upon local experts. Land Securities, for example, commenced operations in Canada in 1956 without such local help and was badly hit by the recession of 1959–61, eventually pulling out at a loss in 1962. Soured by this experience Land Securities subsequently pursued a policy of domestic activity only. MEPC in contrast began operations in Canada in 1954 with a board largely made up of local property experts. This approach allowed the company to weather the depression and by 1963 the Canadian investment return was as high as that in the UK. MEPC increased its overseas expansion entering Australia and East Africa, partially as a result of its UK acquisition programme and in 1971, with local finance moved into Europe, acquiring properties in Belgium and West Germany. Hammerson's first overseas venture was in Australia in 1959. Subsequently the company moved into the USA and Europe, in conjunction with local partners. English Properties was one of the earliest British developers to enter Europe when, in 1965, with local partners, it began office development in Brussels. Activities were later extended to other European cities and to Australia. The company's most important overseas activities, however, came via the acquisition of the British property company, Second Covent Garden. This purchase brought with it control of Trizec, the largest quoted Canadian property company, and in conjunction with Trizec, English Properties later entered the U.S. market.

The organisation of property companies

Most of the major property development firms were formed by individuals or small groups of entrepreneurs. Growth had usually increased the number of people employed, but in such concerns, by comparison with the assets managed, the numbers were extremely small. Indeed, some large property groups still consisted of a mere handful of people.

Structurally, therefore, these companies were quite uncomplicated. Most had developed simple functional systems with different departments dealing with the various functions of the business, while the board, often still dominated by the founder, coordinated activities. This type of structure is illustrated in Figure 6.2.

Source: Extracted from D. Booker, op. cit., p. 34

Figure 6.2   Typical Property Company Functional Structure

The specialised departments covered such activities as the acquisition of new developments prior to approval by the main board; a progress department for administering developments under construction; rent review and lease renewals; service and maintenance for completed developments; and departments concerned with the advertising promotion and letting of properties.

Those companies which operated in a variety of sectors or had diversified geographically usually operated on a slightly different principle, with individual subsidiaries operating as separate units to deal with different types of property or geographic areas. Thus, for example, in Land Securities, City of London Real Property dealt with all City and West End properties. The company's Ravenseft subsidiary dealt with all other properties, while the parent was responsible for raising finance and acquisitions, and for laying down guidelines for the two principal operating subsidiaries. These subsidiaries did not form true divisions, however, since all but Land Securities directors were also board members of City of London Real Property, while Freedman and Maynard continued to control Ravenseft. Each company did its own development planning and Land Securities had no objective screening procedure for fund allocation between the subsidiaries due to the board composition. Similarly English Properties also maintained its Second Covent Garden subsidiary separately in order to deal with town centre and shopping complex developments in the UK and Eire. MEPC operated a number of regional branches in the UK, but these were essentially for managing day to day operations rather than for decision making.[10]

International operations in contrast tended to be managed by local offices. MEPC had a number of regional offices in Canada and Australia and the Canadian subsidiary had a local board which contained a number of main board members. Hammersons had permanent offices in Australia, Canada and the USA while English Properties also operated locally in the USA. European developments were initially managed from London, but as these activities increased in scale local management offices tended to be established.[11]

Board structure varied considerably between the property companies with the entrepreneurial firms tending to have small boards. As entrepreneurs had given way to managers, however, so board size tended to increase. Thus the Hammerson Board had increased from four to eleven with non-executives such as a retired banker and an insurance company chairman joining executives promoted from within. The MEPC Board had expanded from five to fourteen since 1950, due to both internal promotions and positions being offered to senior members of acquired companies. A number of non-executives had also been appointed from banking, insurance, estate agents and the like.[12]

THE CONSTRUCTION CORPORATIONS

Although closely related to property development, the construction companies were substantially more complex and the major firms involved had all pursued the common strategy of diversification and expansion overseas. The diversification moves had usually been by forward integration into property development and backward into the production and building materials and components.

Despite the impressive size of the major companies, the building and construction industry was both highly fragmented and highly competitive as indicated in table 6.2. There was also a high level of risk associated with the industry (which had the highest bankruptcy rate) to which even large companies were not immune. While weather was a large contributor to the risks faced by the industry, the most important difficulties experienced in the post war period had been caused by government which had used the industry as an economic regulator, dampening or accelerating demand according to short term economic policy needs. This feast or famine environment had, therefore, been a primary cause for the companies to diversify their activities in an attempt to improve the stability of operations.

Like property, many of the construction firms were dominated by entrepreneurs or by their descendants. Laing, Wimpey, Taylor Woodrow and, until recently, Richard Costain were all such firms, with London and Northern being created more recently. Most of the large construction companies developed in the interwar period initially as speculative

Table 6.2   *UK Construction Industry Market Shares, 1974*

	Total Turnover £m	UK Construction Turnover* £m	Market Share %
John Laing	246	208	3.7
Geo. Wimpey	358	289	5.1
Taylor Woodrow	229	149	2.6
Richard Costain	193	87	1.5
London & Northern Securities	163	105	1.9
Trafalgar House Investments	281	121	2.1
Wood Hall Trust	259	45	0.8
Total	–	5645	100

* Estimated figures.
Sources: Annual Reports, Central Statistical Office.

housebuilders. During the war they became much more involved in civil engineering contracting, building airfields and power stations, factories and roads. After the war the massive domestic rebuilding programme increased this trend to major contracting, with the main firms often working closely with the developers on rebuilding city centres or for government in the construction of power stations, roads and similar infrastructure projects.

The Laing family business, for example, could be traced back to the eighteenth century, with the present company being formed some 125 years ago. The Laing family still controlled the voting shares and John Laing and Son was a close company. There were still three Laings on the Board – Sir John, who was responsible for building up the company in the 1919–39 period was president, and his sons Sir Kirby and Sir Maurice both previous managing directors, had become chairman and deputy chairman respectively. Taylor Woodrow was formed more recently in 1921 by Frank Taylor (later Sir) as a house building company, going public in 1935. The company undertook its first overseas operation in 1936 with housing developments in the USA and in 1937 with housing developments in the USA and in 1937 the company added contracting and civil engineering. At the beginning of 1974 Taylor, then 68, gave up the chairmanship but remained as managing director.[13]

Wimpey had remained dominated by one individual even longer. Sir Godfrey Mitchell originally acquired control of Wimpey in 1919 when the company was a small road surfacing contractor and developed it into Britain's biggest housing contractor. The Mitchell family still controlled the firm and it was not until 1974 the Sir Godfrey, then 81, gave up the chairmanship of the company. The passing of such a long service leader was the first step to occur at Richard Costain along the path to the only transition from family management among the major construction companies. The company, which began as a family business in Liverpool, was led for 45 years from 1920, until his death in 1966, by Sir Richard Costain. He was replaced by his son, a member of Parliament, who ultimately handed over the chairmanship to Sir Robert Taylor. Poor economic performance, coupled with an attractive property portfolio, led to Slater Walker building a strategic shareholding in the company. This tranche of shares was subsequently placed with Middle Eastern interests which were attracted to the company by its successful contracting operations in the area, while subsequently these interests were purchased by Lonrho.

Diversification into related construction operations
All of the construction companies had diversified their activities to offer a wide range of contracting and building services. The companies had also, to a greater or lesser degree, extended their operations outside the construction business. Firstly, each of the leading companies had moved into property development. Although holding property since 1928, Laing moved extensively into speculative development in the 1950s and by the 1970s was a major developer in its own right. The company had also embarked on speculative development overseas. Taylor Woodrow also entered the market during the 1950s and was an early developer of industrial estates. In addition, the company had also operated overseas in North America, western European and Australasia. Costain, too, had undertaken significant developments in its own right, although the company's strategy had especially emphasised overseas activities. Thus, the company had been an active developer and housebuilder in Canada, Australia and, to a lesser extent, in Portugal. Only Wimpey had never undertaken speculative development on its own. Instead the company had worked in partnership with other developers, providing capital and construction skills. Most important of these was the company's close relationship with the development company controlled by Mr. Harry Hyams, Oldham Estates, in which Wimpey held a 40 per cent interest until 1972.

The companies had also all integrated backward to some extent into the manufacture of construction materials which could be both consumed internally as well as sold to third parties. Laing began manufacturing bricks before the second world war, and after the war expanded into the manufacture of lightweight building blocks, concrete additives and lightweight concrete. The company had also added new services such as specialised plant hire and, since the mid-1960s, the provision of electrical, mechanical and plumbing services. All these activities were operated as independent businesses with only some 15 per cent of their output being consumed internally.

Taylor Woodrow had also added a range of construction related products and services under the Greenham name. Built up since 1945, these included plant hire, ready mixed concrete, aggregates, tyres, tools, some electrical equipment and protective clothing. Other interests included mechanical engineering and the manufacture and sale of prefabricated sectional buildings and structures. Costain, too, had extended into prestressed concrete products, dredging in conjunction with D. Blankevoort of Holland, mechanical engineering and opencast coal mining in the United Kingdom.

By contrast Wimpey had remained relatively undiversified. The company had extended its operations into chemical, mechanical and electrical engineering mainly as a result of construction-generated links with oil companies and overseas contracting. The oil industry had also led to a further major diversification involving Taylor Woodrow, John Laing and Wimpey. All three had entered the market for oil rigs, usually in conjunction with US partners in the first instance, to participate in the capital investment required to exploit Britain's North Sea oil assets. These ventures had not proved over-successful however, since the operating companies had been reluctant to provide the British rig contractors with orders.

The move to international contracting

In 1972 British contractors carried out some £400m of overseas contracts or about 10 per cent of their total output. This activity had been growing rapidly by comparison with domestic construction, but unlike the home market, overseas contracts tended to be concentrated among the leading firms. The overseas activities of the sample firms are shown in table 6.3. Costain had established the highest percentage of its activity overseas, with nearly half its turnover and 60 per cent of profits being derived abroad in 1974. By contrast London and Northern had only a limited amount of international contracting activity.

Like so much of British industry, the construction companies tended to commence their overseas operations in the former Empire territories, especially Canada and Australia, and to a lesser extent, Central and Southern Africa. Since the late 1960s, led by Costain, the British contractors had also been particularly active in the Arabian Gulf. Much of this overseas activity tended to be conducted for local governments and involved major civil engineering contracts for roads, power stations, harbours, dams and other infrastructure development. Such contracts were, therefore, often located in developing countries and while there had been a decline in activity in Africa an increase had taken place in parts of the Far East and Latin America. The British contractors had made only limited penetration in Western Europe, although Laing and Wimpey had

Table 6.3 Construction company geographic analysis of turnover, 1974

	John Laing		Taylor Woodrow		George Wimpey		Richard Costain		London & Northern Securities	
	£m	%	£m	%	£m	%	£m	%	£m	%
UK	208	85	149	68	289	79			139	93
Rest of Europe	27	11	8	4	–	–	{104} 54		2	1
N. America	1	–	23	11	21	6	8	4	–	–
Asia (incl. Middle East)	10	4	28	13	18	5	37	17	6	4
Africa	–	–	–	–	–	–	25	13	3	2
Australasia	–	–	11	5	21	6	23	12	–	–
Other	–	–	–	–	11	3				

Source: Annual Reports

established operations in Spain and speculative housing developments had been built on the Mediterranean.

Conglomerate diversification and construction

The remaining companies involved in construction were different in a number of respects from the relatively long established, family dominated concerns. All three were of much more recent origin being created in the post war period by individual entrepreneurs. As shown in table 6.4, all were substantially more diversified than the major contracting companies, although London and Northern Securities strategy had been to remain largely within the building and construction industry. The companies had also largely achieved their size and diversity as a result of an aggressive acquisition policy, although this was less true of Wood Hall Trust in later years.

The most financially successful of these firms was Trafalgar House Investments.[14] Created by Nigel Broakes, the company was initially involved in property development, where Broakes proved an adept operator of the third schedule loophole. In 1961, the company, until then a quoted investment trust in which Mr. Broakes owned some 43 per cent, became closely associated with Commercial Union Insurance which acquired a 28 per cent shareholding. In return, a number of properties owned by the insurance group were injected into the company, and its name was changed to Trafalgar House.

Rapid expansion followed in property development, including a highly successful acquisition of City West End Properties in 1964. In the same year Trafalgar House acquired its first stake in contracting, with the purchase of Bridge Walker. This move brought Mr. Broakes together with Mr. Victor Matthews, to form a successful management team. A further

Table 6.4 Diversity of Construction Industry Conglomerates, 1974

Wood Hall Trust

	% T/O	% PBT
Overseas Trading	25.4	17.2
Civil & General Engineering	9.7	22.2
Building Estate Development and Contracting	8.4	2.0
Finance & Property Dealing	–	1.5
Materials Handling	3.3	16.7
Pastoral Trading	51.6	25.4
Food Manufacturing	1.6	5.5

London and Northern Securities

	% T/O	% PBT
Construction	64.7	60.6
Building Products & Construction		
Services	18.1	18.8
Metal Reclamation & steel stockholding	17.2	14.2
Other	–	6.4

Trafalgar House Investments

	% T/O	% PBT
Property and Investments	5.2	35.2
Contracting & Engineering	46.2	14.6
House building	8.2	22.7
Shipping and Hotels	37.2	21.5
Industrial and General	3.7	6.2

T/O = turnover
PBT = profit before tax

Source: Annual Reports

series of acquisitions extended property operations and, in 1969, a joint company was formed with Whitbread to exploit the brewing company's property interests. Substantial growth by acquisition took place in contracting with the purchase of Ideal Building Corporation (1967), Trollope and Colls (1968), Cementation (1970) and the Willett Group (1971). The most significant move came in 1971, however, when Trafalgar House acquired the troubled Cunard Steamship Company. This move at a stroke made Trafalgar a leading world shipping company and provided it with a large tax shield for future earnings, due to Cunards accumulated losses and the unused depreciation charges of the Cunard fleet. This acquisition growth strategy pursued by Trafalgar House is further illustrated in table 6.5.

Wood Hall Trust was originally registered in 1919 as the Salvage and Towage Co. Ltd. The company became a quoted shell until it was acquired by Mr. Michael Richards in the early 1950s. In 1952 the name was changed and the company relaunched as a quoted industrial holding company, initially with interests in wines and spirits, merchanting and banking. In 1957 the company acquired Davis Estates, a house building company. In subsequent years further acquisitions extended the company's operations into a wide range of industries including property dealing, bill broking, materials handling, and food manufacturing, in addition to overseas merchanting and contracting and wool trading in Australia. By the end of the 1960s, however, the pace of new acquisitions had slowed markedly and the company began to concentrate on expanding its existing interests rather than purchasing new ones.

London and Northern Securities was also created as a holding company. It was first registered as a private company in 1961, being made public in 1963. The policy of the group was to provide a mechanism for well managed family companies, engaged in or associated with the construction industry, to escape the restrictions of close company legislation and the dangers of estate duty. By providing the umbrella of a publicly quoted company, the private owners could realise part of their capital by selling to the holding company, while still maintaining managerial control. Incentive was provided by the prospect of improving the value of the owner's residual share stakes in their own businesses.

This formula initially proved attractive and by the end of the 1960s London and Northern, led by Mr. J. Mackenzie, had emerged as a significant building and construction group with additional important interests in plant hire, building products, road haulage, commercial vehicle body building and scrap metal recovery. The extensive acquisition programme was pursued and Northern followed a regular pattern. Normally London and Northern would purchase between 60 and 75 per cent of the shareholding of those companies joining the group and allow the existing management to continue to run the subsidiary operations. Like other such groups before it, however, there are serious potential

Table 6.5   Development of Trafalgar House Investments

July 1963	Public flotation – small property company. Gross Assets £3.5m No of employees 6
1964	Acquired City & West End Properties (£4.6m) (property)
1966	Acquired Woodgate Investment Trust (£2m) (property & equity investments)
1967	Acquired Ideal Building Corpn (£4m) (building & construction)
1968	Acquired Trollope & Colls (£13m) (construction & contracting & building components manufacture) Acquired South Wales Concrete Pipe Co (concrete pipe manufacture) Acquired Eastern International Investment Trust
1969	Joint venture with Whitbread to develop the brewing company's property Overseas construction prospects in Caribbean investigated. Development of hotels on own account.
1970	Acquired Cementation Company (£14m) (international civil engineers and bridge builders) Acquired Trans World Hotels Acquired 2 Caribbean Hotels
1971	Acquired Cunard Steamship Co (£27m) (shipping passenger & cargo) Acquired William Bain & Co (South Africa) (construction) Acquired Willett Group (housebuilding) Acquired Lunn Poly (travel agencies & package holidays)
1973	Acquired 40% Dearbern-Storm Corpn ($33m) offshore drilling & oil services)
1975	Gross Assets £382m No of Employees 15,486 (UK only) Structure: Divisional as below:

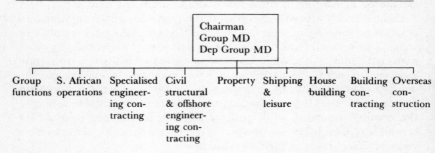

Source: Annual Reports

problems with this strategy and during the early 1970s the need for improved coordination between the subsidiaries, became apparent and led to the introduction of group wide policies especially in areas such as financial control.

The organisation of construction industry firms
Construction companies exhibited a range of organisations with holding company and divisional systems predominating. There were difficulties in

some cases in distinguishing between these, however. Further while significant decentralisation could and often did apply, the largely family or entrepreneurial nature of most of the companies led to autocratic management styles and a close centralisation of key strategic decisions.

In all the companies the different aspects of the construction business tended to be organised into separate operating subsidiaries each of which functioned independently of the others and was a separate profit centre. Inter company trading was usually carried out at arms length. In Wimpey for example decision making was more centralised than in Taylor Woodrow. Wimpey's main board was largely executive, and in close contact with one another in the central office. Below this board, was the board of management consisting of some 38 executives including directors, regional managers and managers of service departments. This body met monthly and reviewed information about all parts of the country. This board had no executive function, however, and could only make recommendations to the main board, which in turn was dominated by Sir Geoffrey Mitchell, who was the final arbiter for all major decisions.[15]

In contrast Taylor Woodrow consisted of over 100 subsidiary or associated companies located in five continents. Each subsidiary operated largely independently of the others. As a result, the parent company structure was described as a non-trading holding company. Each subsidiary had its own board and management with coordination being achieved largely via overlapping directorships. There was no requirement for subsidiaries to purchase goods or services from within the group, although in practice they tended to do so whenever practicable. The company's overseas operations were divided on a geographic basis, with an umbrella holding company usually controlling each centre of operations. Each subsidiary was responsible to a member of the group executive board which comprised some group directors and a number of other senior executives. This board in turn was responsible to the parent board. Control was maintained primarily via a well established system of rules which established the parameters within which subsidiary chief executives could make decisions. In addition the finance and accounting systems provided a tight rein on financial freedom.[16]

John Laing and Costain had adopted more formalised divisional systems of management. Following the appointment of Sir Robert Taylor as Chairman, Costain adopted a divisional structure in 1969, following recommendations from McKinsey and Company. This reorganised the company into two basic units, United Kingdom Operations and International Operations, each with a separate chief executive reporting to a group chief executive. Beneath these two, the organisation was sub-divided on a product basis principally in the UK, and on a geographic basis overseas, each of these sub-divisions being generally treated as a separate profit centre subsidiary.

The organisation of Laing was somewhat similar. Construction work was undertaken by two divisions. A building division carried out all building work in the UK and operated four self contained regions from regional offices. The engineering and overseas division was responsible for all overseas construction while in the UK, it controlled civil and industrial engineering construction through four specialised branches. This division was also responsible for pipeline activities and offshore structures as well as managing plant depots. Property was handled by three closely linked divisions, house building, property development and completed properties. Finally two divisions dealt with manufactured building products.[17] In addition to this structure the company still maintained a number of separate subsidiary companies involved with brickworks, mechanical engineering plant and ground engineering. Separate overseas subsidiaries also operated in Spain, engaged in local construction, in Canada, in property development, and in the USA.

The divisional companies operated in a much more decentralised manner than Wimpey. While extensive decision rules were established to contain the decision making autonomy of operating units within these limits, subunit managers were free to act. The divisional firms also tended to be more developed in central services than the holding companies.

The highly diversified companies engaged in construction operated either holding company or divisional structures. Trafalgar House adopted a divisional structure in the early 1960s, when it began to diversify. By 1968, the company consisted of three divisions, property, quoted investments and contracting. Housing was later spun off as a separate division as contracting expanded; an industrial and general division was set up to deal with sundry activities such as quarrying and pipe making; and the remaining construction division was sub-divided with building, civil and structural engineering, and specialised engineering. A hotels division, set up to aid entry to this sector, was later merged into a shipping and leisure division, following the purchase of Cunard. Finally, an off-shore division was set up to coordinate North Sea interests. Within the divisional structure the operating companies continued to trade under their own names, in cooperation with other group members.

The group executive function was well established in Trafalgar House as were group financial control systems. These were less evident in Wood Hall Trust and London & Northern Securities which operated more pseudo divisional structures. Wood Hall was nearer the traditional divisional structure, with subsidiary companies combined into product based divisions engaged in overseas trading, building, industrial estate development, materials handling, food products and finance and property. In addition the group's extensive operations in Australia were organised in two subsidiaries, one primarily concerned with wool trading, while the other was itself a small divisionalised, industrial holding company.

London and Northern had evolved to become organised into 12 operating divisions based upon common activities and location. Divisional boards had been established; responsible for the operation of the subsidiaries within each division and these reported through their chairmen to head office, and the main board. Divisional secretaries coordinated and monitored the performance and budgetting of the divisions' activities and reported to head office and the divisional boards on these matters. London and Northern had therefore been evolving from a holding company structure toward a divisional system by the gradual introduction of group executive functions.

THE LEISURE PROVIDERS

The remaining four firms were primarily engaged in leisure and similar services. They bore a close relationship in several ways to the property companies and a number of the construction concerns. All were managed by their founding entrepreneurs or by second generation family management. All were essentially post-war creations and had experienced relatively high growth rates in order to make the ranks of the top 100. Finally, all the companies had either developed as a result of interests in property, such as Grand Metropolitan, or had acquired such interests as part of their pattern of expansion. Details of the spread of interests of these companies are shown in table 6.6.

The largest of the private sector service industry firms, Grand Metropolitan[18] owed its position largely to the property and acquisition skills of Sir Maxwell Joseph. The brother-in-law of leading property developer Harold Samuel and an associate of Sir Isaac Wolfson, Joseph began as an estate agent before the war, and after it, began to take an interest in the property potential of hotels. By 1955 he owned six London hotels, but in 1957 he first came to prominence with a bid for the Mount Royal Hotel. After this Joseph became involved in a remarkable series of financial and property deals. These reached a peak in 1962 when Grand Hotels (Mayfair), then better known as the Washington Group and which had previously acquired control of Eglinton Hotels, merged with Joseph's Mount Royal Limited. The rationalised group, later renamed Grand Metropolitan Hotels, went on over the next few years to expand rapidly, largely by acquiring other hotel groups throughout the UK.

The company adopted the policy of concentrating on major cities only and in 1966 Joseph obtained control of the French hotel group, Societe des Hotels Reunis, which owned the Lotti and Scribe hotels in Paris and the Carlton in Cannes. In 1968, Grand Metropolitan acquired the Spanish holding company owning the Madrid Hilton, which was subsequently converted to the management of the British Group. In 1969, major acquisitions were made in New York and Amsterdam, while in the UK a significant opening programme of new hotels was under way. The group added Rome and Brussels to its international coverage in 1971. In 1972 it

Table 6.6 *Diversity of leisure industry firms, 1974*

Grand Metropolitan	% T/O	% EBIT	Ladbroke Group	% T/O	% EBIT	Lex Service Group	% T/O	% EBIT	Trust House Forte	% T/O	% EBIT
Hotels, Entertainment & Catering	28.2	43.4	Gambling & Casinos	91.3	80.0	Vehicle distribution & Servicing	76.2	66.7	Hotels	41.8	54.5
Milk & Milk Products	21.0	11.5	Hotels, holidays & Other leisure	7.7	20.0	Transportation & vehicle leasing	5.3	5.6	Catering	40.8	23.0
Brewing & Distribution	17.4	16.5	Property investment & dealing	1	–	Plant hire	5.3	22.9	Leisure	4.9	9.3
Wines & Spirits	18.2	21.3				Hotels & Travel	11.1	(4.3)	Manufacturing & Other Interests	12.5	20.2
Gambling	14.9	7.1				Personnel Services	2.2	5.4			
						Property	–	4.3			

Key: T/O = turnover
    EBIT = earnings before interest and tax

Source: Annual Reports

started to open a chain of hotels, motels and inns in the UK under the name of Country Hotels. Related diversification also occurred with the purchase of the Bateman Catering Organisation in 1967 and Midland Catering in 1968.

In 1969, however, Grand Metropolitan began a policy of diversification which has led to its emergence as a powerful conglomerate. In that year the company acquired the Express Dairy Company, one of the two largest distributors of domestic milk in the UK and also a manufacturer of dairy products and operator of a chain of some 150 dairy/grocery stores. Also in 1969, Grand Metropolitan purchased Empire Catering, operators of a chain of restaurants and snack bars.

In 1970, the company further extended its catering and entertainment interests by acquiring firstly, Berni Inns, a group which had pioneered the development of licensed steak bars, and secondly, Mecca Limited, the leading British group in entertainment, with activities in bingo, dance halls, betting shops, casinos and sports facilities. The following year saw the company become the first non-brewing family to acquire a leading brewing concern, when Trumans was purchased. Then in 1972, after a hard-fought battle Grand Metropolitan won control of Watney Mann, operators of over 6,000 public houses and owners of International Distillers and Vintners, a major wine and spirit manufacturer and distributor.

The greatest British rival to Grand Metropolitan in hotels and catering was Trust Houses Forte (THF).[19] Also created by an entrepreneur, Sir Charles Forte, the group grew from the 9 milk bars operated by Forte in 1945 to a group operating some 250 hotels around the world, in addition to the Travelodge chain in the USA. Linkages also existed with Travelodge Australia and other hotels in Australasia and the Far East. In addition Forte had similarly built up an extensive range of catering interests and restaurants, principally in the UK. The company also operated a number of motels and highway service facilities in France and Britian as well as being involved in industrial catering. THF's leisure interests included holiday villages, amusement parks, seaside piers, caravan parks and nightclubs, while the group specialised in operating airport catering services and duty free facilities at both airports and aboard cruise liners. Some limited interests had also been acquired in chocolate manufacture and travel management.

The existing group was largely the result of a merger, in 1970, between Trust Houses Limited, a relatively traditional British hotel group led by Lord Crowther, and Forte Holdings which, led by Forte, was especially strong in catering. The expected fruits of the merger did not materialise, however, and by the middle of 1971 there were rumours of board room dissension between the two participants. In November, Allied Breweries made a bid for the company and the board split became public when the group led by Lord Crowther recommended acceptance of the Allied bid after a reference to the Monopolies Commission. Forte, however, fought off the bid and forced the resignation of the former Trust Houses management group, to so obtain full control of the merged group.

The remaining leisure groups were smaller. Lex Service[20] which was originally solely concerned with automobile distribution only diversified in the late 1960s when Trevor Chinn succeeded his father and uncle as chief executive. Under its new chairman Lex expanded rapidly over the next few years into a variety of new businesses including, automobile leasing, specialised truck distribution, road transportation, freight services, heavy plant hire, hotels and property development. By the early 1970s therefore, Lex had become a service industry conglomerate, with a capital employed over twelve times more than that inherited by Mr. Chinn in 1968.

Ladbrokes, created by Cyril Stein, had the fastest growth rate of all the service industry companies investigated. Stein saw the potential of developing a nationwide chain of licensed bookmakers following changes in the UK gambling laws in the mid-1960s. From a base of a small cash betting operation the company was made public in 1967. In the space of the next few years, largely by acquisition but also by new openings, Ladbrokes established a chain of over 1,000 retail betting shops. During its first seven years the company achieved an eleven fold increase in earnings per share – a cumulative growth of over 1,000 per cent, while turnover rose from £39m in 1968 to £255m in 1974. With expansion came diversification and by 1974 Ladbrokes had entered other leisure industry areas including hotels, holiday centres, casinos and property development.

Managing the leisure corporations

All the leisure companies were managed with a divisional organisation structure – an abbreviated version of the Grand Metropolitan system is shown in figure 6.3. The degree of centralisation within these broad structures, however, was somewhat variable. At Grand Metropolitan Joseph operated in a more decentralised fashion than did Forte at THF. In most cases though, each division within the overall corporate framework tended to trade under its own established identity with only Lex and to a lesser extent Ladbrokes endeavouring to create some element of a corporate identity. In the case of THF and Grand Metropolitan, however, such a move would have been abortive since the subsidiary names were often better known than that of the parent. In all the companies it was noticeable that the central office was small in size and performed primarily a monitoring and financial control task. The key strategic decisions, however, tended to be very much the province of the founding entrepreneurs.

Conclusions

The strategies of the property, leisure and construction companies were fairly closely interwoven. A number of the retailers, such as Sears Holdings and Great Universal, also had close personal and ideological linkages with

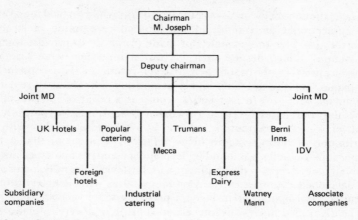

Source: Sewell & Quinn, op. cit., p. 3

Figure 6.3   Organisation of Grand Metropolitan Hotels, 1973

this group, too. Moreover, the banking and insurance sectors had become increasingly involved with firms operating in these industries. Despite this, however, it was notable that as a group these firms were generally completely outside the City establishment observed in earlier chapters. Although some institutional non executive directors were to be found on the board of the odd property company this phenomenon was rare by comparison with the links between the financial institutions themselves. There were probably several reasons for this. Firstly, this group of companies were all relatively recent in origin with the exception of the major contractors. Secondly, they were nearly all entrepreneur or family led. Thirdly, in property and leisure, many of the entrepreneurs were Jewish, thus as with retailing there was a strong ethnic strand in these sectors.

Strategically the firms had shown contrasting patterns. The pure property companies had found no major reason to diversify, save geographically, and even this had been limited. There had been some rationalisation and increased concentration by acquisition during the 1960s, largely as a means of expanding property portfolios, but in the main, strategic change was relatively limited. Indeed, given that financial performance had been more than adequate to permit diversification, the property companies were almost unique in consciously choosing not to engage in wider interests. A major reason for this was the entrepreneurs involved had little interest in the problems associated with expansion, most notable of which would have been the need to manage large numbers of people.

The major construction firms had expanded their range of interests, largely by forward and backward integration and by related diversification into new areas of contracting. Yet while vertical integration had come about as a result of the internal recognition of strategic opportunities these moves were not made primarily to provide internal transactions. Thus, despite their vertical nature they were primarily diversifications in terms of their market interface. The construction companies had also not been highly acquisitive. The industry remained fragmented and growth had largely come as a result of internal efforts rather than purchases. Overseas growth had been stimulated, partially as a result of domestic stagnation, but also as a conscious strategy with the distribution of business again being relatively unusual in that a high proportion of activity was found in developing countries and especially the Arabian Gulf. Property development had, however, generally focussed on the developed countries of the Commonwealth, with joint ventures or extensive local management being a prerequisite for success.

The diversified firms with interests in construction were in many ways more similar to the leisure firms. All had adopted strategies relying heavily on acquisitions, which had accounted for much of the apparent growth achieved. The ability to manage such diversity had, however, been variable. The leisure firms too had expanded largely by acquisition, taking on new activities in new sectors, usually with property connections. With the exception of the construction companies most firms had relatively high gearing. In part this was a function of the property component within the companies. Earnings performance had been variable, partially as a result of the high debt capital structure but also because earnings were not necessarily the correct measure. For property companies, increases in assets per share and the pursuit of capital gains were the primary measure of financial success. During times of rising property prices this strategy proved most successful but in the 1970s, climbing interest rates, which had drastically reduced activity in the property market, also severely undermined the earnings performance of highly geared firms. Moreover, those with a weak cash flow position found it increasingly difficult to service their debt. The highly geared acquisitive companies, despite their diversity, also did not escape unscathed and without adequate cash flow, earnings were sharply reduced by interest charges. For the construction companies the problems were rather different. Their principal problem had been to cope with a highly variable market demand for their services.

Structurally, only the property companies exhibited functional organisations, although some of these too, subdivided on either a product or geographic basis. The property development process however, required few people and thus organisations tended to be relatively simple. The construction companies in contrast, were relatively large employers, although the workforce was mainly widely scattered on local sites. The companies were also more diversified by product and by specialised construction service. Holding company structures were therefore, most common, although in two cases a divisional system had emerged. This structure was the norm among the leisure group, however, which had been amongst its earliest adopters. In all cases it was the conglomerate variant that was used, which featured a small central executive group relying mainly on financial controls to measure subunit performance.

7. Families and Formulas for Retail Distribution

Retail distribution[1] is one of the largest of the service industries employing some 2.7 million people in 1974. Eighteen of the sample firms or organisations were mainly involved in retailing and distribution, twelve of these being primarily engaged in non-food markets while the remainder were principally food retailers. The post war period has been one of great change for the retailing industry, and major multiple retailers, details of which are shown in table 7.1, have generally experienced a substantial level of growth.

The development of modern retailing stems from the growth of urbanisation, resulting from the industrial revolution. The traditional fairs and street markets which were the historic means of distribution declined in importance, and in their place came fixed shops stocking branded goods, advertised by their manufacturers, at prices fixed under resale price maintenance agreements. In addition, a wholesale function emerged which increased in importance as an intermediary between manufacturers and retailers and often took over some processing functions previously done by the early shopkeeper. Toward the end of the nineteenth, and increasingly during the twentieth century, multiple shop groups began to emerge. Such chains grew especially rapidly in the food and boot and shoe trades, where the advantages of mass production or concentrated purchasing power were allied to mass distribution. In 1880 there were 1,564 shops belonging to multiple chains; by 1905 this number has risen to 15,242 and by 1915 to 25,000.

The multiples, although similar in appearance to the single, family owned stores, developed more efficient organisations to control staff, stocks, purchasing, selling and accounting. After the first world war the new pattern accelerated aided by the growth of mass production, the development of road transport, national brand advertising and direct deliveries from manufacturers to multiple retailers, so reducing the power of wholesalers. In the towns, populations began to move toward the suburbs and shops became more widely spread while the multiples moved to take prime positions in the high streets and new suburban shopping parades.

The penetration of the multiples increased and their image gradually changed from an emphasis on lower prices towards an impression of

Table 7.1   Major retail groups 1974 (£m)

Company	Principal Activities	Turnover (£m)	Capital employed (£m)	No of UK employees
Tesco Stores (Holdings)	Operates over 800 grocery stores supermarkets, off licences, furniture stores and cafes mainly in London and S.E., Midlands and North West.	423	78	40,245
J. Sainsbury	Operates 175 supermarkets selling predominantly food in S. E. and Midlands.	446	168	31,146
Fitch Lovell	Operate some 170 stores and supermarkets, also engaged in food manufacture and wholesaling, smaller interests in shopfitting, insurance broking, timber distribution and building materials.	268	46	15,120
Wheatsheaf Distribution	Wholesale distribution of food & other goods from 6 warehouses, 52 cash and carry warehouses & 35 retail stores and hypermarkets.	227	15	5,623
Cavenham	Food manufacture & retailing through over 2,000 stores; confectionery, tobacco & newspaper distribution via around 370 shops; international operations in Europe, North America and elsewhere.	737	300	40,300
House of Fraser	Department store operator with over 130 retail stores in the UK.	297	186	27,820
Debenhams	Operators of 70 department stores 35 supermarkets, 43 fashion stores and 13 retail shoe stores, shoe manufacture.	246	183	33,531
John Lewis Partnership	Operator of 17 department stores & over 50 supermarkets and food stores; manufacturing interests supplying the store group.	237	104	25,301
Marks & Spencer	Operator of 252 retail variety stores in the UK and with linked outlets in Europe and Canada.	722	413	39,480
British Home Stores	Operator of 98 retail variety stores in the UK.	162	72	22,160

The Service Industries

Table 7.1 Continued

Company	Principal Activities	Turnover (£m)	Capital employed (£m)	No of UK employees
F. W. Woolworth	Operator of 1067 retail variety stores & out of town superstores in the UK & a limited number of former Empire territories.	462	269	81,669
The Boots Company	Operators of around 1500 retail pharmacist & variety stores, manufacture of pharmaceuticals, drugs, fine chemicals & toiletries, distribution of agricultural chemicals and related products.	503	233	68,846
W. H. Smith	Operators of 301 stores & 65 station bookstalls, retailing & wholesaling newspapers, books, fancy goods & records, operators of mail order book clubs, limited activities in Europe and Canada.	217	53	19,220
Great Universal Stores	Operators of over 2,000 multiple stores in mens and womens fashion clothing, furniture & footwear in the UK. Activities in travel, mail order, credit finance; overseas interests in Europe & Australia, South Africa and Canada.	692	377	47,615
Sears Holdings	Footwear manufacturer & retailer with over 2000 stores, department store operators, baker & catering, engineering, motor vehicle distribution, betting offices, jewellery & silverware distribution, linen line & laundries, knitwear manufacture. Overseas interests in Europe and the USA.	599	397	65,000
UDS	Operators of over 1200 multiple retail stores in mens & womens fashion wear, footwear & department stores, furniture stores, catalogue & mail order retailing, duty free retailing.	247	181	37,000

Table 7.1 Continued

Company	Principal Activities	Turnover (£m)	Capital employed (£m)	No of UK employees
Powell Duffryn	Manufacturers of a wide range of engineering products including pumps & compressors, boilers, furnaces, hydraulic loaders, materials handling equipment; building services; pollution control services; shipping wharfage, ship owners, freight forwarding, road transport; chemicals; storage; fuel distribution; quarrying; timber & builders merchants; ship bunkering and overseas fuel distribution.	224	71	11,820
Cooperative Movement	Operating over 2500 retail outlets by some 175 retail societies. Activities cover food & non-food retailing, supermarkets, department stores, furniture, fuel distribution & funerals. Retail stores serviced by a wholesale society operating over 200 factories, workshops & warehouses. Other subsidiaries operate banking & insurance services.	1400	n.a.	over 250,000

Sources: Annual reports

quality. Multiple stores became bright, modern and well fitted in the main, while the small shops became increasingly reliant upon local convenience trade. Department stores, which had originated as low markup, high turnover ventures moved up market to serve the needs of the growing middle class. The range of goods offered increased, specialised buying became established, and the stores became fashion leaders, while the stores' own merchandising and promotion policies gave them a growing strength in their relationship with suppliers. The cooperative movement was another specialised multiple trading organisation which emerged at the end of the nineteenth century as consumer protection societies, designed to further the interests of the working class. The growth of this initially local movement in turn led to the creation of a massive supporting wholesale and manufacturing organisation, the largest element of which was the Cooperative Wholesale Society.

The evolution of the retailing industry was temporarily interrupted by the second world war when rationing and the central control of essential commodities left the distribution industry with little to distribute. The introduction of rationing helped to preserve the position of small traders, since for many commodities, consumers were forced to register with a specific store. Price control and mark ups were strictly determined so further reducing the level of competition. These controls persisted for some years, even after the end of the war, as did restrictions on new building. Thus it was not until the early 1950s that significant differentiation again began to develop between retailers.

The war also led to the more efficient use of manpower and the cost of labour ensured that after the war the trend to reduced labour usage continued. This trend was particularly marked in food retailing, where the early 1950s brought the introduction of self service retailing by a few pioneers. This new retailing strategy, which sacrificed personal service for lower prices, was at first resisted due to a dislike of change, the government restrictions on building and the last years of rationing. From 1954 however, when shoppers again became free to shop where they wished, self service stores flourished.

Soon larger stores were developed, and these supermarkets, which offered even lower prices were a threat, not only to the traditional personal service stores, but also to the smaller self service operations. The arrival of self service and supermarkets dramatically fostered the competitive position of a few new multiples, such as Tesco and Fine Fare, and gradually forced change amongst a number of the traditional multiple groups such as Sainsbury, Fitch Lovell, and International Stores. The cooperative societies, in aggregate the largest multiple group but organisationally fragmented, suffered as a result of the spread of self service almost as much as the independent shops. Retail societies were forced to amalgamate or modify their retailing methods while wholesaling became concentrated around the Cooperative Wholesale Society.

Outside of food the change in retailing was less dramatic due in large measure to the continuation of resale price maintenance, which was strongly enforced by many manufacturers, especially those producing branded products. Blanket restrictions on resale price maintenance were removed in 1956, when collective enforcement by manufacturers was abolished under the Restrictive Practices Act. Individual manufacturers however, still had the power to enforce resale prices for their goods, although in the grocery trade the practice quickly broke down as the supermarket operators, and especially Tesco, openly defied the manufacturers. Elsewhere resale price maintenance tended to hold, although competitive pressures gradually mounted as aggressive retailers such as Tesco extended into non-food markets. Against resistance from many manufacturers, in 1964 resale price maintenance was finally outlawed, subject to a procedure whereby the Restrictive Practices Court could grant exemption in special cases. The abolition of price maintenance led to a rapid escalation of retail competition, new forms of discount operations sprang up in many sectors but especially in consumer appliances, and groups, such as the department stores which had tended to be slow to exploit their overall purchasing power, moved to centralised buying and the development of a common corporate identity.

By 1960 self service retailing was well established and shops were being converted at four times the rate in 1950, with the practice extending into other areas of retailing than food. The burden of the high cost of counter service, coupled with a lack of price competitiveness caused a substantial decline in the number of independent retailers as shown in table 7.2. This was especially true in food retailing where competition was fiercest.

Table 7.2   Retail establishments, 1950 – 71

Number of establishments	1950	1957	1961	1966	1971
Total retail	583,132	577,174	577,307	504,412	485,346
Food retail	283,576	275,154	278,454	227,744	201,844

Source: The post war censuses of distribution.

A further trend in the post war period was an increase in average store size. Supermarkets had begun to appear by the end of the 1950s, and as the early versions of these stores gave way to larger units, the food retailers increased the shelf area devoted to non food items, using the principle of low price and high turnover. In 1966 the introduction of selective employment tax, designed to discriminate against workers in the service industries by comparison with the manufacturing sector, enhanced the trend to lower levels of counter service. By 1971 the number of independent retailers had fallen sharply since 1950.

The rebuilding of old town centres, the development of new towns and the growth of new suburban shopping precincts led to further substantial changes in retail structure with the higher rents charged for redeveloped sites encouraging the spread of the multiples. Town centres have remained the principal trading centres for non-food trading and provide the primary location for department and variety stores. Food retailing, however, has become substantially more diversified, with suburban centres which offer superior parking facilities, growing in importance. By the late 1960s the trend toward larger units and the growth of consumer affluence and car ownership had led to a slow, but distinctive move toward out of town centres and the development of the third generation multiple store, the superstore or hypermarket. In the post war period the multiple retail groups have significantly increased their share of the market in all sectors.

Concentration in the main segments of the retail market varied considerably. By 1971, largely by a process of absorbtion, four main groups dominated the department stores. Other areas of high concentration were variety stores, pharmaceuticals and toiletries, and footwear distribution, while, despite major gains by multiples, food, clothing and other segments were still largely fragmented. The position is illustrated in figure 7.1, which reveals roughly the situation after the last census of distribution in 1971, indicating the relative dominance of individual store groups in each of the main market segments.

THE FOOD RETAILERS

A convenient way of differentiating between the major store groups is to divide them into food and non-food retailing, although as will become apparent this differentiation has become increasingly blurred as the food chains have added non-foods while a number of non-food multiples have moved into food distribution.

The largest of the food retailers in terms of sales is Tesco Stores.[2] Led by its founder Jack (later Sir John) Cohen, Tesco was one of the pioneering organisations which first introduced self service operations in Britain. Tesco was also one of the earliest supermarket operators and Cohen gained massive publicity in the 1960s by his defiance of manufacturers in the fight against resale price maintenance.

Cohen began as a market trader in London in the interwar period. A skilled buyer, Cohen initially bought job lots of merchandise which were sold cheaply in London street markets. A relationship with tea importers and blenders T. E. Stockwell, led Cohen to the sale of packed blended tea under the brand name Tesco, formed from an amalgam of Stockwell and Cohen's own names. The success of this venture led Cohen to integrate back into tea wholesaling while still retaining his own retail interests, which were expanded to cover a number of street markets.

During the 1930s Cohen extended into more conventional permanent site retailing partially alone but also with other family members. Moreover, Cohen endeavoured to maintain his street market image of low prices and good value, and flouted resale price maintenance with price cutting methods. By 1933, Cohen was essentially involved with three different businesses, wholesaling and two retail grocery chains. The first of these traded under the Tesco name, while the second was a partnership with Michael Kaye, operating the trade name Bargain Centres (later renamed Pricerite). By the end of the 1930s Cohen had built the Tesco chain to a total of over 100 grocery stores. Further, he had pioneered private label branding, and had integrated back into wholesaling and to a certain extent into food packing and manufacture.

In 1935 Cohen visited the United States and was impressed by the early development of self service retailing. An experiment was conducted in one of Cohen's British stores shortly after the war and following its success,

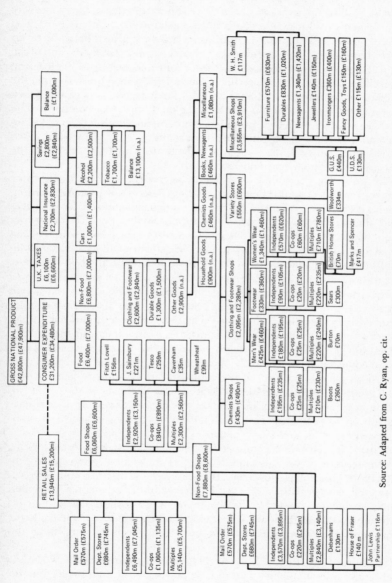

Source: Adapted from C. Ryan, op. cit.

Figure 7.1   Market Strength in Retail Distribution, 1971

Tesco began to convert the majority of its stores. By 1955, 85 per cent of Tesco's 120 stores featured self service, and the company had begun to expand both in the average size of stores operated and in location away from Cohen's traditional strength in and around London.

Geographic and floorspace expansion was accomplished partially by an aggressive policy of store openings but also by acquisition. By the end of the 1950s Tesco operated around 200 stores and had begun to explore the possibilities of extending its product range into non-food lines. In 1960 the purchase of John Irwin and Sons added a further 200 stores in the North West and led to the creation of a new regional operating company. The purchase of Harrow Stores provided the company with valuable knowledge on household goods and furniture retailing, so that in 1961 Tesco opened a major new supermarket in Leicester in which 50 per cent of the floor area was devoted to non-food products.

The publicity generated by Cohen's aggressive war on resale price maintenance was a major factor in building Tesco's low price reputation, which was further enhanced by the use of trading stamps. Growth was rapid, financed largely by Tesco's own suppliers who provided four weeks credit while the company's efficient control systems and warehousing aimed at a stock turn of only two weeks. New store openings were virtually all supermarkets and their average floor area continued to increase. Acquisitions also added to Tesco's expansion, with the purchase of rival supermarket operator Victor Value in 1968, making Tesco the fourth largest multiple in Britain with 834 stores. Further diversification also occurred into specialised Home'n Wear non-food operations, cakes and bakeries (via the purchase of Cadena Cafes) and wines and spirits.

Despite its high rate of growth however the management of Tesco remained highly personalised. Cohen retained strong central control over operations for the majority of the company's development, relying on a small group of dedicated helpers who grew with the business and on his two sons in law. The company did not neglect the development of adequate controls, however, and Tesco were early users of sophisticated computerised financial and stock control systems.

As new aspects of the business developed Cohen initially operated with a holding company organisation based on product or geographic concentration. In 1969, however, the company's organisation was investigated by McKinsey & Co. The consultants advocated increased centralisation and this led to the development of a corporate headquarters to accommodate all the main activities, including non-foods, and led to the creation of centralised functions for buying, marketing, computing and data processing.

The revised structure still effectively divided the business into two halves each under one of Cohen's sons in law, Harvey Kreitman succeeding Sir John Cohen as chairman, being in charge of foods, while Leslie Porter operated as managing director in charge of non-foods. When Leslie Porter succeeded Kreitman as chairman in 1974 a further reorganisation took place which integrated buying and selling operations and divided the company into a series of specific functional activities – retailing, property, buying distribution and administration – while other trading subsidiaries were organised separately. The functions were then divided between two managing directors as shown in figure 7.2.

The origin of J. Sainsbury[3] dates back to 1869 when J. J. Sainsbury opened his first dairymans shop in London's Dairy Lane. The company like Tesco, however, had a well established retail formula which although amended over time remained largely constant in its essentials. Further, Sainsburys remained firmly in family hands, a policy which for a long time inhibited its emergence as a public company.

While Cohens formula at Tesco has been described loosely as 'pile it high and sell it cheap', J. Sainsbury's original concept was to concentrate on the sale of fresh dairy products and provisions in stores carefully designed to ensure cleanliness. The success of this formula meant that by 1914 Sainsbury's had expanded to 114 branches located in an area confined to London and the South East, due to difficulties in the transportation of fresh produce. Sainsbury carefully built up his organisation's reputation for quality and freshness. He constantly sought out producers who were the best in their field and who were willing to rush their produce to his warehouse. At the end of the first world war J. B. Sainsbury, who had been taken into partnership by his father, decided to increase the number of grocery items sold, to introduce 'own label' groceries at a separate counter, and to develop a meat trade. During the interwar period J. B. Sainsbury was also responsible for rapid expansion of the branch network and increases in the size of existing stores to accommodate the larger range of merchandise sold. By 1938, Sainsburys, which had become a limited company, operated 244 branches and the company's self developed training programmes and management systems were already a model for the grocery retail trade.

The war seriously restricted Sainsburys' business which was founded on perishables many of which were subject to rationing. Availability of these lines was severely limited, and in order to enable the branches to survive, alternative products such as canned goods and other groceries were introduced. After the war, the company also decided to capitalise on its reputation for quality and freshness by marketing the majority of products sold under its own brand name. To supply much of this merchandise Sainsburys integrated backward into meat and poultry production, eggs and cooked meats, other lines being manufactured and packed to the company's own specification.

During the 1950s store modernisation and rationalisation of the branch network took place. Self service was gradually introduced, especially for larger, new stores, but by 1959 counter service still dominated being used in 250 of the company's 270 stores. The trend to self service accelerated in

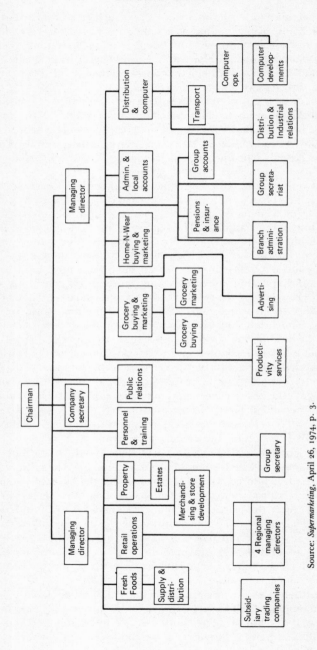

Figure 7.2   Tesco Organisation, 1974

Source: *Supermarketing*, April 26, 1974. p. 3.

the 1960s and, in addition, the company began to expand its coverage into the Midlands and East Anglia.

Towards the end of the 1960s Sainsburys underwent a basic change in strategy. The company moved rapidly to develop supermarkets, using the traditional formula of own label goods, especially fresh food and perishables. Some limited moves into non-food items also took place in larger stores. The trend to supermarket trading accelerated from 1969, the firm's centenary, when John Sainsbury became the fourth generation family member to succeed to the chairmanship. He also ended the company's policy of vertical integration by merging the meat processing and egg and poultry interests with other groups.

In 1972 Sainsburys became a public company, with the majority of shares still held by family interests. Under John Sainsbury, the company's organisation, although still firmly in family hands, became more de-centralised. Earlier generations had traditionally maintained close central control over operations but with the development of computerised control systems greater freedom was permitted to operating managers.

Fitch Lovell[4] was also a family based concern, being created by the merger of two family companies, Fitch and Son and Lovell and Christmas in 1959. These two companies could trace their origins back to the eighteenth and nineteenth centuries, although by the time of the merger the founding family interests had largely disappeared. The new company was formed into four divisions, Lovell and Christmas, general provisions, the former Fitch grocery interests, bakery and timber, these latter two being the result of defensive diversification moves undertaken by Fitch in the 1920s.

By comparison with Tesco and Sainsbury, therefore, Fitch Lovell was substantially more diversified, with interests in food manufacturing and processing and more specialised areas of retailing such as baking and confectionery, poultry and processed meat production, and meat retailing in addition to grocery trading. Expansion came about in large part by means of acquisitions and following one such purchase the company developed its supermarket operations under the Key Markets trade name. Later the company was an early entrant into cash and carry wholesaling, where acquisition was again used as a major mechanism for expansion.

At the time of the 1959 merger, Fitch Lovell operated as a holding company. Gradually an increasing number of central systems were introduced although the major operating companies had remained largely autonomous. The group's retailing interests, however, were closely controlled, although by comparison with the well defined retail formulae established by Tesco and Sainsbury, Fitch Lovells' image remained diffused and diversified rather than concentrated and uniform.

The remaining two retailers mainly concerned with food, Cavenham Foods and Wheatsheaf Distribution, were both recent creations. Cavenham[5] emerged in 1965 as the result of a merger between three food and confectionery manufacturing and retailing companies inspired by Mr. (later Sir) James Goldsmith. After moving out non-food and wholesaling interests, the remaining subsidiaries were subdivided into four divisions covering bakery, confectionery, grocery and wholesaling, each operating under its own general manager and board of directors.

From this base with sales of around £25 million, Goldsmith and Cavenham expanded dramatically over the next decade, largely by acquisition. Many of these moves took place in Europe and especially France, where Goldsmith built up a parallel food and financial services operation. Cavenham itself became a major operator in food retailing in the early 1970s when, following the successful purchase of traditional food manufacturers Bovril, Goldsmith moved to acquire Wrights Biscuits and its subsidiary Moores Stores in 1971 and Allied Suppliers early the following year. Allied, unlike Tesco or Sainsburys did not have a uniform image. Rather the company operated around 1,750 shops under a variety of names. Furthermore most of these stores were small, the company being slow to develop into supermarkets. Following the acquisition by Cavenham, Goldsmith moved quickly to rationalise the group disposing of uneconomic stores in order to recover their property value and improve overall performance.

Although Cavenham remained largely a food manufacturing and retailing concern, it was linked via significant shareholdings and cross interests to other parts of Goldsmith's empire. This embraced a much wider range of activity including pharmaceuticals, liquor, banking, finance, insurance broking and property development. Moreover Goldsmith's operations extended the linkages between Cavenham and Goldsmith's French based mother company, General Occidentale, being shown more widely in figure 7.3. Within Cavenham, the operating companies were arranged into a United Kingdom divisionalised structure, each having its own autonomous board over which the small central staff exerted strict financial control and established policy decision rules, day to day operations being largely decentralised.

By comparison with Cavenham, Wheatsheaf Distribution was a more simple operation. The company was originally established as a subsidiary of flour millers, McDougall Ltd, as an investment holding company. In 1959 the company acquired a wholesale grocery business and shortly afterwards took over those McDougall subsidiaries also engaged in wholesaling. After the merger between Rank Hovis and McDougall in 1962 to form Rank Hovis McDougall, the grocery distribution interests of the new company were consolidated into Wheatsheaf and in 1967, the decision was taken to float these off as a separate public company.

Initially the principal activities of Wheatsheaf were grocery wholesaling, cash and carry warehouses and a limited number of retail stores. Expansion of the company's wholesaling interests followed in the early 1970s by acquisition. In addition, Wheatsheaf established a joint venture

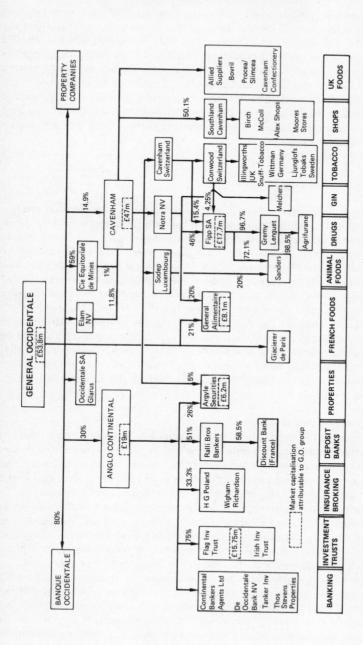

Figure 7.3 Structure of the Generale Occidentale/Cavenham Group, 1972

Source: *Sunday Times.*

in 1970 with S. A. Carrefour, the leading French hypermarket operator, to establish Carrefour hypermarkets in the United Kingdom. By 1974 Wheatsheaf consisted of three principal activities, wholesaling, cash and carry operations and hypermarkets, each of which was managed by a separate management group. Under this semi holding company system each subsidiary operated with its own board maintaining contact with the small central office via the subsidiary company chairman. Meanwhile the central office itself was small and responsible essentially for finance and capital expenditure, maintaining operating control over the subsidiaries via the budgetary system.

THE NON FOOD RETAILERS

The non-food retailers had a number of similarities with the food groups. Firstly, they too tended to divide into the two basic types namely, those which had developed around a specific retail formula such as Boots, Marks and Spencer, and Woolworths, and those which had been created by financially orientated entrepreneurs, usually by a process of acquisition, such as Great Universal Stores and Sears Holdings. A number of the companies operated a combination of these two approaches, consolidating within a particular retail segment by acquisition such as House of Fraser and United Drapery Stores. Secondly, family interests had been or remained strong in many of the companies, while those firms established by acquisition tended to have usually been created by entrepreneurs. Thirdly, over time there had been a steady trend to diversify the product range offered both within existing store operations but also by entry into other areas or retailing.

The department store specialists
The largest of the department store groups was House of Fraser,[6] which was started by the Fraser family in Scotland in the mid nineteenth century and had remained with a family member as chairman ever since. The company began to expand by acquisition from 1927 when the third Hugh Fraser (later Lord Fraser of Allander) succeeded to the chairmanship. In 1948 the company became public and began to develop rapidly, moving to England by purchasing local department store groups and establishing in London via the acquisitions of John Barker and Harrods. Expansion continued until the mid 1960s when a period of consolidation took place following the succession of the fourth Sir Hugh Fraser in 1966.

Despite its rapid growth, organisation change in the House of Fraser did not match the requirements of strategic development. In particular the company failed to integrate the store groups under its control. No coordinated purchasing policy was introduced until 1972, when the previously autonomous store groups were assigned to a region, dependent upon their quality level, and own branded goods were purchased through a central buying system.

Debenhams[7] the second largest department store group had diversified somewhat more than House of Fraser, adding fashion stores, supermarkets, out of town superstores and some manufacturing interests. For more than a century, until 1928, the company was led by the Debenham family after which the company grew largely by a process of acquisition.

During this phase a holding company structure prevailed with a few directors being responsible for running the group of businesses. From 1958, following a change of leadership, the company was slowly reorganised and rationalised, with each board member being made chairman of a small group of businesses and managing director of the principal store within each group. During the 1960s however, Debenhams lost ground, along with other department store groups, to the more labour efficient supermarket traders and other discount groups which began to emerge, by taking advantage of the end of resale price maintenance.

Although Debenhams introduced some central buying in the 1960s there was considerable resistance by the highly autonomous store managers. As a result the company largely failed to exploit its full potential, and allowed the regional department stores to maintain an independent localised image. Further, Debenhams diversified into food retailing, restaurants and catering. However, the company was slow to recognise the future potential of supermarkets, and although experiments were conducted to introduce food into larger department stores, the strong positive sales effect on other departments was not seen until the mid 1960s.

Under new management from 1971, performance improved significantly. as the company increased its food interests, diversified into photographic equipment retailing, and extended back into shoe manufacture and high fashion, all by acquisition. In addition the company closed a number of its uneconomic stores, developed a common usage and store identity around the Debenham name so permitting national advertising, significantly cut back its labour force, and rationalised the range of goods sold toward the middle ground of consumer taste.

In pursuit of this strategy Debenhams have moved into the segment occupied by the John Lewis Partnership.[8] Unlike the other department store groups John Lewis had performed outstandingly well and acquired a reputation for quality, value for money and first class store management. The Partnership traded under a variety of department store names but like Sainsburys made extensive use of own label merchandise, sold under a common brand name in all its stores. The company had also developed a significant food retailing operation, with an image of quality and value for money, again reminiscent of Sainsburys, and operating principally in the South East.

Founded by John Spedan Lewis, the company operated an unusual organisation based on cooperative ownership by the employees. In 1929,

Lewis signed the First Irrevocable Trust, selling his business to the workers in exchange for an interest free loan which remained in the company and was repaid over a number of years. This common ownership structure is illustrated in figure 7.4.

By the second world war, the company operated 18 department stores, 33 foodshops and a number of manufacturing operations supplying goods to the stores. After the war growth continued broadly along the same lines although the partnership's food retailing interests have been converted to supermarket operations. Because no ordinary shares were held outside the partnership little growth had occurred by acquisition and internal growth from store enlargement and new openings proved the dominant method of expansion. Despite the smaller number of stores therefore, the average turnover per unit of John Lewis department stores was significantly higher than for other department store groups. Further, despite its common ownership structure the company had always operated with a strong centralised management team which established trading policy for all the stores. The Waitrose food retailing interests were managed autonomously along lines similar to Sainsbury with a heavy emphasis on quality and private label products constant with the partnership's overall image and philosophy. Central buying was practiced and some 60 per cent of goods were common to all stores.

The organisation of the Partnership worked along clear hierarchical lines although in theory there were no managers and employees, only partners and senior partners. The 'management' team was however made up of senior partners who certainly enjoyed privileges and rewards commensurate with outside store groups and the company was relatively ruthless in its pursuit of quality, with those employees not making the grade, leaving the system.

The variety chains

The doyen of the variety chains was Marks and Spencer,[9] which had developed a unique image for high quality, well designed and attractive merchandise sold at reasonable prices. From its early beginnings as the Penny Bazaar in the late nineteenth century, the small fledgling chain passed to Simon Marks, the son of the founder, and his brother in law, Israel Sieff, in 1915. These two second generation entrepreneurs largely developed the company into a household name and established its successful retail formula.

Contrary to rival variety store chains, Simon Marks decided to concentrate activities in two specific areas, food and clothing and as a result, Marks and Spencer reduced by over 70 per cent the range of products handled, dropping items such as toys, jewellery and sports equipment. Next, concerned about the variations in the quality of merchandise received from suppliers, the company began to lay down precise specifications for all its merchandise. A merchandise development

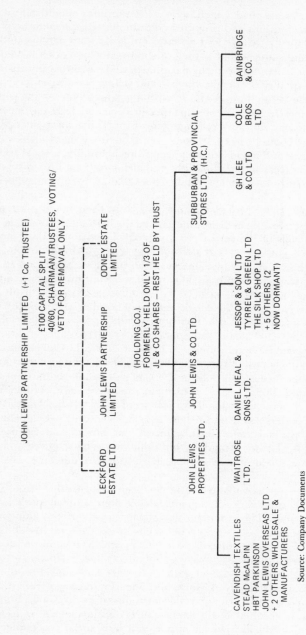

Figure 7·4 The Structure of the John Lewis Partnership

Source: Company Documents

function was established which advocated suppliers should adopt mass production techniques and provided consultancy assistance to help them achieve it. Thirdly, Marks and Spencer only sold merchandise under its own brand name and would not sell any item on which it felt it could not make either a satisfactory return on capital or make a contribution in terms of price and quality. Fourthly, buying and selling were strictly divorced, all purchasing being done centrally with a gradually increasing sophistication, which included both product specification and design, while selling was conducted by the store management. Fifthly, the company operated an enlightened policy toward its employees, providing them with extensive fringe benefits and good working conditions. Finally, the Marks and Spencer stores were austere but light and clean, offering little display and no fitting rooms but always ready to exchange merchandise without question.

The Marks and Spencer formula had over time become almost an ideology which had been deeply inculcated throughout the business. Even the lowest levels of the staff were involved in decision making and the loyalty of the employees had become legendary. During Simon Marks leadership, however, personal intervention in the detailed operations of the business was also common. This trend was continued when, after his death he was succeeded by Lord Sieff. The business remained firmly in the hands of descendants of the Marks and Sieff families although the board did contain a number of non family members.

In the early 1970s Marks and Spencer had perhaps experienced its first major setbacks in attempting to expand abroad. Operations were commenced in Canada, France and Belgium using a range of merchandise similar to that successfully sold in the UK with similarly laid out stores, merchandising policy, staff treatment and the like. Only limited modifications in the traditional formula were made to accommodate local tastes, and perhaps as a result these overseas ventures were not initially successful. The successful translation of the Marks and Spencer formula out of the United Kingdom thus remained to be achieved and might require some relaxation in policies if the desired outcome was to be attained.

The nearest rival to Marks and Spencer was British Home Stores[10] (BHS) which initially developed almost as a slightly down market copy of the larger group. The company was started as a variety chain in 1928, offering a range of goods priced between threepence and five shillings, a formula similar to that of both Woolworth and Marks and Spencer. In 1933, BHS went public and by 1945 operated some 70 stores. In 1956 the company began to experiment with self service and moved more toward the specialisation strategy of Marks and Spencer and away from the wider variety of Woolworths. In 1960 BHS introduced its own housebrand and had gradually eliminated all manufacturers brands except in toiletries.

BHS, unlike Marks Spencer imported a substantial percentage of the textiles it sold and concentrated on somewhat lower prices than its rival. Buying was centralised and prices established nationally, but although high standards were maintained for merchandise by tight quality control, BHS did not involve itself to the same extent as Marks and Spencer, in the business of its suppliers. BHS also maintained a wider range of merchandise than Marks and Spencer and had established a strong position in a number of specialised segments such as lighting and millinery and in some lines of perishable foods: BHS was also more flexible on out of town developments than Marks and Spencer. Whereas the latter remained firmly wedded to city centre cites, BHS had joined forces with Sainsbury in the future development of hypermarket operations. More recently in the early 1970s, therefore BHS had achieved a higher rate of growth than its main rival, partially as a result of improved regional coverage from new store sites but also as a result of sharper pricing and more a aggressive merchandising stance.

The success of these two retail formulas was in sharp contrast to the relatively poor performance achieved by the original five and dime variety store operator, F. W. Woolworth.[11] When Frank Winfield Woolworth finally extended his variety store concept to Britain in 1909 the result was quickly a dramatic success. Expansion was rapid and by the outbreak of the second world war the company had 768 stores and was the undisputed leader in high street trading. In 1931 the British company was floated locally, with its US parent holding a controlling shareholding.

After the second world war progress continued throughout the 1950s, the group's 1,000th store being opened in 1958. Woolworths offered a wide variety of merchandise including food, confectionery, clothing, ironmongery and a wide range of household and stationery items. During the 1960s, however, the rise in consumer affluence meant that the down market position of Woolworths became a handicap rather than an advantage. Further, the company was slow to modernise its stores, some 900 of which remained relatively small, with bare floor boards, mahogany counters and were labour intensive. Management had maintained its faith in the original variety store concept so much so that Woolworths stocked over 50,000 product lines and had developed at least 18 private label brands. In one respect, however, management departed from the conventional formula of low price, high volume. For Woolworths the key element in marketing was profit margin rather than stock turn, with the result that there was serious duplication of the lines stocked and an accumulation of stocks for those lines which although offering high margins, sold slowly.

In 1969, a number of outside shareholders, although unable to obtain control because of the US parent holding, expressed strong criticism of the existing management. A new chairman was appointed who, unlike previous incumbents, made a series of appointments to key positions from outside the ranks of the existing management. Over the next few years many of Woolworths' established practices were transformed, a new public image sought and a gradual increase in the value and reduction in variety of merchandise stocked took place. Store modernisation was accelerated and all were converted to self service or cash 'n wrap. Many of the smaller stores were shut down and, in 1967, Woolworths began to open a range of new out of town superstores under the Woolco name. These stores, all much larger than the average high street stores, sold only one tenth the number of lines held by the traditional shops. In 1974, a further new venture in catalogue discount stores was initiated using a number of the small traditional stores as initial sites. Despite these efforts, however, Woolworths had still largely failed to reestablish its once dominant position and represented a relatively unusual example of a dominant retailer failing to adjust its retail formula to accommodate changing consumer needs.

While Woolworths represented the adoption of a successful US based formula which had failed to evolve adequately, the strategy of the Boots Company [12] represented the successful extension of an American retailing concept. From a relatively specialised retail format centred on the distribution of pharmaceuticals and related products, Boots had developed a successful formula which embraced both small chemists shops offering a limited range of merchandise to large high street variety stores. The company was started by Jesse Boot, a retail pharmacist in the nineteenth century, and went public in 1888. Boot believed that retail margins were too high and operated his business on the principal of offering quality merchandise at lower prices. To assist in this he integrated backward into the production and compounding of a range of pharmaceuticals and toiletries which were sold alongside proprietary products at a lower price. Thus Boots was another example of the successful use of a quality private brand name being used as the basis for establishing a successful retail business. By 1915, the company had expanded to 550 stores largely by acquisition and the range of merchandise sold in Boots stores had widened to include stationery, books, gifts and fancy goods, in addition to the traditional pharmaceuticals and toiletries.

In 1920 due to ill health Jesse Boot sold control of his business to the American, United Drug Company. The Americans were responsible for a number of important changes including the establishment of a basic management structure in contrast to the autocratic style practised by Boot. In 1933, financial pressure in the USA led Boots to be sold back to the British, with Jesse Boot still in control. By 1939 Boots operated a chain of nearly 1,200 shops and had begun to establish a limited presence in New Zealand and other Empire territories.

After the war Boots concentrated its activity on its retail business and, following the removal of building restrictions, embarked on an extensive store enlargement and modernisation programme. Work on pharmaceuticals and drugs also continued however, and extensions were made to the range of products self manufactured and further areas of specialised distribution, such as agricultural sales were developed. In 1967 a major reorganisation took place which decentralised decision making to a divisional system, a new managing director was appointed and other changes made among the senior management. A more aggressive programme of diversification and expansion followed which led to the acquisition of Timothy Whites and of drug makers, the Crookes Group, and two abortive merger attempts with pharmaceutical manufacturers Glaxo and House of Fraser. In addition, further expansion occurred overseas in pharmaceuticals with international activities being consolidated into an overseas division.

Boots retailing operation consisted of two chains. The first of these, Boots the Chemist, according to store size carried a wide variety of merchandise divided into four principal product groups, chemist, beauty/fashion, leisure and home while the second, the Timothy Whites chain, specialised mainly in home products. Boots had moved wherever possible to reduce its labour requirements and apart from the sale of medicines, photographic products and certain specialised departments, no counter service was provided. All the Timothy Whites stores operated on a self selection basis. Buying and distributing was strictly centralised for both store chains and over the past decade extensive development of own brand products had taken place either manufactured by the company or produced to specification.

The final variety chain, W. H. Smith,[13] evolved from an early concentration on publishing wholesaling and bookstall retailing. A family company, W. H. Smith went public in 1950, but profits declined as margins came under pressure during the following decade. In 1958 a major change in retail group management occurred which rearranged operations into a series of 18 largely autonomous areas. Expansion followed both by opening new branches and by increasing the size of existing ones. By the late 1960s new store openings were offering a wider range of merchandise including toys, games and records. In addition centralised buying and promotion were strengthened while a number of bookstalls and small stores were closed down. W. H. Smith's was also the leading wholesaler of newspapers and periodicals in the UK. These activities although providing the group's traditional strength had shown few opportunities for growth in a mature market although reorganisation and the choice of alternative uses for the space available could release valuable additional cash flows. By acquisition and some internal expansion W. H. Smiths have also become the leading operator of mail order book clubs in the UK.

The retail conglomerates

In contrast to the department store groups and leading variety chains which have tended to evolve largely by the exploitation and expansion of a specific retailing formula, a number of companies embraced a series of retail activities forming a conglomerate group of multiple chains which often included significant manufacturing interests. These groups had commonly been created as a result of entrepreneurial actions such as at Cavenham, with acquisition playing a major role in expansion. The important exception to this trend was the cooperative movement which was the most diversified retailing organisation.

Sears Holdings[14] was built up by Mr. (later Sir) Charles Clore in the 1950s and by 1975 operated over 2,000 retail stores, largely involved in the distribution of footwear. In the early 1950s Clore recognised the underlying property value of a number of shoe manufacturing companies which had integrated forward into high street trading. These organisations with their conservative managements and undervalued property were ripe for acquisition. Clore quickly built up a substantial empire of shoe shops and manufacturing operations, making extensive use of the sale and leaseback technique on the property to finance his purchases. These interests were later consolidated into the British Shoe Corporation which operated through several multiple shoe store chains and came to dominate the market for footwear in the UK.

Clore also diversified into mechanical and electrical engineering and other areas of retailing and the service industries, including department stores, specialty jewellery and tableware distribution, hotels and betting shops. Each of these disparate interests of Sears Holdings operated as an autonomous unit, reporting primarily in financial terms to the small central office managed by Clore and a number of close associates.

In addition to Clore and the third Lord Fraser, the early post war period also saw the emergence of two other large entrepreneur led retail conglomerates. Great Universal Stores [15](GUS) was largely created by Mr. (later Sir) Isaac Wolfson who, in 1930, joined the Universal Stores Company, an organisation devoted to catalogue selling to working class families by the use of door to door salesmen. In 1931 the company went public and Wolfson became managing director shortly thereafter.

By a process of acquisition Wolfson dramatically expanded the range of interests of the group, moving into many areas of retailing including furniture, electrical goods, fashion clothing, footwear, mens outerwear, do it yourself, and general merchandise. In addition, GUS diversified into package holidays, mail order retailing, investment and financial services and some sectors of manufacturing. Unlike most store groups Wolfson also expanded overseas, acquiring interests in Sweden, Holland, France, Austria, South Africa and North America.

As a result of its diversity, GUS operated with a divisional structure. Wolfson was one of the first to introduce such an organisation in the UK having observed the structure in practice at Sears Roebuck in the United States. Each major operating unit such as the specialised product, multiple retail chains like furniture, electrical, fashion, mail order and so on, operated largely independently of one another but subject to strict financial controls. In addition, there was some vertical integration between the retail groups and the group's manufacturing interests while the buying of all merchandise was also coordinated centrally.

United Drapery Stores[16] (UDS) was former in 1927 to purchase the businesses of five department stores and a credit drapery business. Liquidity difficulties later forced the Eagle Star Insurance Company to foreclose a mortgage it held and take control of the company. As a result, after a period under Sir Bernard Mountain, John Collier was named as the chairman in 1950. Under Collier the company embarked upon an aggressive acquisition programme which persisted even after his death in 1968, until the early 1970s. The company expanded in particular into mens tailoring via the purchase of Prices Tailors in 1953, and Alexandre the following year. Other smaller groups were added during the 1960s and a proposed merger with the Burton Group was rejected by the Monopolies Commission. In addition, UDS entered womens fashion retailing, mail order and more recently footwear distribution. Overall by the early 1970s, UDS operated around 1,200 multiple stores and 21 department stores, in addition to its mail order and salesman collection operations, the latter being similar to the GUS tallyman activities.

Under John Collier UDS was an early adopter of the divisional form of organisation. The individual multiple chains acted in an autonomous manner and had substantial discretion over the product range stocked. In the mens outerwear operation, however, the business was essentially vertically integrated with 80–90 per cent of sales being produced within the group's own factories.

The Burton Group,[17] like UDS, was also heavily involved in mens outerwear. Built up by Mr. (later Sir) Montague Burton, Burton was one of the earliest manufacturers of mass produced, made to measure suits. By 1952, when Sir Montague died, the company was the world's largest multiple tailor. The death of the founder however, left a managerial vacuum which the company endeavoured to fill with the purchase of Jackson the Tailor, a small multiple chain, in order to obtain its management. The new team of the Jacobsen brothers did little however, to develop internal management skills and by the late 1960s, a further succession crisis developed. This resulted in the appointment of a new chief executive, Ladislas Rice, who proceeded to change the company's strategy and structure in response to a declining profit performance brought on by a market change from made to measure to more fashion oriented ready to wear suits.

The company's retail stores were rationalised and an attempt made to change its conservative image, in order to recapture business among younger consumers who were increasingly the major purchasers of mens clothing. In addition Rice diversified by the acquisition of a series of other multiple chains taking Burton into womens fashion, office equipment, and photographic retailing as well as expansion into continental Europe. These moves did not prove successful however, and Burton failed to achieve any significant economic progress. Further, increased gearing against the groups property interest meant heavier financing charges, such that the group had found it increasingly difficult to maintain an adequate cash position. Structurally, Rice adopted a divisional organisation for Burton as shown in figure 7.5, in a manner similar to that found in the other conglomerate store groups. Each division acted in a largely autonomous fashion although in the case of the menswear division Burton maintained two major chains under the Burton and Jackson brand names as well as subdividing the Burton stores themselves to cater for specific consumer segments. Manufacturing was also divorced from the retail stores and in theory was expected to remain fully competitive with potential outside suppliers. In reality, however, this deliberate attempt to break down the relationship between manufacturing and retailing had been largely unsuccessful in creating two viable profit centres and the future of the two functions still seemed indivisibly linked.

Burton therefore was the unique example among the sample companies of where divisionalisation was clearly unrewarding in terms of improved performance. As shown in chapter 10 this transformation normally results in a sharp improvement in financial results but, in the Burton case this was clearly not so and ultimately Rice was replaced in 1977 as the company's performance continued to deteriorate.

Powell Duffryn was not a typical retailer but was involved in distribution. The company was originally the largest operator of coal mines in the United Kingdom and from this position built up a vertically integrated business which extended into coal distribution by sea and rail, the production of mining equipment and railway wagon production, and the supply of timber. Overseas the company was responsible for operating bunkering facilities in a number of countries. Moreover, Powell Duffryn had also diversified into the storage and distribution of oil products as these came to compete with coal for many fuel markets.

After the second world war the coal mining industry was taken into public ownership and Powell Duffryn found itself cut off from its core business around which all its integrated activities had developed. Financial compensation was not actually paid until sometime later, but rather than return these funds to the shareholders, the Powell Duffryn management decided to invest the funds by an acquisition programme. This activity commenced in the late 1950s and continued apace throughout the early 1960s.

The company began to build up its industrial interests as separate businesses. The timber supply business was expanded by purchase, other fuel distributors were bought, extensions were made into road haulage and bulk liquid transportation as well as many other areas. The company rapidly became a conglomerate operating a set of basically dissimilar businesses. At first the new activities were loosely linked into the group in a

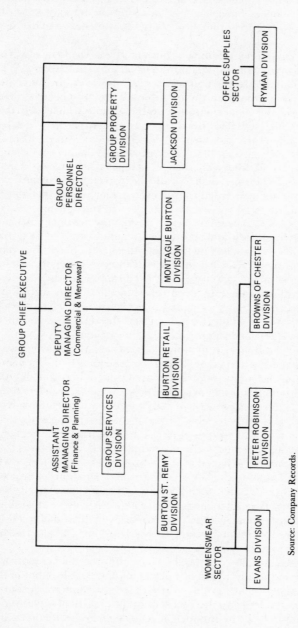

Figure 7.5   Burton Group Organisation, 1973

Source: Company Records.

holding company relationship. An awareness of the deficiencies of this structure developed, however, and following the appointment of a new chairman in 1967 a divisional form of organisation began to be introduced in 1968.

The most diversified retailing organisation was the Cooperative movement, which in total operated around 11,000 shops in England, Wales and Northern Ireland.[18] In the post war period, however, the movement had substantially lost ground to the multiples. This had occurred for several reasons. Firstly, the social environmental conditions which led to the initial inspiration which created the cooperatives had largely disappeared. Secondly, while many members of the movement wanted to match the success of retailers such as Tesco and Marks and Spencer they lacked the resources, skills and, above all, the will to repeat their success. Finally, the organisation of the movement made the presentation of any common image difficult and prevented it from even achieving the buying potential of the combined retail societies which went to make it up.

The Cooperative movement began in the nineteenth century, as a way of providing goods for the working classes at fair prices. The initial retail societies which were owned by their members, usually within a particular region, integrated backward into wholesaling in order to obtain better prices and to supply wider areas. In 1863 a number of the northern retail societies combined to create a central wholesale society for the North of England, which was later extended to cover the entire country. Despite this consolidation of wholesaling, however, the retail societies themselves remained localised and often jealously autonomous.

One result of this local autonomy was that each retail society was free to purchase its goods wherever it chose and consequently the movement as a whole used a vast number of different suppliers and did not therefore concentrate buying power through its own wholesale society. Moreover each retail society was a sovereign body owned by its members. As a result there was no central body able to make changes to the system and any reforms therefore had to pass through a slow process of persuasion. In addition, the management structure of individual societies was controlled largely by committees elected by a small group of the electorate who were ideologically committed. The small size and amateur nature of many such committees made it difficult for the societies to attract and retain high quality retail management. The societies were also inhibited by their close connection with the trade unions which tended to ensure they were slow to reduce labour by moving to self service, and also restricted the autonomy of managers.

The consistent loss of market share by the movement led to a recognition, in the late 1960s, of a need for change. A number of the more forward looking retail societies attempted to modernise. Further, as competition developed in the 1960s, from the growth of supermarkets and self service stores, so the number of retail societies in financial difficulty increased. In 1965 the only central organisation in the movement, the Cooperative Wholesale Society[19] (CWS), therefore produced a plan recommending a substantial reduction in the number of retail societies and the development of a closer relationship between the societies and the CWS including the increased use of the CWS as the central buying organisation for the whole movement.

Unfortunately, the CWS itself, just as the retail societies, was a bureaucratic jungle of committees. In addition many of the manufacturing operations established by the CWS, and which produced some 30 per cent of the goods sold to the retail societies, were antiquated, labour intensive, inefficient and made products of poor design and reliability. The CWS also marketed under a profusion of brand names, and its central buyers were considered by many to be out of touch with consumer requirements and of poor quality by comparison with the buyers in other retail groups.

In 1967 the CWS undertook the drastic step of appointing a new chief executive Phillip Thomas, from Associated British Foods. Thomas immediately set about reorganisation. Other outsiders were introduced and a reorganisation committee devolved control of the CWS to Thomas and an executive board. Uneconomic factories were closed down and the number of retail societies sharply reduced from around 450 to about 175, with the eventual objective of cutting this to 50 regional societies. Unfortunately, Thomas was killed in an air crash before his ideas could fully bear fruit but his work was continued by Alfred Wilson, a Coop man of long standing, but a firm believer in the radical ideas of his predecessor.

The CWS structure was subdivided into a series of trading divisions, each supervised and coordinated by a controller, and sales and profit accountable. In addition a retail and services division was created to advise, cajole and actively assist retail societies to improve their management, marketing and retail skills. The structure is illustrated in figure 7.6. In addition to modifying its structure the CWS led the movement in adopting a uniform brand image under the Coop brand name, initiated a nationwide stamp trading scheme which was extended beyond the movement to the garage trade, aided the establishment of a common modernised corporate store identity emphasising the Coop symbol, and moved to expand the Coop bank into a force capable of competing with the main clearing banks. These moves had not resulted in a marked improvement in the movement's competitive position, but it largely stabilised the situation, while in some areas, such as home freezer centres and hypermarket development, individual retail societies, usually aided by the CWS, had been at the forefront of development.

Conclusions

The retail industry has undergone a substantial transformation in the post war period. For the major retail firms a number of specific strategies can be recognised which have all managed to encompass these trends if they have

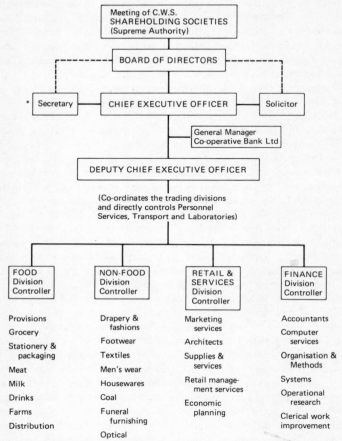

* For all secretarial matters and statutory obligations connected with his office, the
  Secretary is directly responsible to the Board and the Solicitor retains his additional
  function of legal adviser to the Board. For all other matters, they are responsible to
  the Chief Executive Officer, as is the General Manager of the Co-operative Bank Ltd

Source: Cooperative Wholesale Society

Figure 7.6 Organisation of the Cooperative Wholesale Society, 1973

been successful. Firstly, there are those companies which have found a
particular formula which has proved capable of adaptation over time.
These firms tend to have been formed by entrepreneurs and later extended
by subsequent family generations, which have adapted the founder's basic
concepts to modern market requirements.

In addition these firms have all tended to significantly develop private
label brand names which have a reputation for quality, at least on a par

with major brands. Centralised buying has become the rule for success and this is a critical function, largely determing the ultimate profitability of the firm. Retail operations tend to be organised on a regional basis with limited degrees of autonomy for individual store managers. Dependent upon store size, there has been some move towards increased product choice, although there has also been concentration on the precise groups of products handled by stores. Nevertheless, there has been some tendency toward similarity, with food retailers moving into non-food and a number of major non-food retailers moving into food retailing. Expansion throughout the UK has been a major strand in the post war development of many of the store groups, although a few had established a national network prior to the second world war. Very few of these firms, however,

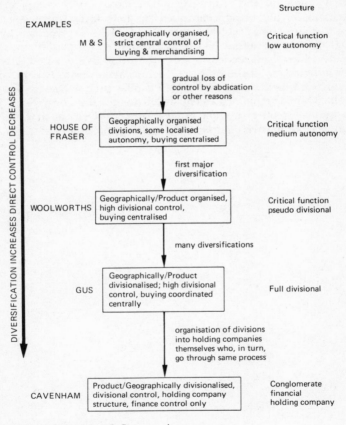

Source: Adapted from C. Ryan, op. cit., p. 93

Figure 7.7   Retailing Organisational Forms

have endeavoured to move internationally, although Boots and Marks and Spencer, have made limited efforts.

The alternative strategy to the family oriented, single formula retailer has been the acquisition oriented strategies of post war entrepreneurs such as Clore, Wolfson, Collier and Goldsmith. The firms created by such men as these have adopted a multiple formula strategy, achieving success by combining groups of similar stores under a common brand name or corporate identity and then realising the potential economies of scale in purchasing. Moreover, these firms have been more aggressive in international expansion, not being confined to a UK oriented retail formula.

In terms of structure, the retail companies offer a variety of forms. The simplest form is a critical function structure, where buying is centralised, while store operations are managed on a regional basis. This structure was normally found in the relatively undiversified family companies. In addition to buying being centralised in these firms, there was clear evidence that strong central control and high involvement by top management in operations had a positive impact on performance. The more diversified firms tended to move toward a divisionalised system as shown in figure 7.7. In some cases, such as Woolworths, where several different retail models operated with a similar product range, however, centralised buying remained and made full divisionalisation difficult. Only when quite disparate product ranges were involved, as at GUS and Burton, was a full divisional system deemed appropriate.

8. The Transport Industries: Strategy, Structure and Political Intervention

A major sector of the service industries has been taken into public ownership. The phenomenon of nationalisation advanced substantially in the post war period with the return of the first post war Labour administration. When the first Atlee government was sworn in in 1945 it came to power on a platform embracing a wide ranging policy of nationalisation, an ideological position which dated back to the formation of the party and of early socialist thinkers, especially Sidney and Beatrice Webb. Despite its socialist parentage however, many of the arguments advanced in favour of nationalisation such as economies of scale; the elimination of wasteful competition and underuse of assets; the need in some industries, to provide a wider social service than to seek mere profit maximisation; the lack of adequate private capital; and the need for military or national security, have also been generally accepted by the Conservative party, despite its ideological commitment to a free enterprise economy.

Since the first industries were nationalised further elements of common policy between the two major political parties have emerged. These industries are now seen as a major tool in national economic policy in areas such as industrial capital investment, prices and incomes and regional policy. The industries have also been perceived as a means of fostering technological innovation. Despite this common ground, however, there are fundamental philosophical differences between the parties which have tended to lead to significant policy reversals when the parties have succeeded one another in office.

Prior to 1945 a number of examples of state enterprise had already been created. From the outset the Post Office had been a department of state while the early utility franchises, although often vested in private hands, were to revert to municipal control after twenty one years. In 1908 the Liberal government of the day created the Port of London Authority as the first major twentieth century act of nationalisation. Then, although a dramatic increase in state intervention took place during the first world war, the next major move was the establishment of the Central Electricity

Board in 1926. The British Broadcasting Corporation was set up in 1923 as a public corporation to control the new medium of radio, and in 1933 the Conservative dominated National government established the London Passenger Transport Board, based on Herbert Morrison's concept of a public corporation. The Conservatives also nationalised coal mineral rights in 1938, and in 1940 set up British Overseas Airways Corporation, the last of the prewar public corporations, to take over from Imperial Airways.

The transportation industries were a high priority for nationalisation by the 1945 Labour government, although land based transportation had been the focus of regular legislation for considerably longer, a major Act being produced at intervals of about every eight years, since 1930. These tended to concentrate on attempts to produce a coordinated policy between road and rail transport while other forms of transport, such as air, inland water and coastal shipping, had been the subject of far less attention. Much has been written about the development of the public sector transportation industries and it is not intended here to duplicate this. Rather the chapter focusses briefly on the key changes in strategy and structure and looks partially at the landbased sectors as a total system. Further, it examines to some extent the key role of political intervention in the strategic decision making process and in the periodic redesign of organisation structures.

THE NATIONALISED AIR TRANSPORT INDUSTRY

The nature of the industry

The air transport industry passed effectively into public ownership when British Overseas Airways Corporation (BOAC) was created by a Conservative government in 1940, largely for strategic and imperial reasons. The return of the post war Labour government resulted in the creation of two further specialised organisations, British European Airways (BEA) and British South American Airways. BEA was to concentrate on European routes while BOAC was to cover long haul operations; British South American was later merged with BOAC in 1949. Each of the nationalised corporations was given a complete monopoly of British scheduled services with no competition between them. This position changed in 1952 when the incoming Conservative government encouraged the growth of an independent private enterprise air transport sector, which has remained to the present day.

The air transport industry is largely an international activity since the economies of aircraft operation make air travel a relatively unattractive proposition over distances of less than 200–300 miles. Nationalisation therefore, can only apply to the air transport industry of a particular country and airlines based in different countries are largely outside the control of a particular government except for journeys in and out of the airspace controlled by each nation state. This sovereignty of each country over its own airspace was confirmed by the Chicago Convention of 1944 and the countries therefore bargain for the use of one anothers airspace, negotiate landing rights for commercial operations and the like. This convention failed to achieve a multilateral agreement for air traffic rights but a further conference in Bermuda in 1946 established a formal set of principles between Britain and the USA governing the important North Atlantic routes.

The Chicago Convention also established the distinction between scheduled, regular fixed price services, and non scheduled operations. Scheduled services which necessitate operators providing a specific service tend to operate with load factors lower than non scheduled flights which can be more adapted to suit demand. Scheduled services have therefore tended to be governed by price tariffs approved by the International Air Transport Association (IATA). During the early post war period, scheduled services tended to dominate air traffic but the high prices fixed by IATA led to the rapid growth of non scheduled services and especially the development of Inclusive Tour (IT) business. This service, which involves the sale of a package of air travel and hotel accommodation for an all in price, has expanded rapidly with rising affluence.

The rapid growth of non scheduled charter traffic for IT and other operations is still to some extent governed by IATA pricing policies. In addition the two systems have developed separately in the main, using different aircraft and even different routes. Changes in aircraft fleets in recent years have, however, blurred the traditional demarcation between scheduled and non-scheduled flights. In particular the arrival in service of large capacity aircraft has led to the placement of IT and affinity groups on scheduled flights in an effort to increase the load factor on such flights.

In addition to fare price fixing, many airlines operate pooling arrangements. This form of control agreement usually involves an equal sharing between the participants of the seat capacity on a given route and joint revenue irrespective of the actual traffic carried by each participant. Governments can and do encourage some pooling agreements and make it a condition of operating on some routes. Governments, too, are usually responsible for the designation of particular airlines as scheduled carriers on routes which use airspace under their jurisdiction.

Over the post war period the traditional differences between short and long haul aircraft economies have undergone a substantial change. In the 1950s over a short range of around 500 miles long haul aircraft operating costs were approximately twice the seat mile rate of purpose built short haul machines. By the late 1960s newer long haul aircraft were becoming as cheap to operate as short haul thus changing the critical factor in aircraft choice increasingly to route passenger density rather than route length.[1]

The development of BEA

Against the background of these overall trends in airline economics the two state owned corporations have evolved. In the early years after its creation BEA was primarily concerned with building its route network. This expanded dramatically and by the mid 1950s most of the major routes in Western Europe had been established. By 1960 the airline's capacity ton miles had reached 237.4 millions with an operating load factor of 65.2 per cent.[2] The Corporation had by this time converted its fleet from the small post war Dakota and Elizabethan propeller aircraft, to larger turboprop Viscounts and, in 1960, started its first pure jet services with the introduction of the Comet 4B.

During the early 1960s BEA began to lose market share as both passenger and overall load factors declined. This resulted from the introduction of the larger and/or faster Vanguard and Comet aircraft and the move by a number of European competitors to introduce pure jet aircraft. In 1964 BEA began operating the Trident, its first second generation, short haul, pure jet aircraft. This was followed in 1968 by the addition of the BAC super one-eleven short haul jet, leading to the progressive replacement of the Viscount fleet, the selling of the Comet 4 fleet and the conversion of most of BEA's Vanguards to freight carrying by 1971. Over the decade of the 1960s BEA's CTM capacity increased by nearly 200 per cent, the number of passengers carried increased from 4.0m to 8.7m and freight ton miles expanded from 16.6 to 45.9m. At the same time, however, despite this significant growth, there was a decline in overall load factors from 65.2 to 54.2 per cent, while the passenger load factor fell from 66.7 to 60.4 per cent.

The organisation of the airline changed to meet the increasing complexity of operations. Initially BEA operated with a functional form organisation as shown in figure 8.1, which illustrates the system existing in 1956. Under the main board was a chief executive reporting to whom were the heads of all major functional departments. Local ground operations located away from London were regionalised under a system of area managers, responsible for the stations along BEA routes within a particular area. As a result of the expansion of the corporation, by the early 1960s over 30 executives were reporting directly to the chief executive. Moreover, the functional departments were operated as cost centres with responsibility for profitability residing only at the top management level.

In 1964, after leading BEA since 1949, Lord Douglas of Kirkeside retired and was replaced by Mr. Anthony Millward. Lord Douglas had combined the offices of chairman and chief executive since the resignation of Mr. Peter Masefield in 1955 and, following his retirement, the two offices were again separated with the appointment of Mr. Henry Marking as chief executive. The organisational deficiencies within the old structure now became widely recognised and with consultancy help from the Tavistock

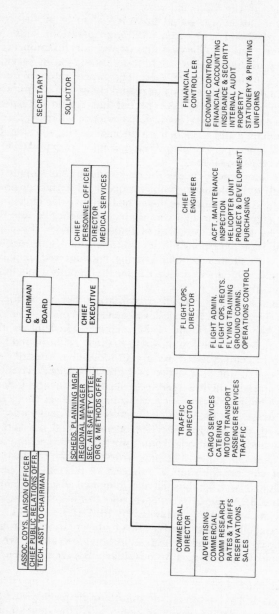

Figure 8.1 BEA Administrative Tree, 1956

Source: BEA Annual Report, 1956/7

Institute, a committee was established in 1966 which led to a reorganisation of the corporation in the following year.

The new organisation was based upon a system of profit centres. A number of the passenger and cargo handling operations, and the area managers, were merged with the commercial and sales function, creating a traffic and sales division, while flight operations, cabin services and London ground station activities were regrouped into an operations division. The Engineering functions were also treated as a separate profit centre. Under the new system it was expected that Traffic and Sales would 'buy' aircraft capacity from the operations division, which in turn would purchase maintenance and services from the engineering division. Central services such as finance, personnel and purchasing were expected to charge for services wherever possible.

The excessive interdependence of the operating divisions made the new structure difficult to implement. Problems occurred with coordination in keeping traffic and sales separate from operations, the checking in of passengers, luggage and the like was the responsibility of one division, while flying crew and aircraft control remained under the control of another. The division of responsibilities led to serious arguments between the 'divisions' with further problems being encountered as a result of schedule planning, which was another separate function reporting direct to the chief executive.[3]

The deficiencies of the revised organisation led to a further reorganisation of the group in 1971, following the retirement of Sir Anthony Millward and the appointment of Mr. Henry Marking as the new chairman. The new organisation shown in figure 8.2 subdivided BEA into ten separate profit centres based mainly on individual aircraft fleets and route groups. For example, the largest of the divisions, BEA Mainline, was to operate and market scheduled services over European and UK internal routes using the main Trident fleet and airbus aircraft as they came into service. By contrast, the BEA Super One Eleven Division was based at Manchester, with the responsibility for operating and marketing scheduled domestic and international routes from Manchester and also over internal West German routes. The new structure also integrated into the mainstream of the organisation a number of related but peripheral activities which had been established and managed as separate subsidiary companies. Thus BEA had been an early operator of regular commercial helicopter services which were managed by BEA Helicopters Ltd., while direct entry into the IT market had led first to the creation of BEA Airlines and later to the development of interests in hotel operations, which were managed through another separate subsidiary, Sovereign Group Hotels.

The development of BOAC

In its early days BOAC assumed the mantle of its predecessor Imperial Airways and an important aspect of policy was 'the development and

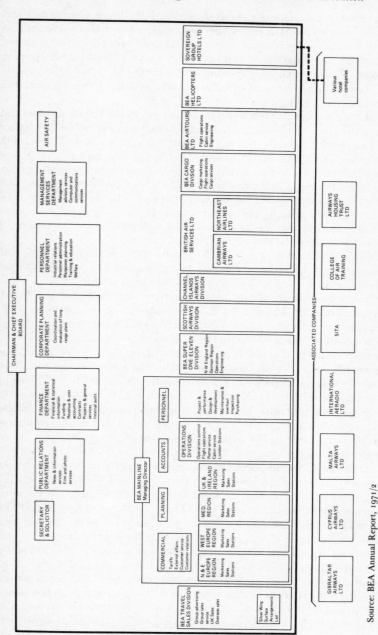

Source: BEA Annual Report, 1971/2

Figure 8.2 BEA Divisional Organisation, 1971

integration of air communications throughout the British Commonwealth and the Empire.'[4] As a result the corporation was heavily engaged in routes which in themselves were not always profitable. In addition investments were made in a series of feeder airlines, usually in developing country areas, which while providing traffic for BOAC's main trunk routes also were a transport and communication system, system within the countries concerned.

The corporation also felt a special obligation to use British aircraft and during the 1950s the fleet was transformed from a heavy post war reliance on American Constellations and Strato-cruisers to Bristol Britannia turbojets and De Havilland Comets. Being the first airline to use new British aircraft meant that BOAC tended to have higher operating costs than its competitors and these were held to be a major reason for poor economic performance during the early 1950s. Certainly the fact that the corporation was initially expected to continue using these aircraft, when later the Boeing 707 became available, did reduce its economies of operation significantly.

BOAC was however, a long haul operator and a high proportion of its operations were scheduled services. The corporation was thus less affected initially by the growth of IT traffic although high scheduled fares led to significant growth in affinity group charters, especially on the North Atlantic. From its London base, the corporation's services were concentrated on three principal areas: firstly to the west, which included North America and the Caribbean, then on to Australia and the Pacific Basin; secondly to the South principally linking the Empire and Commonwealth territories of Africa; and finally eastward, via the eastabout routes through the Middle East, to Asia and the Pacific Basin. Following its merger with British South American Airways, BOAC was also responsible for operating main trunk services to Latin America until this loss making route was eventually divested to the private sector of British aviation as part of the Conservative government inspired reorganisation of air transport in the early 1970s.

During the 1950s the Corporation expanded its geographic coverage. In 1950 the Corporation's main operations involved 56 stations outside London, while by 1960 some 82 main locations were serviced. At the same time capacity expanded from 161m CTM in 1950 – 51 to 577.4m CTM a decade later. Much of this new capacity was the result of the introduction into service of the new large jets, especially the Boeing 707, which not only brought increased speed but additional seat capacity and improved operating efficiency. For BOAC, however, the arrival of the new all jet aircraft brought a serious decline in operating financial performance. Following the withdrawal from service of the corporation's Comets after a series of crashes, BOAC, too, added Boeings to its fleet prior to the arrival of the British built VC10 ordered for delivery in the mid 1960s. In an attempt to maintain capacity usage, the corporation led the way toward a progressive reduction of fares on the North Atlantic and concessionary fares were later introduced in other arenas of operation. Similarly competition for air cargo increased, and BOAC also endeavoured to expand its charter business especially for its surplus propeller aircraft capacity, which due to obsolescence and a depressed market could not be sold off at other than a distressed price. Nevertheless load factors fell from almost 60 per cent in 1950 to 55.7 per cent in 1960–1.

Revenue per CTM fell sharply from 13.2p per CTM in 1960–1 to 9.9p in 1962–3, operating deficits were incurred in the early 1960s with performance in 1960–1 resulting in an overall loss after interest and tax of around £50m. In 1963, BOAC became the subject of a Government review which criticised performance, in particular of new aircraft introduction policy, the management of investments in associated and subsidiary companies, principally feeder airlines, and finally the corporation's organisation and management structure.[5]

As a result of this report a drastic reorganisation of the corporation's board took place. The chairman and managing director both resigned and Sir Giles Guthrie was appointed as chairman with Mr. Keith Granville and Mr. Charles Hardie becoming deputy chairmen. A further five board changes followed in short order. In addition Guthrie clarified two further factors of fundamental importance to BOAC. Firstly, the government agreed unequivocably that the choice of aircraft was a matter for the corporation to decide. Secondly, it was confirmed that the fundamental responsibility of the corporation was to act commercially and any departure in pursuit of the national interest should be the subject of express agreement or at the express request of the Minister. Below board level, the organisation of the corporation underwent only limited change, remaining essentially functional, although operations were subdivided on a regional basis.

Under Guthrie the performance of the Corporation improved sharply, aided by a capital reconstruction which translated part of BOAC's debt structure into a form of equity, Exchequer Dividend Capital. Unprofitable routes were pruned, improved marketing methods were introduced and a significant reduction was made in operating personnel, employees falling from 21,660 in 1961–2 to 18,845 in 1965–6. Capacity expanded by 240 per cent during the 1960s, although the number of passengers flown only increased by 132 per cent from 0.79m to 1.85m. Freight ton miles growth went some way to fill the additional capacity, expanding by 500 per cent, but BOAC's overall load factor continued to fall reaching just under 50 per cent by 1970–1. Nevertheless the improvements in cost and productivity achieved, coupled with a stabilisation of the new aircraft introduction programme, led to significant gains in financial performance, yielding favourable profits for the latter half of the decade.

The 1970s, however, seemed less promising. Increased competition on the North Atlantic again resulted after the introduction of jumbo jets.

Moreover BOAC lost ground due to a damaging pilot dispute which delayed the start of its Boeing 747 services for some 10 months. The 1970s also saw the effective reversal of government policy in allowing BOAC to adopt commericial criteria in its choice of aircraft. As a result the corporation was required to purchase the Anglo-French Concorde supersonic transport which was expected to run at a loss.

The formation of British Airways Corporation

The 1960 investigation into the financial position and prospects of BOAC which led to the subsequent boardroom reorganisation, commented upon the relationship between the two state air corporations. Integration of the two organisations was not recommended but limited linkages were developed in an effort to improve coordination, since the corporations shared station facilities in a number of locations and in part acted as a feeder for one another. One step taken led to the respective chairmen becoming members of both corporation boards.

In 1967 the government set up a further committee of inquiry into civil air transport under the chairmanship of Sir Ronald Edwards.[6] This committee reported to Parliament in 1969, which led to the publication of a White Paper incorporating many of the Edwards committee proposals.[7] The incoming Conservative government in 1970 rejected the increased role visualised for the state sector by Labour and the 1971 Civil Aviation Act incorporated these changes. One major feature of this Act, however, was the creation of the British Airways Corporation to be responsible for the affairs of both BEA and BOAC.

The increased flexibility of new types of aircraft, the extension of the operating range of short haul aircraft to enable them to operate traditional long haul routes, and increased passenger capacity has led to route density becoming the critical factor in aircraft choice.[8] High capital cost also makes high aircraft usage essential and this has led to the increasing use of more flexible machines rather than long and short haul specialised aircraft. The advantages of a standardised fleet were recognised by the Edwards committee which also observed that large airline size could produce significant economies of scale, not merely from fleet standardisation but also from marketing, when widespread coverage was required and when large overall scale was associated with high participation in particular markets. Where these conditions did not exist, however, no advantages were expected. Edwards did not recommend an outright merger between BEA and BOAC but suggested the establishment of an airways board with strategic responsibility over both corporations. In addition the committee visualised the development of a regional airline group, concerned with second level routes.

In the event the government chose to fully integrate the two corporations and British Airways Corporation duly succeeded them in 1972. One of the first duties of the new board was to review all the activities now grouped under its control to determine whether these were organised efficiently or not. A series of special study groups was set up to examine aircraft procurement, route structure, commericial activities in Europe, character operations and other activities. Meanwhile a divisional structure was introduced based on the former corporations, see figure 8.3.

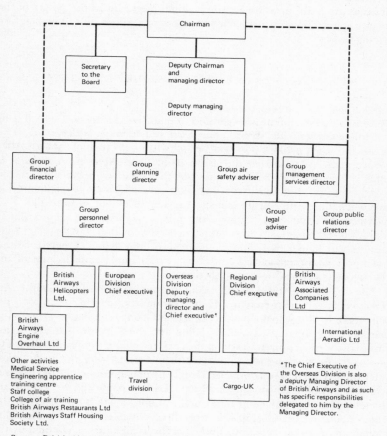

Source: British Airways Annual Report 1973/4

Figure 8.3   British Airways Organisation Structure, 1974

The evolution of the air transport sector reveals that strategic and structural change has occurred largely due to environmental change and to political ideology. The changing nature of the market place, the economics of aircraft type and usage have led to a blurring of the traditional demarcation between long and short haul services. This has ultimately resulted in the reorganisation of the industry from two separate organisations into the British Airways Corporation. The role of political intervention has largely been seen in its influence on the structure of the domestic industry, on the organisations of the public sector enterprises and perhaps most damagingly on the choice of aircraft fleets to be operated. However, unlike with the land based transport industries, the fact that air transportation is international has reduced the power of the government to actively intervene in areas of operational detail such as fare pricing policy.

THE NATIONALISED LAND BASED TRANSPORT INDUSTRY[9]

The first integrated strategy attempt

By contrast government intervention in land based transport which is by definition domestically based, has been much more widespread. This began in the immediate post war period with the return of the first Atlee government. While earlier governments had legislated in an attempt to achieve a degree of coordination among the respective sectors of the land based transportation industry, the first post war Labour government had nationalisation of the entire transport system as one of its priorities. This system embracing road haulage, the railways, buses and inland waterways, was therefore taken into public ownership by the Transport Act 1947 and placed under the unified control of the newly created British Transport Commission (BTC). This creation must rank as one of the classic organisational follies of all time.

The initial operating assets taken in public ownership by the Act consisted of the independent railway companies, together with a 50 per cent stake in the British Electric Traction Group, the major private bus fleet operator. In 1948, Thomas Tilling and the Scottish Motor Traction Company were acquired to add to the road passenger interests of the BTC. However, further major acquisitions of bus fleets were not undertaken since these tended to be controlled largely by urban municipalities many of which were politically dominated by the Labour party and were reluctant to cede control to the centralised organisation of the BTC. Even at this stage, political partisanship began to intervene in a manner designed to obviate many of the economic and even social advantages claimed by the exponents of nationalisation.

In road haulage, however, such political barriers did not exist and the 1947 legislation gave the BTC the right to acquire a monopoly in long distance haulage. Aided by a licencing system whereby hauliers had to apply to the BTC for a permit for carrying goods more than 25 miles other than for their own account the BTC rapidly began to acquire all long distance hauliers. This resulted in the subdivision of the Road Transport executive and by 1951, when a Conservative administration was returned, some 3800 independent haulage operators had been acquired.

The operation of the British Transport Commission

The BTC was thus charged with a massive task under the Act which could be summarised as: – [10]

1. Owning, controlling and reorganising the entire railway system.
2. Acquiring some 3,800 road haulage contractors and creating an integrated public monopoly.
3. Owning and controlling all road and rail passenger transport in and around London.
4. Reviewing passenger road transport facilities for the rest of the United Kingdom and preparing schemes for reorganisation.
5. Surveying the nation's harbours and preparing group schemes for reorganisation.
6. Preparing pricing policies for passenger and freight transport by road and rail.
7. Managing canals, docks, ships and hotels acquired under the Act.

By 1949 the BTC was a massive operation employing nearly 900,000 people with book net fixed assets of over £1,600 million. These assets, however, were severely depleted after the ravages of war, and in the case of many road haulage firms, were almost worthless. Moreover, despite the enormous task involved in establishing a viable integrated organisation, there was a critical lack of management. Only London Transport had any semblance of an integrated management team. The railway companies, which had competed vigorously against each other for many decades, were unaccustomed and even unwilling to work together in harmony while in the plethora of road transport companies, management was often totally non-existent.

Yet the overall organisation for this newly created empire, the BTC itself, consisted of merely five men, only one of whom was under 60, while one was over 70. This group in turn was supported by a central staff of less than 100 people. Further, no decentralisation of critical decision making was allowed the various 'Executives'. The largest unit, railways, was not allowed to borrow money except when specifically authorised by the BTC while its capital expenditure authority was limited to a mere £25,000. At the same time decision making from the Commission was painfully slow.

Reporting to the BTC were four, later five 'Executives', each of which was responsible for a specific area of transport delegated to it by the Commission, thus for example, the railways executive was delegated to run the railways subject to directions from the Commission. These directions initially concentrated on tight control over capital expenditure and appointments, regular monthly reporting and copies of board minutes. The Commission considered itself integrally involved in policy formation although certainly, the railway executive strongly resisted this and treated the Commission's powers as merely constraints to their own responsibility for running the railways. Moreover, the railway organisation was regionally based, according to the original private railway companies and the extension of the management chain and loss of regional identity brought about by the addition of the BTC, was deeply resented.

The road haulage executive also faced serious managerial problems. Initially the new management endeavoured to centralise its structure but many of the regional units were led by entrepreneurs who had been compulsorily brought out. These men were difficult to weld into a bureaucratic structure and the executive soon learned that essential business contracts could not be maintained or adequate levels of customer service provided with rigid centralisation.

Coordination and competition

In 1951 a Conservative government was returned and in 1953 the new government introduced a new Transport Act which significantly affected the position of the BTC. The new Act firstly abandoned the principle of an integrated transport system and limited the BTC to providing railway services for the country and a coordinated system of passenger traffic in the London area. The Commission's road haulage interests were to be returned to the private sector and a disposal board was set up for this purpose. In the event this task proved more difficult than expected and by 1956, when the disposal board itself was wound up, some 9,000 of the original 35,000 goods vehicles offered for resale remained unsold. This residue was therefore vested in a publicly owned road haulage contractor, British Road Services, to compete with the private sector.

The Conservative legislation also changed the organisation of the railways. The separate railway executive was disbanded and a number of its members appointed to the BTC where they were given functional advisory responsibility and a measure of overall authority. Day to day operational control of the railways was then delegated to six regional managers, creating a structure which in many ways resembled that of the former independent companies.

This new organisation was not successful, however, and within 15 months further changes were introduced. Statutory area boards were established in January 1955 to supervise each region and these were in turn supported by the creation of a substantial bureaucracy, encompassing advisory bodies, specialised committees, sub commissions and central staff agencies. This revised structure was thus both complicated and slow in operation; nevertheless, it persisted for some seven years to 1962.

The 1953 Act also relieved the railways of the necessity to publish their non-negotiable rates for both passengers and freight. This common carrier code, imposed on the railways since Victorian times, had resulted in the rapidly growing road haulage industry picking off the best freight contracts while leaving the non-economic loads which, under law, the railways were obliged to accept. After 1953, therefore, the railways were able to offer more competitive freight rates for specialised loads. In addition a major re-equipment programme was introduced at a cost of £1,240m designed to modernise the railway system.

Nevertheless, the competitive position of the railways continued to deteriorate and when the Select Committee on nationalised industries reported critically on railway modernisation in 1960 yet suggested no solutions, the Government appointed its own specialised advisory group. This group, the Stedeford Committee, which included Dr.Richard Beeching, a senior executive with ICI, was charged with specifically reviewing the operations of the railways. After the committee had reported privately Dr. Beeching was appointed as Chairman of the BTC, a position which he held until legislation was prepared based on the conclusions of the Committee.

The return to separate organisations

The final result of the Stedeford Committee was the introduction of the 1962 Transport Act which ended the attempt to manage an overall series of transport operations under unified management. This new legislation abolished the BTC and replaced it with 5 separate Boards responsible for each of Railways, London Transport, Docks, Inland Waterways and a catch all holding company to run road haulage, provincial buses, hotels and Thomas Cook, the travel agents. Each of these boards was permitted 'the maximum practical freedom of operation in its own commercial fields' with the Ministry of Transport holding overall responsibility for coordination between the specific businesses and for resource allocation of investment funds. The capital debt structure of the BTC was also divided between the new boards and, in the case of British Railways, a portion of the debt was suspended and carried no interest.

1. The British Railways Board. With the dissolution of the BTC, the railways, packet ports and ships, and hotel and catering services collected by the original railway companies, were made over to the newly created British Railways Board (BRB). The new organisation was responsible for six basic services namely; property letting, the railways being a major property owner; hotels and catering which included catering services for the travelling public; docks, harbours and wharves which operated facilities for British Rail shipping services; shipping, which was principally engaged in cross channel ferry activities; and the railway passenger freight operations. As can be seen from table 8.1 the railway services contributed well over 70 per cent of the BRB's revenue and also accounted for the large persistent deficits incurred in the early years after separation.

Each of the new separated boards was granted some discretion in designing its own organisation. As a result, British Railways, where

Table 8.1 British Railways percentage gross receipts and profitability by activity, 1964–74

	1964		1967		1970		1972		1974	
	% Receipts	Gross Profits* £m	% Receipts	Gross Profits £m	% Receipts	Gross Profits £m	% Receipts	Gross Profits £m	% Receipts	Gross Profits £m
Railways	87.9	(73.3)	87.0	(97.4)	87.0*	39.6	86.6*	7.7	84.6	(106.4)
Shipping & Hovercraft	4.3	5.1	5.0	4.6	5.1	3.8	5.5	3.1	6.2	(2.3)
Docks Harbour & Wharves	0.5	0.2	0.6	0.3	0.6	(0.1)	0.6	0.1	0.9	0.0
Hotels & Catering	4.8	1.3	5.4	1.0	5.2	1.0	5.4	1.8	5.1	(0.3)
Property	2.0	7.4	2.4	8.6	1.9	7.4	2.2	8.6	2.0	15.0
Commercial Advertising	n.a.	0.6	n.a.	0.6	n.a.	0.8	n.a.	1.1	n.a.	1.4
Total	100	(62.5)	100	(86.5)	100	51.7	100	24.9	98.8	(92.6)

* Includes government grants for uneconomic railway ratio
Source: British Railways Annual Reports.

Dr. Beeching assumed the chairmanship, was divided into the BRB and seven, lower level, but also statutory, regional boards. The BRB itself was composed of 13 members, 8 of whom were full time and responsible for specific functions. Each region had its own management team consisting of a general manager and the heads of functional departments. This group, together with a few part time local members, made up the regional board. The regions were, however, granted a considerable degree of operational and marketing autonomy, but all major policy issues were the concern of the BRB.

Under Beeching a radical reorganisation of the railway system was proposed in 1963 in an effort to make it economically viable. The main changes proposed by Beeching included the discontinuation of many stopping passenger services and the closure of many small stations; concentration on main trunk route inter-city services for passenger traffic; reduction of uneconomic freight services by the closure of local stations; the development of liner train services for dense freight movements; concentration on company trains for specialised freight; and the rationalisation of the composition and use of the railway's road haulage fleet.

The Conservative government accepted Beechings plan despite massive public protest, especially over the closure of uneconomic local passenger services. However, the proposals proved too radical for the Labour government which succeeded the Conservatives in 1964. As a result therefore, initial government acceptance was reversed by the incoming administration and many loss making services were retained on the grounds of social rather than economic benefits. Within 18 months of the introduction of the Beeching plan, the major objectives for the railway system had been reversed. Beeching resigned in 1965.

2. The Transport Holding Company. The second main descendant of the BTC was the Transport Holding Company, (THC), established by the 1962 Act. The THC's main activities were the original road haulage and road passenger interests of the BTC, although there were also limited manufacturing interests producing trucks and buses for the road transport subsidiaries, and travel agents, Thomas Cook and Sons. Unlike its predecessor, the THC operated as a commercial holding company and was consistently profitable throughout the period of its existence as shown in table 8.2. The company also maintained a relatively aggressive acquisition policy as indicated in table 8.3, moving into the European market via the purchase of the Dutch company, P. E. Boers International, and Anglo Continental Container Services. By the time it was disbanded in 1968 THC was the leading British road haulage company operating some 27,000 vehicles and holding around 7 per cent of the market.

The road passenger market was much more concentrated than road haulage and THC was dominant in rural markets save for the interests of British Electric Traction, a private sector holding company. These

Table 8.2   Transport Holding Company
Gross profit by activity (£ million)

Activity	1962	1963	1964	1965	1966	1967	1968
Road Haulage	3.5	4.7	7.3	7.0	4.9	3.0	3.8
Road Passenger(a)	6.9	6.7	7.3	6.9	7.7	6.9	14.4
Shipping	0.4	0.7	0.5	0.7	(0.3)	(0.3)	(0.7)
Travel & Tourism	1.3	1.4	1.7	2.0	1.6	0.7	1.2
Manufacturing	0.2	–	0.2	0.3	0.2	0.1	0.2
Ass. Companies (Investments)	2.5	2.5	2.7	2.7	2.4	2.3	0.2
Total	14.8	14.0	17.7	17.6	14.3	10.0	16.3

(a) In 1968 includes B.E.T. which became fully owned and was transferred from Ass. Co. status.

Source: K D Worthing op. cit p. 79

Table 8.3   Acquisition record of the Transport Holding Company by market sector

Activity	1963	1964	1965	1966	1967	1968
Road Haulage		2	10(a)	13	1	
Road Passenger	3	5	6	1	2	45(c)
Travel & Tourism					2	1
Manufacturing			2(b)			
Total of Co's	3	7	18	14	5	46
Cost (£ million)	1.2	1.0	8.5	4.2	2.6	47.2

(a) includes Tayforth Ltd who had several subsidiaries and numbered 1500 vehicles
(b) includes 30% of Park Royal Vehicles Ltd which was acquired by a share deal with British Leyland who received 25% of the other manufacturing companies
(c) All of the 45 companies came with the B.E.T. Group which was acquired for £46.9 million

Source: K D Worthing op. cit. p. 79

activities were finally acquired in 1968, leaving THC with some 42 per cent of all passenger service miles and 32 per cent of bus passengers. The remainder of the market was held by London Transport and other major municipal undertakings, together with many small private operators.

The THC operated as a holding company with the boards of each of the subsidiary companies being directly responsible to the THC board. Initially there were 91 subsidiary companies but these were subdivided into 16 loose market and regional groups each with a chief executive who helped to coordinate policy and objectives. In addition interest grouping federations were established to provide specific staff services. Corporate staff remained small, although it was expanded in 1966 to include freight and passenger planning functions.

The second strategy of integration

The 1964 Labour administration with a parliamentary majority of only 4 did not have either time or sufficient political strength to undertake any other major reorganisation of the transport system during its term in office. A new government White Paper was however produced which, coupled with the introduction of national indicative planning, reflected government thinking. First, it was considered land transport was still in urgent need of modernisation and since investment funds were scarce, an integrated policy was necessary. Second, the problem of traffic in urban areas was considered to be of priority with solutions favouring a reduction in the use of private cars and increased use of an integrated public transport, road and rail network. Third, and crucially, social as well as economic objectives were expected from the public sector. Based largely on these principles following reelection in 1966 with a working majority, the Labour government drew up the 1968 Transport Act.

This new legislation did not as some expected, attempt to recreate an overall agency such as the BTC. Instead, the new government considered that it was necessary to treat freight transport as an economic service to industry and organise it on national lines, while passenger transport should be more closely linked to community life which had important local social implications. The Act thus produced a new shuffling of responsibility for transport strategy, and further reorganisation of the structures involved in managing freight, bus and rail transportation.

As a result, therefore, the Act created the National Freight Corporation by combining the road haulage interests of the Transport Holding Company, national carriers, the road transport interest of British Rail, and a controlling interest in freightliners, which was the containerised rail freight system built up after Beeching's proposals for railway reorganisation. This new corporation was given two principal statutory obligations. Firstly, to provide a properly integrated freight service by both road and rail throughout the U.K. and secondly to ensure that, wherever it was efficient and economic, goods were carried by rail.

Following the reorganisation of freight, British Rail still retained responsibility for marketing and operating freight traffic originating by rail such as full train loads of steel, coal and the like and company trains. In addition British Rail was to concentrate on long distance, inter-city travel, while local rail services became the responsibility of a series of new Passenger Transport Authorities (PTAs).

These PTAs, of which there were initially four, serving the conurbations of Liverpool, Birmingham, Manchester and Newcastle, were principally appointed by the local authorities in the areas concerned, although one seventh of the membership was appointed directly by the Minister. London Transport, less its rural bus services, was also made over to the Greater London Council in 1968 in a similar manner to the PTAs.

Within their areas the newly created PTAs were responsible for negotiating with British Rail on the provision of local rail services and the fare structure for these services. In addition the PTAs acquired local municipal and state owned bus companies, and acted as the passenger licensing authority for their area, thus ensuring some measure of control over the remaining private bus operators.

In British Rail the changing external relationships were accompanied by an internal reorganisation. At the end of 1969 a report prepared by McKinsey and Company on the reorganisation of British Rail was accepted by the Minister. Under the Transport Act of 1962 the Board comprised mainly full time members, each of whom had specific functional or executive responsibilities and had chief headquarters executives reporting to them. The board was also responsible for policy formation issuing directives to the regions and for monitoring performance in their functions. The main operations of British Rail were the responsibility of the regional general managers, who were normally also the chairman of regional boards composed of assistant general managers and some part time members.

The new structure converted the railways board into a largely non-executive group in order to give greater emphasis to overall corporate planning, policy making and longer term activities. Beneath the board British Rail was subdivided into a series of separate product market based businesses each the responsibility of a chief executive, railways itself being further subdivided on a regional and product basis as shown in figure 8.4. Under the new structure the Chief Executive (Railways) was a member of the British Railways board and directed the Railway Management Group, which brought together the executive directors at BR Headquarters who covered the major departmental functions and the regional general managers who remained responsible for field management. The Chief Executive (Railways) was also directly responsible to the main board for his performance while the chief executives for other business areas were firstly responsible to the boards of the various separate business areas.

Bus transport too was reorganised. Outside the major conurbations the 1968 Act centralised all other rural bus services into a newly created National Bus Company (NBC). This organisation took over the 91 subsidiary bus companies owned by the THC less some which were transferred to a separate Scottish transport holding company. The manufacturing interests of the NBC were later merged into a joint company with British Leyland in 1970. Under the Act the NBC was placed under a statutory obligation to integrate its services, not only with local PTAs but also with the Scottish Transport Group and the BRB. This integration was to be achieved by the creation of regional committees, and

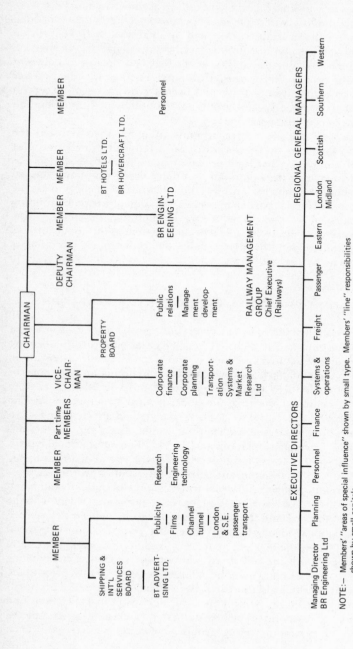

Figure 8.4 British Railways Organisation, 1971

NOTE:— Members' "areas of special influence" shown by small type. Members' "line" responsibilities shown by small capitals

Source: British Railways

in some cases interlocking board memberships as shown in figure 8.5. Like the BRB, too, the NBC was required to operate social rather than economic services, especially in rural areas, and in addition, had to provide replacement services for discontinued railway passenger services. As a result of much pressure the ability of the NBC to operate a coherent marketing and profit policy was strictly limited. Further, in order to cover these costs, as with railways, there had been a growing need for central government to provide special grants and subsidies to camouflage an unsatisfactory economic performance.

The return of a Conservative administration in 1970 reduced the emphasis, so favoured by the socialists, on a fully integrated transport system. For almost the first time no new major piece of legislation was introduced to change the organisation of land based transportation yet again. The new government, however, did intervene in an effort to use the public sector concerns as part of an overall economic strategy. By limiting price increases, in an effort to reduce the level of domestic inflation, the Heath government severely affected the economies of the transport companies and helped them, especially the railways, to accumulate massive deficits by the mid 1970s.

THE TRANSPORT INDUSTRIES AND POLITICAL INTERVENTION

With the exception of the 1970–4 Conservative government each new post war administration had introduced major legislation radically affecting the strategy and structure of the total system of land based transportation. In summary these major legislative changes, the timing and the governments which made them are shown in figure 8.6. In addition there were many lesser changes, affecting the strategy and structure of specific subcomponents of the total system. Such changes had affected the nature of objectives, organisation, leadership, pricing, licensing, marketing, financial policy, industrial relations and the like. The international nature of the air transport industry has reduced the involvement of government, but there has also been significant political intervention in this sector.

These constant strategic and structural changes especially in land based transportation enforced by legislation, has often been inconsistent with the objectives established and frequently appears to have been determined largely by political ideology rather than any economic and /or social rationale. Further, the lack of any form of stability has made the task of management almost impossible. In addition the process of introducing legislative change itself has often been largely a failure. Thus, prior to the introduction of major legislation, it has been usual to put up trial proposals in the form of Green or White Papers for discussion in Parliament and modification in committee before ultimately emerging as completed legislation. On occasion steering groups or committees have also been

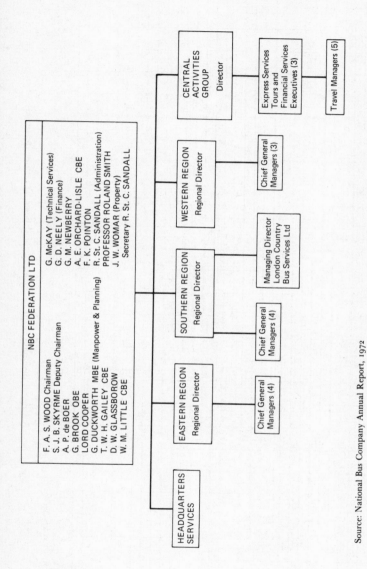

NBC FEDERATION LTD

F. A. S. WOOD Chairman
S. J. B. SKYRME Deputy Chairman
A. P. de BOER
G. BROOK OBE
LORD COOPER
G. DUCKWORTH MBE (Manpower & Planning)
T. W. H. GAILEY CBE
D. W. GLASSBOROW
W. M. LITTLE CBE

G. McKAY (Technical Services)
G. D. NEELY (Finance)
G. M. NEWBERRY
A. E. ORCHARD-LISLE CBE
F. K. POINTON
R. St. C. SANDALL (Administration)
PROFESSOR ROLAND SMITH
J. W. WOMAR (Property)
Secretary R. St. C. SANDALL

HEADQUARTERS SERVICES

EASTERN REGION Regional Director
— Chief General Managers (4)

SOUTHERN REGION Regional Director
— Chief General Managers (4)
— Managing Director London Country Bus Services Ltd

WESTERN REGION Regional Director
— Chief General Managers (3)

CENTRAL ACTIVITIES GROUP Director
— Express Services Tours and Financial Services Executives (3)
— Travel Managers (5)

Source: National Bus Company Annual Report, 1972

Figure 8.5   Management Structure of National Bus Company, 1971–2

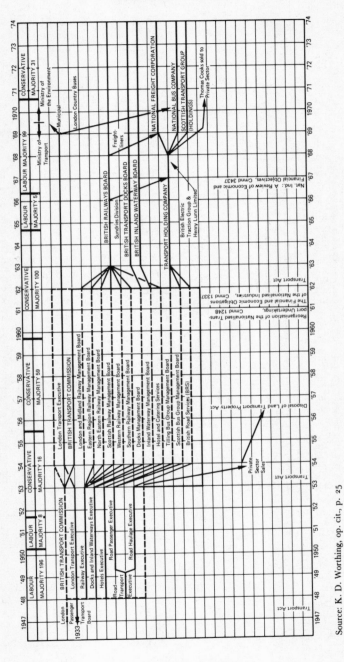

Figure 8.6   Structural Evolution of the Nationalised Land Based Transport Industries

Source: K. D. Worthing, op. cit., p. 25

asked to analyse specific situations and recommend on policy, which further delayed the preparation of legislation. While such procedures did allow for the opinion of outside pressure groups and other interested parties it appears that it has been the influence of political aspirations which in general dominated the ultimate decisions.

The severe delays in the introduction of legislation has perhaps caused as much damage to the establishment of a viable strategy and structure, consistent with whatever objectives were chosen, as inconsistencies in the ultimate legislation itself. As Sir Reginald Wilson commented in 1968 on the winding up of the Transport Holding Company 'to spend 3 long years under virtual sentence of dismemberment and exposed to the backlash of political controversy, distraction and intervention, is hardly conducive to proper and profitable development of a business undertaking'.[11] In the 21 years between 1947 and 1968 it is estimated the organisations involved in land based transportation spent no less than 13 years waiting for major Transport Acts and then reorganising after them. By comparison, the airlines were not as seriously affected by major reorganisations until the creation of British Airways, which brought the two state airlines together. Earlier structural changes were confined largely to internal reorganisations which took place within both BEA and BOAC, in their early years, when significant route changes brought corresponding transformations in organisation.

Once established, however, the major Transport Acts provided the framework within which management of the nationalised land transport industries had been required to act. In general, the decision making autonomy delegated to management had been extremely small. Virtually all critical decision areas such as objectives, marketing and pricing policy, social obligations, structure and organisation, financial structure, relationships with other public and private industries, industrial relations, mangement development and the like were subject to ministerial approval. In addition Treasury approval was usually needed on disposals of reserves and surpluses, capital expenditure, salaries of board members, and accounting procedures. While the air corporations were subjected to many of these controls, the mode of ministerial intervention tended to be somewhat less direct except in the critical area of aircraft procurement. Although ministerial directives were clearly possible under nationalisation, pressure tended to be exerted behind the scenes so that changes in policy did not appear to be made by ministerial intervention.[12] Nevertheless such intervention was made and had severely affected the performance of the corporations, notably with the purchase of the BAC one eleven, the VC10 and Concorde. These aircraft had all been foisted on the reluctant corporations, which would have preferred to purchase more commercially suitable aircraft.

The railways in particular had experienced excessive misguided ministerial intervention. Although railway management could be assigned some of the blame for the system's generally appalling post war performance, this criticism was more true for the 1950s than for the 1970s. Governments, however, had positively encouraged the uncommercial attitudes of the railways. Until the 1960s no attempt was made to define the role expected of the railways and to establish economic criteria. There was virtually no policy guidance and objectives shifted between social and economic goals which were mutually inconsistent. Nevertheless successive governments persistently interfered with the day to day running of the railways. As the Permanent Secretary to the Ministry of Transport told the Select Committee on Nationalised Industries, 'Over the years in relation to the railway industry something has gone terribly wrong.'[13]

Road haulage, too, received significant government intervention, based largely on political ideology. This had occurred in part because of the natural competition between road transport and the railways. This desire for competition reduction and coordination provided the focal difference between the two main political parties with Labour seeking to maintain the viability of the railways, while the Conservatives had insisted on competition between road and rail. The THC thus came under government attack during the 1966 Labour administration for the very success of its commercial policies which increased the threat to the railways' declining freight traffic. The NFC therefore, was statutorily obliged to ensure that goods were carried by rail whenever such carriage was 'efficient and economic'.

Over time, there had been some slight movement to increase the level of autonomy granted to the managers of public corporations. For example, the first two Transport Acts laid out in great detail, although as events proved, inconsistently with the strategy, what the organisation of the various management bodies should be. Thus, whenever even relatively minor changes were made, a reference back to Parliament was required. More recent legislation has provided the relevant Board with a statute and then charged it with the responsibility for designing an appropriate structure to fulfill the statutory obligations, only reporting back to Parliament on the course chosen within a specified time. Nevertheless, the fact that Parliament itself, at best was based on a five year span and the conflicting ideologies of the two principal parties has meant that a high degree of uncertainty tended to persist as to questions of precisely what the management objectives were, what were the assets to be managed and how and by whom. This uncertainty, stated in general, started during at least the last two years of any parliamentary term, and often continued into the next term if a change of government occurred which wished to introduce change in the system.

The impact of ministerial control

A further significant cause of uncertainty stemmed from the power of ministers to make change in the appointments and conditions of the boards of management. Here there was virtually no scrutiny by Parliament of ministerial power which covered the actual appointments of board members, salary levels and length of contracts. Appointments had thus been usually for 4–5 years ensuring some continuity between parliamentary terms, since although ministers held the power of dismissal this had only rarely been used. Persistent defiance or ideological differences were thus usually eliminated by non renewal of appointments. Changes in government were therefore marked by substantial changes in board membership and in particular the position of chairman within the first two years of a new administration.

Appointments to the board of a public sector corporation and to the position of chairman thus formed part of a political patronage system which did not necessarily result in the appointment of the most suitable leadership for the management task at hand. Nevertheless, that a patronage system prevailed has been an implicit reason why salary and emoluments paid to board members were lower than in private industry, to avoid corruption.[14] Apart from control over appointments, ministers also had the power to issue 'directives of a general nature'. This power had however, seldom been used, being restricted essentially to national emergencies. In addition, ministers had exercised influence via their contributions to and appointments of advisory committees to the corporations, as well as by personal contact with management.

In the main, however, it has been pointed out that ministers remained somewhat distant from their responsibilities and that much of the determination of policy was established by contact between the boards and senior civil servants. Differences in management style did remain, however, between Conservative and Labour ministers,[15] with the latter working more closely with the boards and becoming more involved with day to day management. Conservative ministers in contrast maintained a more distant relationship but applied the controls and sanctions they held much more rigorously.

The role of Parliament

The main source of parliamentary information on the transport industry was the annual reports prepared by the various corporations, which after prior ministerial approval were submitted to the House for debate. Since the information required was too voluminous for discussion on the floor, after 1953 the reports were reduced in size and the all party Select Committee on Nationalised Industries was established.

This committee, which was empowered to investigate any aspect of the public sector, has over time prepared some 50 reports for presentation and discussion by the full assembly. Many such reports have been critical of the public sector in terms of its management and policies. One such, on ministerial control, was especially critical, the committee finding 'a sense of confusion', and a general lack of clarity about purpose, policies, methods and responsibility.[16]

To combat these findings the committee proposed 10 guiding principles for the role of the central administration in relations with the state owned enterprises namely: –

1. The ministries main concern should be 'the public interest'.
2. Ministers should exercise a 'broad oversight'.
3. Nationalised industries should otherwise be left free.
4. There should be clear demarcation of responsibilities between the minister and the boards.
5. Control should be strategic rather than tactical.
6. Control should not be wholly formal.
7. Both ministries and the nationalised industries should be publicly accountable.
8. The measure of management should be against the duties allocated to them.
9. Improvement in management should be the first objective, but the ultimate sanction of dismissal should be maintained.
10. Proper exercise of control should depend on the attitude and relationship between ministers and board members.

While some of these recommendations were adopted in the transport corporations others were noticeably absent. As with many of the other committee reports on subjects from pricing to capital investment policy, political expediency appeared to overtake objectivity and in each case governments of all shades appeared to have accepted those parts of reports which suited their purpose while rejecting the rest. The danger with such a philosophy is clear in that failure to establish consistency between objectives, strategy and structure by introducing only partial solutions, will frequently end up with a negative impact from those recommendations which are implemented.

Financial performance and fiscal control

BOAC was the first of the public corporations to incorporate Public Dividend Capital in its capital structure on which a variable dividend or none at all could be paid according to performance. In the event, although this capital reconstruction substantially reduced the corporation's interest payment outflow, the improvements in performance achieved by management actually contributed more to the Exchequer than if the old structure had been maintained. During the late 1960s, with favourable conditions, BOAC performed well. In order to purchase American aircraft, however, the corporation was forced by the Treasury to resort to foreign currency loans. This form of intervention had perhaps discriminated against the corporation since, although a major dollar earner, these funds were not usable for aircraft purchases nor had the corporation been allowed to use official dollars for its purchases unlike the independent airlines. As a result therefore, performance had suffered especially as the sterling exchange rate deteriorated.

While the performance of BOAC proved good by international standards, the performance of BEA was much less so. In part this could be attributed to the use of a suboptimal fleet, contrary to the desire of management, but other factors had also contributed. Thus, BEA was slow in moving into the fast growing IT market, was slow to react to the changing character of the scheduled and non scheduled sectors, and had been much less able than BOAC to contain the growth of its overhead structure and in particular its labour force. As a result BEA consistently failed, albeit marginally, to achieve the financial objective of 6 per cent on net assets after interest and depreciation, set for it for the quinnquennium to 1967–8. Similarly an increased target of 8 per cent for the following quinnquennium was also not met, despite some improvement in performance, contrary to world trends, during 1968–70.

With the sole exception of the Transport Holding Company, the objectives of each of the land transport corporations had been to 'ensure that its revenues and those of its subsidiaries were not less than sufficient to meet their combined charges properly chargeable to revenue account taking one year with another', 'to make proper provision for the depreciation and renewal of assets' and 'to establish and maintain a general reserve'. Apart from the Transport Holding Company and the National Freight Corporation, none of the remaining corporations had achieved these objectives. The industries had therefore, been shored up by writing off capital debt, deficit finance, or since 1968, by grants made for agreed uneconomic public services.

Prior to 1959 all capital for the land transport sector was raised by the issue of Treasury Guaranteed Transport Stock, which was subsequently replaced by fixed interest long term Treasury loans. Despite the claims by many of the boards over time that a proportion of their debt should be financed by a form of government equity this had been rejected by the Treasury. Further, the boards have had no freedom in the area of financial structure.

An annual allotment of capital was established by the minister in conjunction with the Treasury and a level established above which formal ministerial approval was needed by the boards. The level of allotment had varied sharply with the state of the economy, and in recent years allotments had been drastically changed within a specific year as well as between years. In addition, the Treasury also assessed major capital proposals, using standard procedures such as discounted cash flow, sensitivity analysis, and a specified rate of return. Despite such scrutiny, however, the lack of understanding by both ministers and the Treasury, neither of which necessarily knew the industry, permitted wrong investments to be made. Further, the uncertainty created by rapid change in capital availability, caused by short term political expediency made any form of rational long term financial planning exceptionally difficult.

Conclusion

Analysis of the evolution of the nationalised transportation system in Britain over the period some 25 years since its inception revealed a history of almost constant change in one or more of either objectives, strategy or organisation. What could be observed in the total system was the perpetual intervention by the political party in government in response to its own ideology or short range political goals. This, more than any concept of management competence, (and even this is conditioned by the political patronage system of senior appointments) must be held responsible for the inferior performance of most of the operating companies in the transport industries in achieving their objectives.

Nor was there any indication that such interventions would cease, since ideology apart, neither major party seemed sure of what they wanted of the managers they appointed. Rather the only factor which seems certain was that each would do differently from the other. Clearly this continual intervention, with its relative frequency, constant reorganisations and changes in top management, has been highly damaging. Yet even when this has been pointed out and measures to eliminate the problems proposed by Parliament's own watchdog committee, they have largely been ignored by those actually in power. On the basis of the experience of the transport corporations there would seem little support for the further extension of public ownership, without due regard to ensure that such enterprise is managed by those to whom it is entrusted rather than the politicians. These should keep their short run political strategies to themselves, rather than imposing them on the assets of the nation.

9. The State Monopolies

While in general the transport industries although nationalised still operated in a competitive environment, a number of key service industries were effectively state owned monopolies in their main areas of operations, although peripheral activities such as the sale of appliances in the case of gas and electricity or carriage of parcels in the case of the Post Office were open to competition. This chapter explores the strategy and structure of the main state owned service monopolies, the gas and electricity supply industries and the Post Office, which in 1973 were responsible for the employment of some 693,000 people, had sales of £4355m, and completed the year with a combined deficit of £56.4m (this being entirely attributable to the Post Office). By 1974, however, all the industries were in deficit as a result of inflation and government policy of price restraint.

Strategically, the monopolistic state corporations were by their establishing legislation severely constrained in the markets they were able to serve. No major strategic change had therefore taken place in terms of the product market areas they served. As a result of their monopolistic position, however, competition was limited principally to substitution products. Further, the public corporations themselves were often unable to retaliate against such competition because of the strategic restrictions placed upon them. Nevertheless, substantial change had occurred in the cases of electricity and gas, and to a lesser extent in parts of the Post Office. The gas industry, for example, was totally transformed by the discovery of natural gas, while the development of nuclear energy, natural gas and oil burning had significantly changed the traditional coal based generating policy of the electricity supply industry. The Post Office had, perhaps, changed least and by 1974 was still highly labour intensive, with technological change being mainly observed in telecommunications. Like the transport industries, the state monopolies had also been subject to substantial political and other pressures which had often led to structural modifications, sometimes for ideological reasons, but also in the interests of improved efficiency and better management.

The measurement of financial performance in the public sector is exceedingly difficult. As was the case in the transport industries, from the early 1960s financial targets were generally laid down for profits plus interest as a percentage of net assets employed, since no equity capital was involved and interest payments thus essentially replaced earnings for equity. Prior to this, firm financial targets were not set and the industries operated with only a relatively vague break even requirement. This, in itself, presented no problems in analysis, however, the industries had been progressively subjected to political intervention in commercial policy such that prices were artificially constrained. Thus, in the mid-1970s in particular, deficits were accumulated which could not necessarily be attributed to management actions. In reality, both gas and electricity generally met the financial targets established for them, although the financial state of the Post Office had progressively deteriorated. Nevertheless, there were signs that managerial efficiencies had certainly not matched the best achievements of the private sector and increased costs perhaps tended to be transferred to increased prices more readily than they would have done if monopolistic conditions not prevailed.

However, these industries each form an essential part of an industrial society, and in many respects clearly lend themselves in terms of natural economic efficiency toward a monopolistic situation. Clearly, too, if potential exploitation is to be resisted there is a strong case for public ownership, or at least strict public scrutiny, as is found for example in North America where, although remaining largely in private hands, the utilities are subject to public control. The return of the first post war Labour administration, committed to a programme of nationalisation, thus led naturally to the inclusion in this programme of the main domestic utilities, gas and electricity, despite the fact that both were already publicly owned by municipal as distinct from central authority. The postal service was formed as a department of government and the development of telecommunications was placed under the control of this service which, at the end of the war, remained a civil service department.

At the end of the war it was apparent that reorganisation of the utility supply industries was both necessary and desirable, and public ownership was not seen as merely a doctrinal response by the socialists. Nevertheless, the industries were already strongly bound by public controls due to a basic reluctance on the part of Parliament toward any form of private statutory monopoly. Thus, although both industries had initially developed in private hands, the original operating franchises had contained agreements whereby they might at some time be acquired by public authorities.

THE ELECTRICITY SUPPLY INDUSTRY[1]

The rapid growth of electricity consumption resulting from increased industrial usage as a replacement for steam, in particular after the first world war, indicated that the early supply industry was both insufficient and expensive. A commission was appointed, therefore, to investigate the industry, and this enquiry led to the Electricity (Supply) Act 1919, which established the Electricity Commissioners who were expected to secure, regulate and supervise voluntary reorganisation in the industry. A further review of the industry in 1925 recommended the establishment of a Central Electricity Board to operate and manage a national grid for the wholesale supply of power. These recommendations were included in the Electricity (Supply) Act 1926 which established the Board under the supervision of the Electricity Commissioners. While ownership of generating stations remained with the electricity companies, the Board established the level of production required and purchased power supplies which were redistributed to local companies by an interconnecting high tension grid system, built up over the following ten years or so.

The creation of the national grid led to improved efficiency and quality in that the number of smaller, less economic generating stations was substantially reduced, and a standard supply frequency was established. The 491 generating stations in 1926 had been reduced to 171 connected by the grid system in 1938[2].

While supply was subjected to increased centralisation, as a result of the establishment of the grid system, distribution remained fragmented, with some 562 separate organisations, two thirds of which were owned by local authorities. The McGowan Committee was established in 1935 to investigate electricity distribution and recommended the creation of a regional policy sometimes under the leadership of a publicly owned undertaking, sometimes under private ownership. These recommendations were not accepted however, and no further changes occurred until the end of the second world war.

Nationalisation

The industry was nationalised in 1947. An organising committee was set up, and with the passage of the Electricity Act 1947, the supply industry of England, Wales and Southern Scotland was taken into public ownership. The existing 560 municipal and private electricity undertakings were then integrated into fourteen Area Electricity Boards which shared responsibility for the retail distribution of electricity to consumers. Responsibility for generation and main transmission, together with central co-ordination and policy direction, rested with the British Electricity Authority (BEA). In the North of Scotland, generation became the responsibility of the North of Scotland Hydro Electric Board, established in 1943 to develop hydro-electric resources. This Board acquired the local distribution undertakings under the 1947 Act and became responsible for all public generation, transmission and distribution in the north of Scotland. Consultative councils were also established in each of the local area boards as a result of the Act, to safeguard the interest of consumers and protect the general public interest.

The organisation adopted after nationalisation, therefore, was basically functional, with production being the responsibility of the central authority while marketing and distribution remained on an area basis.

The autonomy of the area distribution organisations was, however, strictly limited. The BEA was responsible for raising all finance, and all capital requirements of the area boards were first submitted to the BEA for evaluation and approval. Acceptable capital expenditure requests were then incorporated into an industry investment programme for submission to the ministry and the Treasury.

Thus, as with the transport companies, the initial structure adopted to implement the policy of nationalisation was one of complete centralisation of all critical decision making. Unlike in transport, however, this structure was more appropriate, in that there was a clear need for central coordination and control, in view of the interdependence of the regions and based on the centralisation of production via the grid system. Where this was less appropriate as in Scotland, although largely for political reasons, the area board remained responsible for both distribution and generation.

The managers of the new system did however, tend to give the industry a production or engineering bias. Prior to nationalisation the engineers were required to obtain approval for capital expenditure from local boards of directors, followed by scrutiny by the Commission. After the re-organisation the area boards were manned largely by industry professionals and so, too, was the central authority, apart from the chairman and one deputy chairman who was a former civil servant. There was thus a lack of checks and balances in the evaluation of capital spending programmes, since government itself was ill-equipped to adequately examine proposals put forward by the Authority. Nevertheless, after the war the supply industry was in poor shape to meet both existing and new demand. Generating capacity was short, transmission and distribution networks inadequate, and supply breakdowns were common. The problem was compounded by the extreme demand fluctuation on both a 24-hour and a seasonal basis. The difference between peak winter demand and summer low offtake was, and is, some 400 per cent while average winter demand is around 55 per cent above that for the summer.[3] These dramatic differences in load mean that substantial standby capacity is required in the industry to satisfy peak demand.

During 1947–57, generating capacity thus doubled as a massive reequipment programme was put in hand to meet demand requirements. However, it was not until the mid-1950s that capacity additions began to exceed increases in demand. Since the development time for new capacity to be brought on stream averaged three years, there was also a requirement for the industry to project the long term demand pattern. This, in itself, presented serious difficulties despite relatively well developed forecasting systems, and until the early 1960s forward projections tended to significantly underestimate expected future demand.[4]

Then, in the early 1960s, indicative planning was attempted in Britain when the government established the National Economic Development

Office, which endeavoured to plan for a higher national economic growth rate. At the request of government, the electricity industry based its forecast of capital plant requirements to 1966, on the assumption that target growth rates would be achieved. In the event these forecasts of national growth proved substantially over optimistic, and as a result planned generating capacity investment proved similarly too high, since demand tended to closely reflect actual economic growth rate.

In 1965 a new national plan was prepared by the incoming Labour government with a somewhat lower expected growth target. Again the industry was requested to plan on the basis of the plan being met, and a forecast of 54,000mw maximum demand was therefore accepted as the level of demand expected for 1970−71. In the event, again this was wildly optimistic as the British economy was subjected to severe deflation, and by 1970−71, demand had only reached 38,600mw. As a result the electricity industry was left with a substantially larger investment programme than necessary, and while some of this was subsequently deferred, there was no doubt that bad economic forecasting had a deleterious effect on the industry's ability to earn its target rate of return.

The evolution of organisation
While strategically the period to the mid-1950s was largely concerned with adding capacity to meet demand, early structural change was limited despite the return of a Conservative administration in 1951. In 1954, some decentralisation occurred when the South of Scotland joined the North, in breaking away from the BEA. A new authority, the South of Scotland Electricity Board was established, responsible for the generation and supply of electricity for the remainder of Scotland not covered by the North of Scotland Hydro Electric Board. Most of the functions of the Minister of Power were, at the same time, transferred to the Secretary of State for Scotland for these two authorities. Some increased consolidation at area board level was also implemented, and the name of the BEA was changed to the Central Electricity Authority.

In 1954, the Herbert Committee was formed to investigate the organisation of the industry.[5] This committee recommended a re-organisation which would establish a central authority with a small, but expert staff to supervise and control the plans of a Central Electricity Generating Board (CEGB). This body would be responsible for the generation and transmission of electricity in bulk to the area boards, which would become more autonomous. Members of the new central authority were to be drawn from outside the industry so as to provide a check and balance. Serving board members from within the industry were ineligible for membership of the new central body. The Conservative government, however, did not accept this recommendation in full, and in the Electricity Act 1957, an Electricity Council was established along the lines of the Gas Council which had been set up in 1948 when the gas industry had been nationalised. This body was a quasi federal organisation. It was made up of the chairman of the 12 area boards, three representatives of the CEGB, and six independent members, including the chairman and two deputy chairmen, appointed by the minister, as shown in figure 9.1. This organisation, with minor amendments, has persisted since 1957. The Council's specific responsibilities were largely in the area of finance, including forecasts of demand for investment planning and consideration of tariff proposals although the responsibility for establishing the all important bulk supply tariff from the generating board to the area boards remained with the CEGB. Other responsibilities included research coordination and industrial relations which were conducted on a national level. Finally, the Council provided the main mechanism for consultation between the industry and government, and acted as spokesman for the industry in the external environment generally.

The Council met monthly, although to improve detailed considerations three standing sub committees were subsequently established on industrial relations, commercial policy and research which then reported their findings to the full Council. Capital planning was a responsibility of the Council and started with demand forecasts over a period of 5 to 7 years ahead. Three independent estimates were prepared, one for each of the area boards based on local knowledge, a forecast by the CEGB based on an estimate of the role of electricity in future national energy demand, and a third by the Council's own advisory staff, based on trends in the main sectors of consumption.

From these forecasts the Council decided which estimates should be used for planning purposes. The CEGB was then able to draw up its programme for generating capacity construction and corresponding transmission capacity, while area boards planned the expansion of distribution networks. These investment programmes were reviewed and consolidated by the Council before submission to the minister for approval.

Finance was arranged by the Council after approval of capital plans for England and Wales. Some 50 per cent of capital requirements were met from internal funding, the balance coming from external borrowing by the Council on behalf of the industry. Long term capital came mainly from direct advances by the minister, after Treasury approval, and in addition, during the 1970s from overseas loans. Short term finance was provided direct from the banking system or superannuation funds.[6]

The area organisation

The area boards became fully responsible for the distribution networks and for retail sales of electricity to consumers after the reorganisation. In addition they performed contract work and sold appliances through their showroom network. The membership of each of the boards consisted of a chairman, deputy chairman, and from four to six other members, and the chairman of the Area Electricity Consultative Council, all appointed by

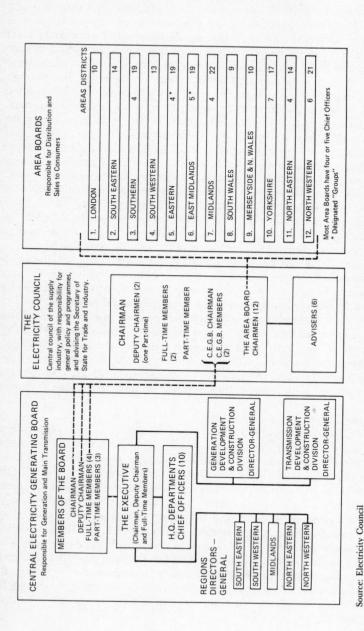

Source: Electricity Council

Figure 9.1   Organisation of the Electricity Supply Industry in England and Wales

the minister. In general, some of the members were part time with the chairman and his deputy full time. A typical area organisation is shown in figure 9.2. Ater nationalisation the organisation below area board level consisted of a further series of subdivisions into 'sub-areas' which in turn were broken down into districts. During the late 1960s alterations were made in individual areas in an attempt to improve efficiency. In a number of areas, districts were merged, in others a two-tier structure was created with no sub-areas and districts reporting direct to the area headquarters.

The area boards, through their retail tariffs, were responsible for ensuring that the whole of the costs incurred in purchasing and distributing electricity and profits required to meet financial targets, were recovered. Each board prepared its own standard retail tariffs for its four main classes of consumers, industrial, domestic, commercial and farms. These tariffs were designed to recover the approximate costs of supply for each of these respective groups. The tariff structure had consistently favoured the domestic consumer. While industrial tariffs included an automatic fuel price adjustment whereby electricity went up as soon as coal prices increased, domestic prices were usually only raised after a substantial delay. In no small measure this could be attributable to political rather than economic motives, and thus while industrial rates increased by 88 per cent per unit between 1950 and 1970, domestic prices only rose by 60 per cent.[7] Partially as a result, domestic sales have grown at a higher rate than industrial, and by 1974 domestic sales represented the largest single electricity market. It was also the least controllable when the industry was in supply difficulties. The growth in domestic demand, although partially a function of underpricing, was also due to the growth in electric appliances and the industry's attempts to break into the central heating market with storage heating based on offpeak supplies.

The Central Electricity Generating Board
The CEGB owned and operated the power stations and main transmission lines, and was responsible for bulk supply to the area boards. The only other direct consumers were for rail haulage or traction or where specifically authorised by the ministry. Membership of the CEGB consisted of a chairman, deputy chairman, four full time and four part time members appointed by the minister and organised as shown in Figure 9.3. After its formation in 1957, the CEGB in turn, was decentralised by dividing its activities into five regional generating and transmission bodies, each responsible for operating their area in line with the requirements of the headquarters based national grid control. Further, significant changes in generating sets and power stations and the introduction of new fuels, in particular nuclear energy, led to the design and construction of new power stations being transferred to three project groups responsible direct to headquarters.

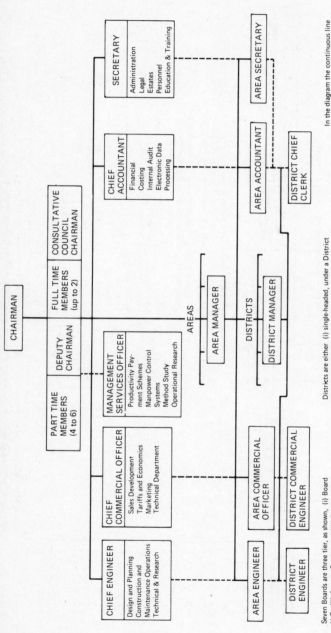

Seven Boards are three tier, as shown, (i) Board H.Q.; (ii) Area or Group; and (iii) District : five are two tier, (i) Board H.Q.; and (ii) District.

Districts are either (i) single-headed, under a District Manager, or (ii) double-headed, having no District Manager, the District Engineer and District Commercial Engineer each reporting direct to the Area Manager or Board H.Q.

In the diagram the continuous line represents the line of command; the broken line the functional staff channel of communication.

Figure 9.2 Area Electricity Board Organisation

Source: Electricity Council

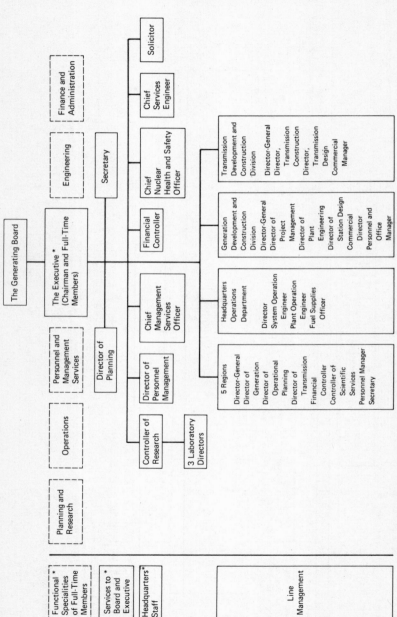

* Members of the Executive will be assigned to particular areas of functional interest and these may be varied from time to time by the Board

* Headquarters' Staff Departments provide a service to the Board and the Executive, and, in addition, supply specialist services and guidance to the whole of the Board's organisation.

The impact of technology

After the second world war, power stations were being built with individual generating sets of 30–60mw. Set size had since increased rapidly by stages, and by the early 1970s new conventional power stations were largely based on 500mw units, four of which were usually used for each new station. Further increases were still being developed, with 600mw sets entering service in 1973. Although these larger sets were expected to yield greater thermal efficiency, initial setbacks with the 500mw sets reduced the rate of progress. Nevertheless, significant overall improvements in average efficiency had been made since nationalisation as a result of new plant, although by the mid-1970s the CEGB still operated some old generating capacity with low thermal efficiency. This older plant was brought on stream as part of a merit order system whereby the least efficient plant was started up progressively to meet peak load conditions. All power stations were ranked according to fuel costs per unit of electricity generated and as new plant was added, so it displaced the least efficient, older plant which was taken out of base load generation.[8]

By the mid-1970s, conventional steam generating plant still accounted for nearly 90 per cent of output, the majority of which was fuelled by coal. Although there had been progressive conversion to oil burning during the late 1960s and early 1970s, the onset of the energy crisis brought a renewed lease of life to coal, the use of which in the past had been often artificially protected by government. Total generating capacity by 1973 had risen to some 61,087mw, while the average system load factor was around 56 per cent.

In 1955, the first commercial nuclear power programme for the United Kingdom was announced in the face of an expected fall in coal availability. This initial programme was subsequently expanded because of the Suez crisis which demonstrated the political uncertainties of continuity in oil supplies, and then later contracted on the easing of fuel supplies, ultimately ending up composed of nine stations with a design capacity of 5,000mw, the last reactor being commissioned in 1971. This first generation of nuclear plants proved to be relatively expensive in the face of improvements in the efficiency of conventional generating plant and ubsequent developments in nuclear technology.

A second nuclear programme was announced in 1964 based on advanced gas cooled reactors. These new stations, although of higher capital cost, and fuel costs lower than the earlier Magnox reactors, and seven such reactors were in design or construction by the early 1970s. Since low fuel cost was an essential determinant of loading, the nuclear reactors tended to assume constant 75 per cent base load positions from commissioning, and the 10 per cent of electricity generated from this type of plant was expected to form the main contribution to base load generation in the future. By the 1980s nuclear plant, and especially new breeder reactors, were expected to take over much of the increased generating load despite political pressures and the accountancy techniques of the industry, which had tended to militate against the high capital cost nuclear plant in favour of increasingly expensive, in fuel price terms, coal fired stations.

Pricing, profitability[9] and politics

The performance of the electricity industry is summarised in table 9.1. Until 1961 the financial objectives established for the industry had solely been that revenues earned should not be less than sufficient to break even taking one year with another. In the 1961 White Paper on the financial and economic obligations of the nationalised industries,[10] new proposals were introduced which established three main objectives. Firstly, the industry was required to earn surpluses on revenue account after interest and depreciation based on historic costs, such that any deficits over a five year period should be covered. Secondly, reserves should be increased to cover the difference in depreciation required using a replacement rather than a historic base. Finally, sufficient reserves should be added to allow a contribution to be made to capital development and safeguard against premature obsolescence.

Table 9.1   Performance of the Electricity Industry 1960–74

	1959/60	1965/6	1970/1	1971/2	1972/3	1973/4	1974/5
Sales (£m)	634	1094	1540	1743	1931	1982	2656
Total Sales (Billion units)	102	138	174	178	191	190	196
Profit after interest (£m)	–	85	(56)	(23)	2	(176)	(258)
Internal financing ratio (%)	48.4	46.6	52.6	70.2	77.6	63.0	48.3
Return on average net assets (%)	–	7.0	4.1	5.1	5.8	3.0	2.3

Source: Electricity Council Annual Reports.

Prior to 1961, the industry overall had been achieving the first two of these targets, but the performance of the CEGB and individual area boards varied widely with most making a loss in several specific years. In March 1962 it was agreed that the supply industry as a whole would endeavour to earn a gross return, composed of depreciation, interest and profit after interest, of 12.4 per cent on net capital employed for the five years to 1966–7. This overall objective was then subdivided into specific targets for each area and the CEGB, such that the total produced the desired overall return. Individual targets were established on the basis of earlier financial performance by individual area boards, expected future capital requirements, and modified in the light of non economic obligations. In general, an attempt was made to make area rates of return more uniform. The CEGB on the other hand was expected to earn almost half the required surplus, this representing a significant policy change, since historically the supply operation had been expected to charge out so as to earn only a low profit.

The target rate of return was not achieved. The shortfall was caused essentially by restrictions imposed on pricing freedom caused by a price freeze and period of 'severe restraint' applied across the economy by central government. This was compounded by the technical method of calculating the asset base, which included work in progress. This rose rapidly over the period, as capital investment increased in line with the expectations of the abortive national plan, and new plant commissions were delayed, making the increased surpluses required to meet an escalating asset base rapidly more difficult to achieve.

Because pricing freedom was restricted, negotiations between government and the industry on new targets were suspended and year by year objectives were set for the next two years. New financial objectives were then established for the five years to 1973–4 for the industry to earn a net return (interest and profit after interest) of 7 per cent on average capital employed over the period. This compared with 6.7 per cent over the earlier quinquennium on the same accounting basis. Further, the new target was applied to the CEGB and each of the area boards.[11]

As inflation quickened in the 1970s, these targets rapidly became meaningless, however. The industry was severely restricted in applying the tariff increases necessary to recover increased operating costs, and by 1971, for the first time since nationalisation, a deficit of £56m was incurred. Increases were also restricted in 1972–3 as part of the Conservative government's policy to keep inflation levels down. At the end of 1973 the industry was caught by massive increases in fuel prices brought on by the oil crisis and subsequent wage demands by the domestic coal industry, resulting in a substantial deficit in 1974.

The artificial manipulation of the industry's performance by central government made measurement of the performance progressively more difficult. Moreover, it meant substantial fluctuations in the industry's ability to finance its own capital needs. In 1963 internally generated finance accounted for some 48 per cent of new capital invested, and it was hoped this would rise to about 69 per cent by the end of the decade. In the event, the percentage of internal finance remained low during the mid-1960s, and slumped to under 40 per cent in 1967 during the price freeze.

In the second quinquennium gross return initially improved, and with a decline in capital spending requirements as demand estimates were revised down in line with actual expectations rather than the nebulous forecasts the industry had been asked to accept under the National Plan, the ratio of internal capital increased dramatically. Under the second period of price restraint, however, this ratio again began to slump and increased demands were made upon the Treasury.

The overall performance of the industry since nationalisation has thus been reasonable in many respects. The aberrations in performance in the main seem to be attributable more to poor economic management on the part of the government than to the managers themselves. Although demand forecasting in the late 1950s was relatively poor, this was in part understandable given the complexity of long range forecasting, but some criticism of the domestic tariff pricing which exacerbated demand expectations, can perhaps be levelled. In the 1960s and early 1970s, however, industry performance has been seriously affected by short run government policy, interference into pricing policy by forcing demand estimates on the industry which resulted in excess capacity, and on the continued influence over fuel policy in favour of coal or less economic nuclear designs. These, more than any actions of management, are the primary causes of poor performance. Further, this style of ill-informed intervention for short range political objectives can be expected to have an undesirable effect on the long run strategic options of the industry and through it on the ancillary manufacturing industry based suppliers.

THE GAS INDUSTRY

Nationalisation and rationalisation 1949–60
The development of the gas industry in the post war period demonstrated many similarities to electricity, although it also possessed some unique features. Gas was one of the last areas for nationalisation by the post war Labour administration. Since then, it has been subject to a total transformation which changed it from a position of relative decline to being an increasingly important factor in national energy policy. Prior to nationalisation the gas industry, which had been in existence for over a century, was similar in many respects to the electricity industry. Production and supply were in the hands of private and municipal authorities servicing local regions as statutory monopolies. Although sales of gas had continued to grow in the interwar years, the industry's relative importance was declining as electricity became the dominant energy source for lighting, and proved a competitive threat for cooking and heating. Gas appliances, too, improved in efficiency further reducing potential demand.

An official report, produced in 1945,[12] concluded that much of the industry was composed of small, thermally inefficient plants, many of which were within the range of larger works capable of producing gas more economically if an extensive local and area grid system were built. This report served as a basis for the Labour government's nationalisation plans to which the industry, unlike others, offered no resistance. As a result, gas was nationalised in 1949 and since a national distribution grid for gas was considered impracticable, the initial structure chosen was based on regional organisation.

Twelve statutory regional boards were established, each of which was separately appointed by the minister for Fuel and Power. Unlike other regional bodies in nationalised industries these boards were responsible to and reported directly to the minister. Each board was largely autonomous, being required to conduct its business to fix tariffs to ensure at least a break even position, and for the development of its own capital expenditure programme. A federal Gas Council was established, composed of a chairman, and deputy chairman appointed by the minister, together with the heads of the twelve area boards. This council was primarily responsible for capital borrowing to finance approved area investment programmes and for advising the minister on matters of general policy pertaining to the industry. In addition industrial relations and the research, education and training programmes of the area boards were coordinated centrally.

As normality returned after the initial post war shortages, it became apparent that overall demand for gas was static and between 1950 and 1960 gas sales increased only marginally. Domestic sales, the largest market for gas, actually declined, although some increases in sales were made to industrial and commercial users.

The primary need for capital spending in the industry was thus one of modernisation. In the first ten years after nationalisation the number of gas works was more than halved, as small inefficient plants, were rapidly closed down. Existing large plants were extended or new plants built and a substantial system of local mains was built to link producing units together.[13]

Nevertheless, capital expenditure became increasingly difficult to justify as demand fell. Further, the costs of gas to the domestic consumer increased by over 65 per cent in the 1950s, much more than alternative fuels such as electricity, which over the same period rose by only 25 per cent.[14] This was largely due to the fact that gas was essentially a two-fuel product. In the manufacture of gas by the carbonisation of coal, both gas and coke were produced. The process also required good quality coking coal which was more expensive than the small coal suitable for electricity generation. Supplies of coking coal also became scarce, due to a shortage of suitable seams and competitive demands from the growing steel industry.

The economies of the industry thus depended not only on the sale of gas, but also on the return obtained from the sale of residual coke left after carbonisation. With the introduction of the Clean Air Act in 1957 it was hoped that the gas industry would become a major supplier of smokeless fuel, and so obtain a reasonable return from its coke production. However, by the late 1950s, sales began to fall and considerable stocks began to accumulate.[15] The economies of the industry based on producing both coke and gas thus became increasingly vulnerable. The problem was compounded by the fact that the carbonisation process was capital intensive and had high running costs such that economic efficiency fell sharply unless a high load could be maintained. This made it difficult for the industry to economically meet the differences in seasonal loads expected of it.

The failings in commercial policy

After nationalisation, the area boards, which were largely made up of engineers, first turned their attention toward increasing the production efficiency of the industry. Commercial policy was notably neglected. Demand forecasts were substantially over optimistic due partially to the decreased competitiveness of gas for the domestic market and also to an almost total lack of marketing effort. No promotional tariffs to encourage usage were introduced until the late 1950s with sales being usually made on a flat rate or under a block tariff in which the first high price block was often in excess of the normal level of consumption.[16] Further, the principle of varying charges to consumers on the basis of the cost of supply was not practiced by the area boards which, because of their autonomy, operated a confusing mixture of tariff structures according to individual interpretations of the original Gas Act.[17]

The requirement that the industry only need to break even, also encouraged the boards not to seek a high rate of return on borrowed funds. The statutory requirements of the industry did, however, make the measurement of return on investment difficult since almost 50 per cent of capital investment was required to meet safety and quality obligations. It was thus not until the introduction of improved financial objections for all nationalised industries in 1961 that high returns were actually sought or achieved.

The move away from coal

The need for the industry to move away from coal had become apparent by the mid-1950s, and experimental schemes were begun in this direction. A number of possibilities were explored, which failed to satisfy the basic need until in 1962 Imperial Chemical Industries announced the discovery of a new naphtha based route to the production of ammonia, which as a by-product generated large volumes of clean gas. By 1963 the Gas Council had developed methods for enriching this to produce gas at pressure, and a new plant based on the ICI/Gas Council process was announced.[18]

The case against coal was now clear and even the 1964–66 Labour government accepted this, although anxious to protect markets for coal.[19] By 1969, 84 per cent of total gas-making capacity was based on oil gasification compared with 6.7 per cent in 1961. In the interim period the number of gasworks was more than halved while over 1,000m cubic feet per day of carbonisation plant was written off. Coal consumption declined from 22.0m tons in 1961 to 9.3m tons in 1969. At the same time oil consumption for gasification rose from 236,000 tons to 5.9m tons.[20]

The switch to oil gasification resulted in a substantial increase in capital spending. During the 1960s new oil gasification plants were rapidly introduced and manufacturing plant expenditure rose from £15.4m in 1961 reaching a peak of £115.2m in 1968. Mains expenditure, too, increased as high pressure oil gasification made supply through a mains distribution system from relatively distant production sites, economic. New mains laid totalling 1644 miles in 1961 had risen to 3300 miles in 1969, much of the new system being for bulk supply which increased the degree of area integration. Finally, the change in technology allowed the industry to reduce its labour intensity with the numbers employed dropping from 127,000 in 1960 to 120,000 by 1969, a large decline in operating employees being partially offset by increases in staff and white collar workers.[21]

The impact of marketing strategy
In 1962, the Gas Council made its first appointment of a 'commercial officer', 'to co-ordinate the commercial and promotional activities of the Council and of the Area Boards'.[22] Until this time marketing effort in the industry had varied from area to area, with no successfully established image of gas as an attractive alternative fuel, especially for domestic use. Marketing and promotion in the industry in general was extremely weak, although in the late 1950s the Council had initiated improved designs for domestic gas appliances in conjunction with appliance manufacturers. This initiative had led to the production of a range of new space heating appliances which were to form the basis of the industry's resurgence.

Demand for gas in the domestic market began to accelerate from 1962-3 as sales of new space heating appliances and gas fired central heating installations took off. Total demand grew from 2,923.5m therms in 1962-3 to 4692.4m therms in 1968-9, while domestic sales more than doubled from 1493.3 to 3010.8m therms.[23] Backed by good institutional advertising, gas began to take on a new growth image.

The quality of marketing support increased throughout the industry led by the efforts of the Gas Council which supervised the institutional advertising campaigns and organised marketing training for the area boards, and began to coordinate market research and local area marketing programmes. The role of marketing increased significantly as the industry began to shake off its engineering bias. In 1968 a full time member was appointed to the Council to head up a newly established marketing division responsible for the development of a marketing strategy for the industry as a whole, coordinating plans of area boards and developing new markets.

The increase in domestic demand was also encouraged by the introduction of promotional pricing tariffs by which the more gas existing consumers used, the lower the average price of gas became. This revision in tariff structure, although stimulating demand, had significant, and to some extent unfortunate, side effects. Firstly, it resulted in a gradual decline in the level of income per therm received, and secondly, it shifted the pattern of demand increasingly toward a seasonal peak load during the winter months. This increased peak in turn forced the rate of capital investment to rise, so reducing the level of plant usage from around 75 per cent in 1960 to about 60 per cent in 1970. Taken together, these two factors thus had a significant negative impact on the industry's rate of return on capital invested.

The arrival of natural gas

The change in technology to oil gasification which had led to the revitalisation of the gas industry was proceeding rapidly in the mid-1960s when, after several years exploration, commercial strikes of natural gas were made in 1965 in the North Sea. By mid-1966, despite its still rising level of investment in oil gasification plant, the Gas Council was committed to the construction of a national 1,250 mile high pressure pipeline grid for the distribution of North Sea methane. By the summer of 1967 the early finds had made the North Sea basin one of the world's main offshore hydrocarbon exploration areas and two more major gas fields had been discovered. Crude estimates indicated some 30 trillion cubic feet of gas recoverable reserves, or enough to supply more than three times the average existing daily usage of the entire gas industry for over 20 years.

The magnitude of the discoveries had a dramatic effect on the gas industry. Capital spending on oil gasification plant began to be wound down or abandoned and at the same time a massive new spending programme was planned to ensure the phased conversion of every existing gas appliance to the direct supply of natural gas through a developing national grid system.

The scale of this new planning activity was beyond the limits of any individual area board, and as a result the power of the central Council began to increase. In 1966, three new central departments were established to cover coordination and planning, production and supplies and special projects. The first of these coordinated capital expenditure programmes, reviewed the area plans and liaised on behalf of the Council with central government. Production and supplies was responsible for the production, transmission and storage of gas undertaken by the Council which was itself responsible for dealing with the oil companies on North Sea gas. The Special Projects Group was responsible for negotiating sales agreements of gas from North Sea operators and represented the Council at hearings with the government on the future development of resources on the continental shelf.

The following year, two further central units were created to plan for the receipt and sale of North Sea gas, one to coordinate plans for appliance conversion and the other an operations research department. At the same time the Council's marketing unit began to discuss with manufacturing industry the possibilities of rapidly increasing penetration in industrial markets as North Sea gas became available.

During 1967, the first supplies of gas from the North Sea came ashore and it became apparent that reserves were sufficient to completely replace all manufactured gas. By 1975 it was estimated that natural gas would supply some 15 per cent of Britain's total energy needs, and the Council and area boards planned to receive and distribute 2,000mcfd by 1971–2 rising to 4,000mcfd by the mid-1970s. Under the terms of the Gas Act 1965, the Council would buy the gas from producers and sell it to area boards on the basis of a uniform tariff, subject to variations in load factor. Thus, within the space of two years, the strategy and structure of the industry was completely transformed and the role of the Council had become one of being the only producer of gas, with the area boards responsible for local distribution and maintenance in a similar manner to the area electricity boards. In addition, the Council itself moved into the exploration business with the formation of a new subsidiary Gas Council (Exploration) Limited to undertake exploration and development activities both on shore and in the North Sea.

The new role of the Council was spelled out in the several new Acts affecting the industry in the 1960s, but most notably the Gas Act 1965 and the Gas and Electricity Act 1968. This legislation confirmed the growing tendency to centralisation, with the Council becoming responsible for the acquisition of gas from the North Sea, and its supply to area boards and direct to consumers approved by the minister. In addition to its traditional duties, the Council was also to promote and assist the coordinated development of gas supplies in Britain.

By mid-1969 the major capital investment programme for manufacturing plant by oil gasification was completed, and no further orders for production equipment were contemplated.[24] The trend to the centralisation of major managerial functions continued. Regular long term planning for capital development extending ahead over 10 to 15 years began. In 1971, a corporate plan for the industry was produced. The Council began to investigate industry wide central purchasing and stock management, rationalisation and coordination of area and central computer facilities began, and an international consultancy service was established to exploit commercially the industry's inherent expertise. The Council also began to take an active role in direct marketing of bulk gas to industry which represented the major potential market for natural gas. Industrial sales increased by 47 per cent in 1970, showing the first effects of natural gas. During the period from 1965–6 to 1971–2, the size of the central office increased dramatically from 220 to 2561 people.

The formation of the British Gas Corporation
By 1971–72, North Sea gas accounted for 56 per cent of gas sales and the need to centralise the industry's operations had become fully recognised.

In 1972 a Bill was introduced by the incoming Conservative government which completed the process of structural change with the proposed formation of a new public corporation embracing the total industry.

The British Gas Corporation was established with a board consisting of a chairman and not less than ten nor more than twenty others. In reality, the chairman, deputy chairman and other members of the Gas Council were all appointed to equivalent positions in the new organisation, and the appointment of regional chairmen also became the responsibility of the Corporation. Each regional chairman was responsible for the conduct of corporation business within his region, subject to central policies, directives and decisions. Each regional unit was a management unit responsible for the supply of gas to customers, particularly the domestic sector, and the sale, installation and servicing of appliances.

The corporate headquarters maintained the functional form of organisation developed by the Gas Council with activities divided into production and supply, finance, economic planning, marketing, personnel and research and development. In addition, the central office was largely responsible for the continued rapid growth of bulk gas sales to industry which by 1974 had risen more than five-fold compared with 1968–9 to 5,300m therms.

By 1974 the massive conversion of the gas industry was largely complete. Natural gas made up 82.5 per cent of gas supplied directly and a further 11 per cent for enrichment and reforming, while coal based gas plant produced only 0.5 per cent of gas supplied.[25] The pace of market growth was slowing again, too, as new offshore gas discoveries dwindled with the movement of exploration to search primarily for oil. Nevertheless, gas had within a decade established itself as a major energy source while further offshore finds promised to maintain a high rate of progress for the future.

Financial performance of the gas industry
Recent financial performance is illustrated in table 9.2. Despite the dramatic improvement in the prospects for the gas industry, financial performance in the post war period was only poor to moderate. With the establishment of financial objectives for the nationalised industries in 1962, the gas industry was set the target of an average 10.2 per cent gross return over the quinquennium to 1967. In the event, this was not achieved, in large part because the industry was forced, via changing technology, to rapidly increase its level of capital invested. Thus, in the mid-1960s, the rate of return began to decline, and in 1967–8 reached a low of 7.7 per cent gross return during the time of the Suez crisis and a government policy of price restraint.

In 1969 new objectives were established for the industry of a seven per cent return on net assets, excluding depreciation, for the quinquennium to 1974. Again this target was not achieved. This was due to several factors. Firstly, the second technical change to natural gas left the industry with a

Table 9.2 Performance of the Gas Industry 1960–74

	1959/60	1965/6	1970/1	1971/2	1972/3	1973/4	1974/5
Sales (£m)	388	529	696	787	897	970	1204
Total Sales (million therms)	2540	3484	6133	7992	10180	11487	12932
Profit after interest (£m)	(2)	11	1	15	6	(42)	(42)
Internal Financing Ratio %	58	44	28	47	85	92	76
Return on capital employed %		5.4	6.2	7.2	7.3	5.4	5.5

Source: Reports of the Gas Council and British Gas Corporation.

considerable amount of nearly new oil gasification plant which was originally scheduled for depreciation over an expected life of twenty years. Hence the industry was faced with a large running depreciation charge which reduced net profitability. Secondly, a high rate of capital spending was still required to convert to natural gas, so increasing both the asset base and depreciation charges. Thirdly, the Conservative government's price constraint policy resulted in a net trading loss of £41m for gas in 1974. Nevertheless, while these factors were largely outside the industry's control, its own marketing policies contributed to the poor performance. In the early 1960s the move to promotional tariffs as a mechanism for developing domestic space heating sales led to progressive development of a seasonal peak in demand, requiring additional capital investment. At the same time this tariff structure produced a lower marginal and average income per therm while marginal costs of peak production were increased. From 1969 the trend to a lower average income per therm was accentuated by the development of bulk sales to industry and over the period from 1964 to 1974 average revenue per therm declined by some 25 per cent from 9.42p to 7.05p per therm.

As a result of the relatively weak financial performance and heavy capital spending, the ratio of self generated finance declined markedly during the 1960s from around 50 per cent to a trough of 17 per cent in 1967–8. By the early 1970s however, the main expenditure for North Sea gas distribution and conversion was essentially complete, and the industry seemed likely to be largely self sufficient in terms of meeting capital needs until the late 1970s.

THE POST OFFICE

The Post Office, unlike gas and electricity, has always been publicly owned. In 1974 with a staff in its various operations of over 415,000, the Post Office was the largest single service industry employer. In addition, it tied with the railways as being the most consistent loss maker of the public enterprise sector in the post war period. While in some ways such losses were inevitable due to the labour intensity of its operations and the high need for social service, the Post Office had suffered extensively from the dead hand of bureaucracy. It was probably the least reactive of the public enterprises in adjusting its strategy and structure and to adopt modern methods of management.

Originally established as a state monopoly in 1657 as a component of the state, the Post Office was the oldest nationalised enterprise and had added telecommunications and a savings bank to its original franchise of mail carrying. In addition, the Post Office had evolved as a primary service and distribution system for government, in its dealing with the public. These important activities, while taking a substantial amount of counter time, had traditionally contributed nothing to profitability. Until the post war period the Post Office was a profitable operation. After the second world war rapid increases in costs and inflation tended to erode profits and many postal services had become lossmakers which were sustained for political and social reasons.

Organisational and financial evolution

The early profitability of the Post Office meant that it provided a useful revenue producing vehicle for the Treasury since the industry was a direct civil service department, and its head, the Postmaster General, a minister of the crown as shown in figure 9.4. By the beginning of the 1930s, however, with the addition of new services, and in particular the rapid growth of the telephone system, it was becoming obvious that the Post Office was also a major business.

A government committee was therefore established to review the Post Office and it recommended that the intervention of the Treasury into the finances of the service should be strictly reduced and the Post Office recognised as a commercial undertaking. As a result, a fixed annual contribution was set from the Post Office to the Treasury, with any earnings over and above this being left at the disposal of the Post Office for investment in the more effective management of its business. In addition, the committee recommended that the powers and responsibilities of the head office should be reduced and in 1936, the organisation was modified to introduce a regional responsibility. In the event the degree of devolution given to the regions was strictly limited, and the Post Office continued to remain essentially centralised with the power of strategic decision making resting heavily with the minister and his central team of civil servants. Further, no recognition was taken of the product market differences between postal and telecommunications operations which were clearly becoming distinctive as telephone usage expanded.

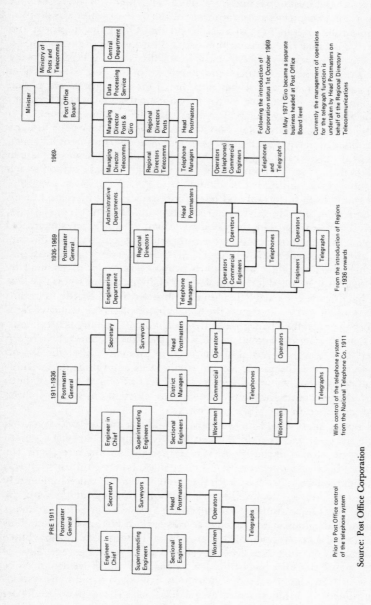

Source: Post Office Corporation

Figure 9.4 The Development of the Organisation of the Post Office

Surprisingly perhaps, the post war Labour administration did not influence the organisational and financial arrangements of the Post Office and it was left to a Conservative administration to re-examine the position with the publication in 1955 of a report on Post Office development and finance.[26] This new report recommended a return to the pre war position with the financial relations between the Post Office and the Treasury being modified to increase the financial independence of the Post Office. Under the new arrangement, which was introduced for a trial five year period from 1956–7, the Post Office made a £5m contribution to the Treasury with the balance of any earned surplus available for reinvestment.

It was also recognised that Post Office services had largely become uneconomic. In particular, the cost of new telephone equipment had risen at least $2\frac{1}{2}$ times over the 1939 level. At the same time a massive increase in capital spending was required to satisfy the rapid growth in demand which had resulted in a waiting list of 380,000 by 1955. Wage rates, too, were rising rapidly both for postal and telephone services and increased tariffs were, therefore, introduced to improve revenue. Despite these changes, however, close linkages with the Treasury remained, and as a result critical investment in telephone exchange equipment was cut back in the late 1950s, although telephone installations increased sharply from 5.4 to 8.3m.

Further, the Post Office added to its problems of under investment by failing to grasp the need for technological change. In the 1920s the Post Office had formed a cartel like relationship with the British telecommunications industry which gave the five main suppliers the exclusive right to supply the need for Strowger electro-mechanical exchange equipment. These five contractors, known as the Ring, shared the contracts between themselves, and were relieved of any need to innovate. After the second world war when requipment for improving and enlarging the telecommunications system became necessary, the Post Office and the Ring both decided against converting to the faster, more efficient crossbar switching system developed in the USA and Sweden.

The new system would have meant substantial change and retooling and the decision was therefore taken to stay with the Strowger system originally developed in the 1890s. When, therefore, in the late 1950s, the Post Office belatedly moved to invest more in exchange equipment, it was considered too late to catch up with the rest of the world which had largely converted to crossbar technology. As a result, in conjunction with the Ring, the Post Office attempted to introduce a new all electronic exchange system, and an experimental exchange was built at Highgate Wood. This proved a total disaster, opening and closing on the same day in 1962. Since no alternative system had been developed to cover the eventuality of failure, the Post Office was thus left facing the 1960s with a massive increase in telephone demand and no new exchange equipment system.

The failure to get this critical strategic decision right was in no small part due to the Post Office's continued severe structural deficiencies from its status as a civil service department. It continued to remain highly centralised, politically inspired and a virtual desert in terms of modern managerial skills. There was no marketing function, little consumer awareness, inadequate finance and accounting skills, no management development, inferior and tardy decision-making and too much bureaucracy.

The move toward corporation status

In 1961 the final links with the Exchequer were broken by the Post Office Act 1961 which gave the Post Office a new financial status. It remained a government department directly represented by a minister, but its financial arrangements became similar to those of the nationalised enterprises. Over the five year period ending in 1967–8, a financial target of a net return of 8 per cent was established for the Post Office in similar fashion to the targets set for other nationalised concerns.

In 1965 the Post Office was brought within the orbit of the Parliamentary Select Committee on Nationalised Industries which carried out a further enquiry into its operations. During the course of this, the Labour government of the day made the decision to change the Post Office into a public corporation. The government's proposals were, however, not published until 1967 and legislation to introduce the new corporation was not introduced until the 1968–9 Parliamentary session, with the new Corporation coming into effect in October 1969. Thus from the point of intention to make a structural change, some 4 years elapsed before this came into effect.

Apart from the changing relationship with the Treasury, significant internal organisation changes were made in the mid-1960s. Recognition of the managerial deficiencies present led the Post Office to call in McKinsey to undertake a fundamental examination of its organisation. The consultants recommended that the differences between the strategy needs of posts and telecommunications be recognised and the organisation decentralised into two separate product divisions. This was implemented in 1967, both in the headquarters and at regional level where the local organisations were split into two separate units, each under a separate regional director. In addition, a marketing function began to be introduced, corporate planning undertaken and new commercially oriented services developed such as a national data processing service, improved philatelic facilities, and a national Giro cash transfer service.

The Post Office Corporation

The structure of the Post Office Corporation was similar in many respects to that of other public enterprises. The board was composed of up to twelve members appointed by the minister with a chairman who might be either full or part time. Initially the board had eight members, four of whom were

brought in from outside the industry, while a fifth came from the Union of
Post Office Workers.

The new management inherited an organisation in financial difficulties.
While telecommunications had met the 8 per cent financial target
established over the quinquennium to 1967 – 8, the postal business had not.
Over the five years 1968 – 9 to 1972 – 3 new targets were fixed. For postal
services the new target was to earn a surplus of 2 per cent on expenditure
over the period, while for telecommunications, a target of 8½ per cent was
set.

In fact, the postal business made a loss of £6m in 1968 – 9, and despite the
controversial introduction of a two-tier postal pricing system, it was
obvious before the corporation had been formed that the losses would
worsen in 1969 – 70. Despite attempts to modernise and increase the
capital intensity of postal services by automatic sorting and the like, the
industry remained labour intensive since, in the end, it needed the
postman to physically collect and deliver mail. Costs, therefore, continued
to rise at an accelerating pace as inflation and wage rates increased. At the
same time the volume of mail handled was nearly static, making it
necessary for the new corporation to continuously seek price increases in
postal rates to compensate for rising costs. Nevertheless, the postal business
made more losses as the 1970 – 4 Conservative government inhibited public
sector price increases. In addition, parcels, postal orders and money order
services all lost money. Even telecommunications, which had traditionally
been profitable, made a loss in 1972 – 3 which increased in 1973 – 4. These
losses incurred as a result of government policy as with the other public
sector industries, were then largely written off by means of 'compensation'
payments from the Treasury. The artificial economics of this political
policy thus made a complete nonsense of the establishment of rational
financial targets for the nationalised enterprises.

Financial performance
The financial performance of the Post Office in the post war period has
progressed from being a positive asset to the Exchequer to becoming a
serious liability. In part, this decline was inevitable in view of the
increasing cost of labour in what will always remain, at least for the postal
service, a labour intensive industry. Since financial targets were established in the early 1960s, postal services have consistently failed to meet any
targets assigned it. A summary of recent performance is shown in table 9.3.

Despite the inevitability of the declining financial fortunes of the postal
services, the problems were compounded by structural weaknesses and
managerial ineptitude. Until the mid-1960s the industry was subject to
capital starvation, overcentralisation and a lack of acceptance of virtually
all progressive techniques in management. Since that time the industry
had endeavoured to improve itself by extensive investigation by select
committees, outside consultants and the like. There still seemed a long way

Table 9.3 Post office financial statistics 1960–74 (£m)

	1959/60	1964/65	1969/70	1970/71	1971/72	1972/73	1973/74
Postal							
Income	217.9	273.6	405.5	379.1	516.1	516.3	631.4
Expenditure	203.9	293.2	430.3	451.7	528.7	603.8	688.9
Profit	6.4	(19.6)	(24.8)	(72.6)	(12.6)	(42.5)	(57.5)
Profit margin as % of expenditure	3.0	(6.7)	(5.8)	(16.1)	(2.4)	(7.0)	(8.3)
Fixed assets net	55.1	99.6	179.2	209.5	229.0	237.8	254.8
Capital expenditure	7.0	13.6	27.3	34.3	29.9	27.5	26.3
Telecommunications							
Income	238.5	372.9	652.2	785.7	884.1	1002.3	1160.5
Expenditure	224.0	333.2	590.9	692.2	826.1	1012.0	1221.9
Profit	14.5	39.7	61.3	93.5	58.0	(9.7)	(61.4)
Profit margin as % of expenditure	6.5	11.9	10.4	13.5	7.0	(1.0)	(5.0)
Fixed assets net	746.9	1174.6	2265.0	2564.0	2961.8	3397.3	3885.3
Capital expenditure	93.9	173.7	451.4	426.2	537.3	622.9	694.7
Return on capital%	7.8	8.6	8.4	9.8	8.6	6.9	6.4

Source: Annual Reports

to go, however, and the changing role of political intervention had inhibited, rather than encouraged, the direction of change.

Conclusions

The utilities and the Post Office represent an interesting group of large concerns which are constrained in an important strategic sense. They are all unable to essentially broaden their product range or increase their geographic coverage. The major strategic opportunities then result from increased usage, which might be obtained from stimulating an overall increase in demand or by substitution competition, or by significant changes in the production technology of providing the service. In both gas and electricity there are notable examples of the latter point, gas undergoing two dramatic transformations; firstly, from coal generation to oil gasification and secondly, to natural gas. Changes in the production technology of electricity generation have been more evolutionary, but again have seen the emergence of a multifuel sourcing policy embracing both oil and nuclear fuels. The Post Office can perhaps be looked at as two separate businesses, with telecommunications being subject to similar changes in production by the introduction of new switching technology, although the postal system has had relatively limited real change.

The ability of the various industries to take advantage and manage the technological changes has been variable. In many respects the gas industry, which underwent two great changes inside a decade, must be said to have performed exceptionally well, especially in view of what would appear to be an organisation which was late in being adapted to changed circumstances. In electricity, change was less well introduced and the decisions on the choice of production mix were far from optimal. While this could be partly attributed to managerial deficiencies, probably due largely to structural faults, the most serious cause of poor performance was inept political decision making, which, in the 1960s, twice foisted the industry with seriously inaccurate demand forecasts and which also made choices on production capacity largely in response to political objectives, rather than a sense of long term optimal fuel policy. In telecommunications the key decisions were also made wrongly. Again, political considerations were important, but poor managerial performance must also be considered largely responsible.

In all cases it is notable that the industries, with the possible exception of gas in recent years, have been notably weak in commercial and marketing management. They appear dominated by production technology and slow to adopt commercial policies aimed at improving economic performance. In all cases the introduction of even the marketing concept has been relatively recent and there is no evidence that this is yet readily accepted in all cases. The industries' monopolistic position has therefore been used less for exploitation that to mask inefficiency and a lack of attention to serving consumer needs.

Structural change has largely been in predictable directions. Thus in gas, an initial series of semi autonomous regional authorities has given way to a centralised production system with the regions being confined to servicing and distribution as production technology has moved in this direction. Electricity, where a national generating system had been established earlier, has a similar structure although has yet to combine the distribution and production operations into a central corporation. The Post Office has gradually evolved as two businesses which have increasingly grown apart, leaving an uneasy structure which can probably be expected to be divided at some future time. When change has occurred, then it has largely been consistent with strategic change. However, the speed of decision making has been painfully slow. Thus the desirability for a structure such as that of the Gas Corporation was apparent several years before it was actually recommended and finally implemented. The move to the Post Office Corporation was indeed virtually recommended over 30 years before implementation. The political mechanism for introducing structural change thus appears to be inept.

Finally in performance terms, none of the industries have been outstanding. Lacking any form of financial target until the early 1960s there was little economic discipline. Since that time, although targets have been introduced, they have rarely been achieved. This is partially due to a lack of commercialism on the part of the enterprises which, lacking the spur of adequate external competition, have perhaps demonstrated a critical disadvantage of the bureaucratic monopoly. More importantly, however, poor performance has been the result of inept political intervention which has too often sacrificed economic viability for short term political expediency.

10. The Process of Strategic and Structural Change

In the post war period the service industries have experienced substantial strategic and structural change. The main directions of this change and the financial performance associated with particular types of strategy and structure were examined in chapter 2. This chapter seeks to explore the process by which the service industry corporations have shifted their strategies and structures. It seeks to find discernible patterns and examines the financial consequences of a number of them. Finally, the chapter concludes with a brief review of the similarities and differences between the strategic and structural evolution of service and manufacturing industry firms in order to generalise the pattern of corporate development across the spectrum of business enterprise.

The process of strategic and structural change observed among the service industry corporations does not seem to be a smooth evolutionary process. Rather change tends to take place in relatively sharp discontinuities. These are followed by periods of consolidation when the new pattern adopted as an outcome of the period of turbulence gradually evolves until a new turbulent phase ensues. This process is depicted in figure 10.1 which illustrates a common but by no means exclusive evolutionary path.

In the early life of the business enterprise its initial strategy is established by the founding entrepreneur. If this is successful the firm grows, usually to the point where the entrepreneur needs to delegate. At this time an organisational crisis often develops due to the difficulties entrepreneurs have in delegating decision making powers to subordinates. In part, this seems due to perhaps common personality traits of entrepreneurs which lead to the adoption of an autocratic paternalistic management style and the single minded pursuit of a particular strategy which permits little deviation. Further, such strategies often rely substantially on ill-defined heuristics which for the successful entrepreneur usually belie the need for a formalised systematic planning system. As a result of their management style, however, a common structural weakness experienced by entrepreneurs is the presence of subordinates who are seldom strong

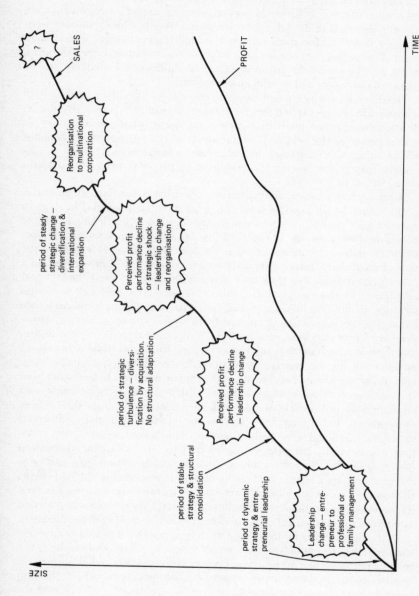

SIZE

TIME

SALES

?

Reorganisation
to multinational
corporation

period of steady
strategic change –
diversification &
international
expansion

Perceived profit
performance decline
or strategic shock
– leadership change
and reorganisation

period of strategic
turbulence – diversi-
fication by acquisition.
No structural adaptation.

Perceived profit
performance decline
– leadership change

period of stable
strategy & structural
consolidation

PROFIT

period of dynamic
strategy & entre-
preneurial leadership

Leadership
change – entre-
preneur to
professional or
family management

Figure 10.1 The Process of Strategic and Structural Change

personalities in their own right. Not unnaturally therefore management succession is often difficult. However, very successful entrepreneurs are usually able to and do delegate operational details while retaining tight strategic control. Moreover, these individuals tend to operate with a small team of very close confidantes who, while not dominating the relationship, bring to the executive group a range of skills complementary to the heuristic flair possessed by the entrepreneur.

However, for many entrepreneur led companies increasing size results in a leadership change. When this event takes place it often proves traumatic. A major reason for this is that such a change is usually involuntary. It occurs often by the relatively sudden exit of the entrepreneur, brought about a dramatic change in corporate fortune which leads to the replacement of the existing leadership, or by physical incapacity brought on by death or old age.

After such a change of leadership, provided a satisfactory financial performance is still possible from the original entrepreneurial strategy, a maintenance policy is often pursued. This applies in particular when the founding entrepreneur is replaced by his direct descendants. Unfortunately, there is no guarantee that the founder's offspring will have the flair of the father. Indeed because they are educated and brought up in a privileged environment they may actually be quite without the feel and sensitivity to the environment which created the original successful strategy. Professional management, too, will often pursue a maintenance strategy, especially when promoted from within the organisation. However, entrepreneurs tend to recognise the weaknesses in their subordinates and those in a position to actually specify their successors, tend to introduce outsiders to the top management position. Surprisingly, perhaps, these choices are not always successful but the individuals tend to be drawn from the traditional British elite background with a privileged upbringing, and education at public school followed by Oxford or Cambridge. Those entrepreneur led service firms with non-executive chairmen conformed closely to this model. One positive feature of introducing elitist managers is that it potentially provides access to be City and financial institutions where as seen in chapters 3 and 4, close personal relationships and cross directorships are a significant feature of board composition. Entrepreneurs themselves as seen in chapter 2 were notably drawn from socio-economic backgrounds quite different from the traditional City elite and their formal and informal links with the financial institutions were therefore restricted.

In the event that a maintenance strategy is possible a period of strategic stability tends to ensue, the duration of which is conditional on the firm's relative performance in the market place. However, as market maturity is eventually reached and financial performance begins to tail off, the firm becomes increasingly vulnerable to possible competitive attack and the attention of corporate raiders. On recognition of the declining performance the normal corporate reaction is to again change leadership as an essential precursor to a period of strategic turbulence. The shipping companies provided perhaps the best example of this.

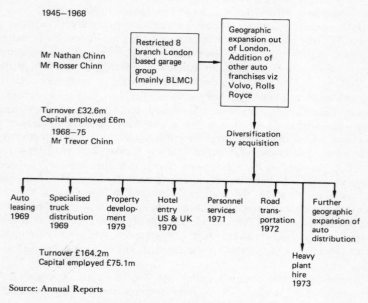

Source: Annual Reports

Figure 10.2   Evolution of the Lex Service Group, 1945–74

The potential impact of leadership on strategic change, is also clearly shown by the case of Lex Service Group. The strategic evolution of the group is illustrated in figure 10.2. Over the period 1945–68 the company was led by Mr. Nathan Chinn and Mr. Rosser Chinn. From a small garage trade and car distribution business located in London, the company grew to a major automobile distributor, operating mainly throughout the south, west and north west of England. By 1968 turnover had reached £32.6 million. Then Mr. Trevor Chinn succeeded to the chairmanship and a marked difference in strategy rapidly followed. Mr. Chinn embarked upon a series of acquisitions which took Lex into a variety of new service industry activities over the next eight years with turnover expanding more than five times while capital employed increased over twelve fold.

Strategic change under these circumstances is normally one of product diversification in an attempt to move into new markets which provide growth opportunities no longer available in the traditional business. Because for most firms the need for change is belatedly recognised, acquisition is almost invariably the chosen method of entry to new markets in order to overcome the internal lack of skills needed to develop new businesses. These acquisitions are almost casually tacked on to the parent company. No significant structural modification tends to take place, with the newly acquired operating units usually continuing a largely autonomous existence, subject only to loose central financial control.

The resulting holding company structure ultimately proves to be unsuitable to the task required of it, although the time interval before this is recognised may well be long, dependant upon the strength of competitive pressures and hence the need for efficiency. Belated recognition is thus usually triggered by a relative decline in financial performance which is often sudden and unexpected. Such a decline, in turn, may lead to external pressures being applied from such areas as a dissident shareholder group, an unwelcome take-over bid or merely a loss of favour in the stock market.

Again a precursor to structural reform is always a change of leadership. There were no examples of structural reform taking place without a prior leadership change. In the service companies this almost always meant a change in company chairman, although on occasion where the chairman's role was non-executive, the leadership resided in the office of the chief executive and change took place in this office, as with Burton Group. The most drastic transformations developed usually under the stress of a bid situation or shortly thereafter, when a board split could occur leading to a sudden change of a large group of directors, as at P & O and Trust Houses Forte.

The normal course of structural reform was to adopt a variant of the multidivisional organisation or, where diversification was more limited, a critical function system was sometimes appropriate. Such change often took place with outside help from management consultants, and as with manufacturing companies, McKinsey and Company stand out as being of particular importance in fulfilling the role of an external catalyst. It has been suggested before that the role of the external consultant in such situations is to provide a series of essential skills which the executive group inside the corporation itself lacks.[1] In addition, the outside professional advisers provide the çhanging firm with a series of technical systems for control, planning and management information, required to manage the new structure and which are also not available from within. While these reasons almost certainly exist it does also seem that the external change agents perform another role.

Since it has already recognised that change is necessary, is it not possible that the task could be completed from within the firm with only the techniques and systems being imported as necessary? This question needs to be asked since so many executives from firms which have undergone reorganisations state that the consultancy reports did little but confirm management's own opinions. While consultants do provide valuable inputs not necessarily available from within the firm there is also probably some truth in the observations of executives. It would thus appear that another aspect of the consultants' role is to perform the less pleasant task of removing those executives which the new leader does not want as part of his team. As a result of reorganisation, substantial changes usually take place within the ranks especially of the executive members of the main board. Indeed within a period of two years after a major reorganisation among the service industry firms it was not uncommon for up to two thirds of the main board executive team to have been changed. The consultants thus seem to perform an essential political role as well as a strictly technical function, helping the new leader to build an executive team of his own choice which owes political allegiance to him.

Following the adoption of a divisional structure, further diversification tends to proceed as a regular and systematic event since the firm is now organised to naturally permit this. The main strategic change now tends to be the pursuit of international growth. While product and geographic diversification often take place concurrently, the systematic pursuit of a multinational strategy does not necessarily occur during the period of strategic turbulence preceding reorganisation. It usually only takes place after reorganisation, when like activities tend to be grouped together in divisions, that attention is turned to firstly, the restructuring of international interests and secondly, their development into a global strategy.

Geographic expansion leads ultimately to further structural change. This pattern tends to be more evolutionary than revolutionary and there is no example of a change in top management being a necessary prerequisite to adaptation of the multidivisional structure to cope with growing international complexity. Conflict certainly occurs, which builds up internal pressure for reorganising. However, this tends to be restricted to the divisional level and centres on the conflicting demands of adapting to the needs of local markets while coordinating activities between national markets. In particular, there appears to be a growing trend for a recentralisation of strategic decision making as more firms begin to adopt a strategic portfolio approach. Moreover, improvements in technology and in particular computer systems, are allowing significant recentralisation of the international finance function to cope with foreign exchange risk, political uncertainty and global cash management needs. As a result, therefore, international treasury management is tending to become a critical function, which by its intervention makes the measurement of geographic and product based profit centres increasingly difficult.

The role of acquisitions in strategic change
We have observed throughout the service industry companies that acquisition provides an extremely important mechanism for achieving strategic change. When acquisition is not a component of an original strategy it usually forms an integral element in the strategic change process after a period of steady state. The trigger which sets off such a process can

have a variety of origins. In the colonial merchants it was a gradual realisation that local nationalist pressures would necessitate a strategic relocation of assets and operations. In the clearing banks, it was the intervention of new competitors in the form of the American and merchant banks as well as relaxation of the rules on mergers by the Bank of England.

For a few firms the environmental change was such as to fundamentally change the total business. In the case of Powell Duffryn for example, nationalisation of the company's coal mining assets led ultimately to the award of substantial cash compensation. The desire for corporate survival proved extremely strong and rather than return this money to the shareholders the company embarked upon an extensive acquisition programme.

This is illustrated in table 10.1 which shows the numbers and product market sectors of the acquisitions undertaken by the company from 1960 on, and classifies them according to their category of diversification. Horizontal mergers are those with companies engaged in a market area the company itself is already involved in. Vertical acquisitions are those involving a potential or actual supplier in the case of backward integration, or a potential or actual customer in the case of forward integration. Concentric acquisitions are those of companies engaged in sectors clearly related, but not the same as, those in which the firm is already operating, while conglomerate mergers are moves into areas where there is no relationship to the existing activities.

Initially Powell Duffryn spent heavily on acquisitions as the company sought for a new raison d'etre. In particular, the company expanded its fuel distribution interests so as to become the largest solid fuel distributor in the UK. Closely related moves into the distribution of other fuels such as oil, followed, while the activities of the solid fuel depots were expanded by adding building materials distribution. The builders merchant business was then supplemented by additional horizontal mergers. Similarly the company's original coastal coal shipping interests were expanded by additional purchases of shipping and wharfage firms. Then, as an extension of its warehousing and wharfage interests, came the moves into road transport. Yet, despite this effort to rebuild a major corporation based upon the peripheral activities after the core of the original business had been suddenly separated from them, conglomerate mergers were also used as part of the process.

Relatively comprehensive acquisition data was available in detail for 57 of the firms on which financial information was also obtained. Over the decade from 1964 these firms made a total of 374 acquisitions which are shown broken down by acquisition category in table 10.2. In addition the firms themselves were subdivided empirically into 3 classes, according to the number of acquisitions made as defined in chapter 1. Those firms making 10 or more purchases were deemed to be aggressive acquirers, those making between 3 and 10 purchases moderate acquirers, while those

Table 10.1 Powell-Duffryn Limited – Acquisitions – 1960–75

Products	Type of Acquisition												Total
	1960–1965				1965–1970				1970–1975				
	H	V	R	C	H	V	R	C	H	V	R	C	
Timber & Builders Merchants	7	2											9
Quarrying				3						1			4
Engineering	1				3	2			3				9
Building Services													
Contracting	1											1	3
Shipping & Wharfage	3		1		1								6
Transport	3				1				1				3
Fuel Distribution	2	1											4
Pollution Control													
Oil & Chemical								2			2		4
Storage					1								1
Miscellaneous													
Motor Engineers & Distributors	2												2
Total	18	3	2	3	6	2		2	5	1	2	1	45

Key: H = Horizontal; V = Vertical; R = Related   C = Conglomerate
Source: Annual Reports

Table 10.2   Relationship between acquisition type and corporate acquisition rate

Acquirer Type	Acquisition Category				Total	No. of Firms
	H	V	R	C		
Aggressive (<10)	83	12	90	66	251	15
Moderate (3–10)	39	3	50	17	109	21
Passive (>3)	7	–	4	3	14	21
Total	129	15	144	86	374	57

Key: H=Horizontal Acquisition;
     R=Related;
     V=Vertical
     C=Conglomerate

involved in 3 or less acquisitions were classified as passive.

The aggressive firms were in fact responsible for some 67 per cent of all the acquisitions made compared with 29 per cent by the moderate acquirers and 4 per cent for the passive companies. Moreover, the aggressive firms showed a distribution different from the others in the types of acquisition made. Passive acquirers mainly undertook horizontal purchases of like businesses while for aggressive and moderate acquirers such moves represented only about a third of the total. Moderate acquirers, by contrast tended to undertake mainly diversification moves (46 per cent) into related business areas. While aggressive firms also made a substantial number of related diversification purchases (36 per cent) they made a significantly greater number of conglomerate moves, these accounting for over 26 per cent of the total.

Because of the importance of acquisitions as a mechanism for achieving strategic change the financial performance characteristics of the three corporate acquisition rate categories were compared. These results are shown in table 10.3. As can be seen, the results suggest significantly different performances according to the number of acquisitions made. As might be expected the highest rates for all the growth variables are achieved by the aggressive acquirers. The difference is particularly marked in the absolute growth rates in assets and sales, indicating that high rates of acquisition are the main way of building a business quickly. However, the aggressive acquirers do outperform other firms in both earnings per share and assets per share growth, although the difference between aggressive and passive acquirers is much less marked.

After the aggressive acquirers, the passive acquirers tend to perform next best. It can be argued that these firms are in relatively attractive markets,

Table 10.3   Financial characteristics of acquisition rate categories

		Acquirer Type				
		Passive (> 3)	Moderate (3–10)	Aggressive (< 10)	Average	F
GEPS	Mean	24.03	13.77	29.42	21.89	
	t	0.531	−2.091	1.433		5.071
	α	–	0.025	0.10		0.01
GAPS	Mean	13.28	16.30	18.81	15.92	
	t	−1.073	0.142	1.005		1.474
	α	0.15	–	0.20		–
RBIT	Mean	19.17	16.03	16.51	17.11	
	t	1.038	−0.628	0.319		1.186
	α	0.15	–	–		–
RAT	Mean	10.41	6.57	7.32	8.28	
	t	1.972	−1.481	−0.822		5.691
	α	0.05	0.10	0.25		0.01
G SALES	Mean	16.21	16.96	42.01	23.26	
	t	−2.512	−2.154	4.080		20.12
	α	0.01	0.025	0.0005		0.01
G ASSETS	Mean	15.22	16.11	40.82	22.18	
	t	−1.440	−1.197	2.342		8.620
	α	0.10	0.15	0.025		0.01

Note: The *t* statistic here tests the difference between an estimated category mean and the overall mean. The F statistic tests for equality of all category means and the significance level is shown for each financial variable below the corresponding F value. α measures the significance of each respective t ratio.

where rates of return are especially high and where growth is sufficiently satisfactory to make it unnecessary for them to change strategy. By contrast the worst performances are achieved by those firms undertaking a moderate number of purchases. These firms tend to be those which are reacting to environmental pressures. They have reached product market maturity or have been subjected to external threats to which acquisition is seen as a potential solution. The aggressive acquirers on the other hand, tend to act upon their environment. For them acquisition becomes an integral component of strategy and they therefore adjust their internal skills and structure to assimilate new purchases.

Acquisition rate is also related to leadership type as shown in table 10.4. The majority of entrepreneur led firms have used acquisitions as a major feature in their growth strategies and it is these firms which almost exclusively make up the aggressive acquirers. Family managed firms have tended to be either moderate or passive acquirers as, too, have those companies managed by professional executives.

The financial implications of strategic and structural change
For a number of companies it was possible to examine the financial

Table 10.4   Relationship between leadership type and company acquisition rate

Acquisition Rate	E	F	M	Total
		Leadership Type		
Aggressive	13	–	2	15
Moderate	3	7	11	21
Passive	2	5	14	21
Total	18	12	27	57

Key: E = Entrepreneurial;   F = Family;   M = Managerial

consequences of particular strategic and structural changes. For seven companies the before and after financial performance data was available for a change from the dominant business category to the related business category. In addition, for 16 firms the financial consequences of a change from a holding company to a multidivisional organisation could be examined. These were the only two change situations where the number of firms available for study before and after the change was sufficiently large to make the results meaningful.

To be acceptable for inclusion it was considered critically important that a reasonable elapsed time should have occurred after the change. This was taken as being four years, this being considered to be the minimum reasonable period when a trend in the financial growth variables could be discerned since the immediate effect of structural change, in particular, tends to tail off over several years.

The results obtained from this analysis are shown in tables 10.5 and 10.6. The tables show the estimated mean values for each of the financial variables in each strategic or structural state before and after change. The

Table 10.5   The impact of strategic chance

	GAPS	GEPS	RBIT	RAT	G SALES	G ASSETS
Dominant Business						
Mean	4.24	2.89	12.13	5.77	11.68	10.16
Related Business						
Mean	8.93	21.71	17.61	8.10	20.73	19.81
t statistic	1.819	1.957	3.005	5.640	2.558	1.710
Significance level	0.10	0.05	0.025	0.005	0.025	0.10

Values of means are those obtained from raw sample data. The *t* statistic is a measure of variance between the distributions for the dominant business and related business strategies.

significance of the difference between the two means is measured by a paired *t* statistic. In testing with matched pairs of before and after effects in the same company instead of taking the differences between the sample means of the two groups, the differences in the observed values for each pair is calculated. The *t* test statistic then becomes the mean pair difference. Although the distribution of the individual pair differences may be unknown, the same distribution is assumed to apply to both with the test hypothesis being that the two distributions are not different. To both cases, but especially in the case of structural change, very high significance levels were observed for differences between financial performance before and after change.

The change from a dominant business to a related business strategy in the companies where data was available tended to occur relatively sharply rather than gradually. Often this was brought about by one or more acquisitions. Over the next few years, after the change these firms on average experienced a sharp improvement in their level of sales and assets growth, similarly return on capital both before and after tax showed major improvements. Most significant, however, was the impact on earnings per share since the effect of both faster sales growth and an improved rate of return effectively acted to lever earnings per share which exhibited an average growth over seven times higher.

Table 10.6   The impact of structural change

	GAPS	GEPS	RBIT	RAT	G SALES	G ASSETS
Holding Company						
Mean	4.31	2.39	10.71	4.20	10.52	11.07
Multidivisional						
Mean	13.20	32.42	16.45	6.64	28.51	28.12
t Statistic	3.58	4.608	3.113	2.822	5.042	3.54
Significance						
Level	.005	.005	.005	.005	.0005	0.005

Values of means are those obtained from raw sample data with no correction for industry variation. The *t* statistic is a measure of variance between the distributions for holding company and multidivisional structures.

The effect of change in the multidivisional structure was even greater. This was somewhat surprising since the effect of this type of reorganisation which is usually brought about with the help of external consultants, is often said to be behaviourally disfunctional. Certainly it is common that substantial attrition occurs at board level and among the ranks of senior management. Nevertheless, for all the financial dimensions measured, on average, sharp improvements in performance were recorded. Growth in sales and assets are seen to almost treble, the rate of return on capital before and after tax is improved by more than 50 per cent, growth in assets per share reveals a three fold increase while earnings per share improves more than 14 times. In part this improvement is due to new management capitalising upon the accumulated slack which has been built up over the years, thus a revaluation of property is a normal post reorganisation procedure. Nevertheless, there is little doubt that a genuine improvement in operational performance also occurs and this is at least partially sustained, certainly into the medium term.

Service and manufacturing industries compared
The evolution of service industry businesses has formed the basis of this book. What are similarities and differences between the service and manufacturing sectors in strategic and structural terms and how far are managerial models, developed primarily from manufacturing industry data, relevant for the service industries? To some extent it is possible to make this analysis by a comparison with an earlier, but similar, study of leading UK manufacturing firms which makes the trend amongst these organisations apparent.[1] The evolution patterns of strategy and structure for major manufacturing companies are shown in Table 10.7 and when compared with table 2.2 it is immediately apparent that a number of similar trends can be discerned.

In 1950, the diversification make up of the two populations is very similar in both cases with 75 per cent of companies in the single and dominant business categories. Among the diversified categories the number of colonial merchants led to a slightly larger number of service firms being categorised as conglomerate as compared with manufacturing firms. As with service industry firms the multidivisional structural form was little known among British manufacturing firms in 1950, being found in only 13 per cent of the population. It was found mainly in the related businesses companies (29 per cent) and, despite the large numbers of dominant business companies, very few (11 per cent) had adopted a divisional organisation. This difference between the two populations was caused almost entirely by the fact that the manufacturing industry population contained a number of foreign owned corporations, mostly with North American parents, and 8 of these firms had already adopted the divisional structure. As with the service companies there did not appear to have been many great organisational innovators in British manufacturing industry as Chandler had found emerging in the 1920s and 1930s in the United States.[2] This failure by British companies to either develop or import the multidivisional form may perhaps in some part be attributed to the relative protection and isolation of the British environment during the interwar period.

The predominant structures to be found throughout British industry in 1950 were therefore, usually either functional systems or variants of the

Table 10.7 UK manufacturing corporation strategy and structure relationships 1950–70[1]

	1950				1960				1970			
	F	HC	M	Total	F	HC	M	Total	F	HC	M	Total
Single Business	25	4	2	31	10	5	3	18	5	–	3	8
Dominant Business	18	15	4	37	9	17	9	35·	2	7	25	34
Related Businesses	7	8	7	22	3	14	21	38	1	10	42	53
Conglomerate	–	2	–	2	–	4	1	5	–	3	3	6
Total	50	29	13	92	22	40	34	96	8	20	73	101

[1] Increase in column totals for different time periods due to new entrants joining the population

Key: F=functional structure;   HC=holding company;   M=multidivisional structure.

Source: Adapted from D. F. Channon, *Strategy and Structure of British Enterprise*, op. cit. p. 67 and research data not previously published.

holding company, both of which were to be found in all categories of diversification. The holding company reflected the relatively 'amateur' British approach to management which was still more bound up with an elitist class system rather than a meritocratic professionalism. It was normally found associated with a degree of diversification. However, a few loose associations of companies in manufacturing and among bankers, insurance and retailing concerns, operating services dealing and competiting with another in similar markets were observed.

The pace of diversification in manufacturing industry proceeded significantly faster than in the service industries, and by 1960 the related businesses category was already the largest single group, representing 41 per cent of the total. By contrast little shift occurred among the service industry corporations as diversification proceeded more slowly. This difference is partly explained by the competition of the post war world coming first to the manufacturing sector.

At the end of the 1950s, as the post war sellers market ended after the Korean war, manufacturers awoke to find themselves faced with a sharp increase in competition. At home legislation was clamping down on monopolistic and restrictive practices, new competitors in the form of aggressive US firms were establishing themselves, while overseas, the formerly protected markets of the Empire were rapidly disappearing with decolonisation, and Germany and Japan, in particular, were proving significant competitors. In the service industries these pressures were not as strong, the banking markets were still largely specialised and officially cartelised through the Bank of England; insurance, too, was largely cartelised with tariff systems existing in general business and only limited attempts being made to diversify marketing efforts. Retailing firms were competing, but were more concerned with store rebuilding and increasing regional coverage, for, surprisingly perhaps, there were still few national chains. Further, resale price maintenance prevented aggressive pricing policies, while self service operations were still in their infancy.

As a result of the moves to greater diversification manufacturing firms were much quicker to adopt more professional management practices and by 1960, 34 per cent of the population had a divisional structure. In the individual strategic categories, 55 per cent of the related businesses and 26 per cent of the dominant business companies had found and adopted a multidivision organisation. Some of these new diversifiers were still in a transitional phase, where the structure represented a somewhat hybrid form, frequently containing elements of a prior functional form represented in particular by the presence of a line marketing function at board level. In this respect such firms resembled the critical function structures which were to appear among service industry firms. The new structure was not adopted in a random fashion, but tended to be concentrated by industry, appearing first in the high technology chemical and electrical engineering industries.

The situation in 1970 saw considerable gains in the number of diversified companies in both populations. The related businesses company had become the major strategic group accounting for 53 per cent of manufacturing firms and 45 per cent of service concerns. A number of differences were also apparent between the two sectors. In manufacturing industry the number of single business firms had shrunk to a mere 6 per cent, and there were signs that even these could, in several cases, be expected to leave this category in the future. The service industry companies however, were apparently stable single business concerns which had opted for this strategy as a matter of choice and had little real pressure to change.

Secondly, the dominant business category in the manufacturing sector still represented 34 per cent of the population and the category showed relatively little decline from the aggregate 40 per cent figure of 1950. Further, investigation revealed that while the dominant category was a transition phase for many companies, there did exist a hard core of stable dominant business strategies in manufacturing industry. In particular firms engaged in drink, tobacco, power machinery, oil and integrated metal and minerals production had shown little attempt to diversify (although the tobacco companies were later to move on toward a conglomerate strategy). For these industries a number of general characteristics could be observed such as high entry barriers to new competition, low growth and profitability, limited transferable technology, and a tendency to integrate capital intensive operations. Companies engaged in these industries thus had little strategic choice, in that earnings generated were all needed to maintain the existing strategy, and no extra was available for diversification.

In the service industries these characteristics did not exist, except in the public sector corporations which were really the only high capital using industries. Other dominant business service companies tended to be in this category as a matter of choice as for example in insurance, banking and retailing. As a strategic category, therefore, the dominant business classification is much less meaningful. However, the stability of the public sector and the clear choice of such a strategy in other industries makes it useful to keep. Further, while for some service dominants this strategy is a matter of choice, the public sector corporations, apart from their obvious political ownership difference, do exhibit characteristics very similar to the manufacturing dominants – namely poor economic performance, high capital requirements (although the industries themselves tend to be large employers) and integration, with a high level of fixed costs. Like the manufacturing dominants, the public corporations tend to be the losers of the industrial economy and although usually essential, require close state involvement to maintain their existence. However, although the remaining dominant business service companies were perhaps voluntarily maintaining their position the same tendency to inferior financial performance was apparent. In part, this was perhaps due to a relative security of position and invulnerability to competition. A further factor may well be leadership, which on balance appears to be passive among the dominant business concerns.

Thirdly, the number of conglomerates present in the two populations, although small, is significantly larger in 1970 among the service industries. In researching manufacturing industry the fact that no conglomerate movement had appeared in the UK, as it had in the USA, was noticeable, although given similarities in stock market conditions this seemed somewhat surprising. One explanation now possible is that the British conglomerate movement emerged primarily in the service industries rather than in manufacturing. Indeed, apart from the colonial merchants, most of the British service conglomerates in 1970 were rapidly created by entrepreneurs, using acquisition strategies based, in particular, on the discovery of underused assets, notably in property.

Structurally, by 1970 the multidivision form dominated manufacturing industry being found in 72 per cent of the companies. This rapid increase during the decade, was in large part due to dissatisfaction with subsequent performance after adopting a diversification strategy. This then led to transformation from a holding company to a divisional organisation. Further, the structure was usually introduced with the aid of external consultants. This structure was still much less common among service industry firms by 1970. Diversification moves were still very recent, and indeed true competition was also relatively new in many sectors of the service industries, thus the pressure for efficient management systems was perhaps less than among manufacturing firms. Evidence to support this argument based on interviews dealing with internal management practices revealed that information, planning and control systems were poorly developed among many service companies, even by 1974. Where change to a divisional system had occurred, however, it had taken place mainly after 1968, and as with manufacturing companies, consultants were frequently used. Consultants were also used extensively in the insurance industry in the late 1960s and early 1970s and here structural reform led to the introduction of profit centred, critical function structures even among diversified concerns.

In the service corporations where profit centred organisations were introduced there was, in general, a much greater concentration on geographic boundaries rather than product, although it was common for both to be present. Retail groups, for example, usually divided their stores into regional groupings, either serviced or managed by regional management groups, who were sometimes profit accountable. The clearing banks and a number of other financial corporations also tended to regionalise their operations. In the public sector regional structures were also common, although in the utility industries production had come to dominate in gas and electricity, thus creating essentially critical function structures. This emphasis on geographic semi-divisionalisation in service industries is interesting in that it provides evidence which tends to support Salter's[3] argument in favour of geographic organisational forms as a definite state in corporate development. By contrast, in manufacturing industry in both Britain and the USA such structures are rare.

As with manufacturing firms the period resulted in a substantial increase in international operations. Surprisingly, perhaps, this tended to be very recent among the service companies in a number of industries, although the colonial and commodity merchants, some insurance companies, and most of the construction companies became international very early. The banking firms were relatively recent adopters of direct international activities, previously being content to work on a representative or associate basis with overseas banks. Exceptions to this were the British overseas banks which had originally set out to operate clearing bank operations in former Empire territories.

The adoption of a multinational strategy had a significant impact on organisation among both manufacturing and service industry firms. While early overseas ventures, especially to the former Empire territories, tended to be allowed great autonomy, as domestic structures and management systems were revised, so international subsidiaries came under increased central direction. Among the service companies this usually took the form of the creation of an international division in the first instance. However, where overseas activities were extensive relative to the home market, area or nation based divisions tended to replace the international division.

Although direct comparison between manufacturing and service firms was not available for the last period to 1974, the continuation of the trends already apparent was indicated. Overall, therefore, the service industry data supports the basic concept that firms do evolve through a series of distinct strategic stages, and that the crude strategic categories noted in the study of manufacturing industry are a useful descriptive device for service industry corporations. At the level of detail, however, product market diversity is not a sufficient substitute for corporate strategy and further indicators are clearly needed to bring predictive power to the analysis of individual firms.

Structurally the manufacturing industry based model proved less satisfactory. Although each of the three main structural categories was found to be relevant, it was necessary to modify them to adequately cover the examples observed. In particular one entirely different form was observed, the critical function structure. Further geographic oriented structures were found to be especially important in a number of industries. This is perhaps not as surprising as it might appear at first sight, since service industry firms have no 'manufacturing' operation to provide a central focus, but rather the major assets are located in the 'selling' or distribution function. Thus, while regional disposition of the sales force in manufacturing is common, in the classification of structure the fact that this function is small in terms of people and assets tends to ensure it is subsumed below the hierarchical level structural theorists are concerned with. By contrast, in service industries the situation is reversed. It is in the interface with the environment such as the branch bank, retail store, regional utility service and the like, that most people and assets are found. This operation thus requires substantially greater managerial inputs to coordinate these activities and to ensure their efficiency. Correspondingly, therefore, these activities dominate the managerial hierarchy and the differences observed occur.

It is not possible to compare the impact of these variables on financial performance in the manufacturing sector nor to compute the influence of factors such as leadership, level of overseas activity and rate and type of acquisitions undertaken. These have all been shown to have apparently significant influences upon the financial performance of corporations. Moreover, the variables themselves are interrelated with the main structural and strategic categories. Much further analysis is therefore required to improve our understanding of corporate evolution, but some indicators of what corporate life will look like in the main service industries in the post industrial age have hopefully been provided.

References

CHAPTER I

1. J. K. Galbraith, *The New Industrial State*, Signet Books, New York, 1968, pp. 81–2.
2. A. D. Chandler, *Strategy and Structure*, Anchor Books, New York, 1966, p. 51.
3. Ibid p. 11.
4. L. Wrigley, 'Divisional Autonomy and Diversification,'Unpublished Doctoral Dissertation, Harvard Business School, 1970, p. 50.
5. See for example D. Channon, *The Strategy and Structure of British Enterprise*, Macmillan 1973; G. Dyas and H. Thanheiser, *The Emerging European Enterprise*, Macmillan, 1976.
6. B. R. Scott, 'Stages of Corporate Development Part 1', Unpublished Paper, Harvard Business School, Boston 1971.
7. L. Wrigley, op. cit.
8. J. Stopford, 'Growth & Organisational Change in the Multi-national Firm,' Unpublished Doctoral Dissertation, Harvard Business School, 1968.
9. L. Franko, *The European Multi-Nationals*, Harper & Row, London, 1976.
10. This statement is not strictly accurate, examples of critical functions can be found in manufacturing for example the central determination of crude oil prices in an oil company or centralised buying of coffee in a firm such as General Foods.
11. I am indebted to Henry Minzberg for this observation who made it following a discussion between us on the critical function structure.
12. See for example P. Selznick, *Leadership in Administration*, Harper and Row, New York, 1957.
13. See for example R. Cyert and March, *The Behavioural Theory of the Firm*, Prentice Hall.
14. See D. F. Channon, *Strategy and Structure of British Enterprise, op. cit.*, p. 129.
15. Richard P. Rumelt, *Strategy Structure and Economic Performance*, Harvard Graduate School of Business, Boston 1974, Chapter 3.
16. 'The Times 1000, 1973–4,' *Times Newspapers* London 1973.

CHAPTER 2

1. See Sir Isaac Wolfson, 'The Growth and Development of the Great Universal Stores Ltd', unpublished paper delivered at the London School of Economics.
2. For a full description of the development of the Sears structure, see A. D. Chandler, *op. cit.*, Chapt. 5.
3. In the case of insurance companies premium income was used as a substitute for sales level.

4. See for example M. Gort, *Diversification and Integration in American Industry*, Princeton N. J. Princeton University Press 1962 pp. 74 – 7, see also statement of Donald F. Eslick, Hearings before the Senate Committee on the Judiciary Subcommittee on Antitrust and Monopoly, Economic Concentration, Part 8 pp. 4996 – 5026.
5. R. Rumelt op. cit. Chapt. 3.
6. In two cases the founding entrepreneur was in the process of handing over having accepted a position of lifetime president. These companies were treated as entrepreneurial.

CHAPTER 3

1. Much of the material used in this chapter can be found in extended form in the companion volume to this book which deals specifically with the strategic and structural development of leading financial services institutions. D. F. Channon, *British Banking Strategy & The International Challenge* Macmillan, 1977.
2. Report of the Committee on the Working of the Monetary System, Gmnd, 827 (HMSO 1959).
3. Detailed consideration of these banks is found in chapter 5.
4. See Chapters 3 & 7. *British Banking Strategy*, op. cit. for a detailed description of the changes occurring among the clearing banks.
5. *British Banking Strategy*, *op. cit*; see chapters 4 and 7 for a detailed analysis of the development of the leading merchant banks making up the Accepting Houses Committee.
6. The subsequent collapse of Slater Walker Securities in 1975 – 6 took place after the research was largely completed.
7. S. G. Warburg was not a new corporation, but its merger with the traditional Seligman Bros. gave the new bank entry to the Accepting Houses Committee.
8. See *British Banking Strategy*, op. cit, Chapter 5 for a full description of the secondary banking collapse of 1973 – 5.
9. C. Mansell, 'The Banker in Bowring', *Management Today*, August 1972, p. 55 – 61, 110.
10. See especially D. Robinson, op. cit, p. 106 – 9.
11. See for example, R. Whitley, 'Commonalities and Connections Among Directors of Large Financial Institutions', *Sociological Review*, Vol 21, No. 4., Nov. 1973.

CHAPTER 4

1. H. McRae & F. Cairncross, *Capital City*, p. 131, Eyre Methuen, 1974.
2. *British Banking & Other Financial Institutions*, HMSO, 1974, p. 102.
3. With 'assurance' there is no uncertainty that the event against which one is assuring will occur. The only uncertainty is when, say, death will take place. On the other hand, in general 'insurance' it is possible that the event against which cover is sought may never take place.
4. G. Clayton, *British Insurance*, Elek Books, 1971, p. 232.

5. A notable exclusion was the Cooperative Insurance Company, which is an integral component of the Cooperative movement and one of the top 10 insurance companies. We experienced some difficulty at first in dealing with the companies as individual entities. Relatively few have been written up as case studies and the like and in particular organisational differences with the manufacturing sector were hard to differentiate at first. As a result we actually interviewed a large proportion of the companies and since their structures were given in confidence that section of the chapter dealing with this topic does not specify which firm is used as an example of a given structure. For details concerning particular companies see M. E. Ogborn, *Equitable Insurances*, Allen and Unwin, London, 1962,; P. G. M. Dixon, *The Sun Insurance Office*, 1710–1960, Oxford University Press 1960, A. Moreton, 'Norwich Unions Big Balancing Act', *Director*, November 1974; G. Foster, 'Legal and General's with profits policy', *Management Today*, August 1972, p. 62–7, 108; G. Foster, 'How the GRE Grew', *Management Today*, August 1974, p. 50–9.
6. Clayton op. cit., p. 235.
7. See for example Clayton ibid p. 253–266, and 'Which' Supplement on Life Insurance.
8. Clayton, op. cit., p. 267.

CHAPTER 5

1. B. Holder, 'Booker McConnell Ltd.', unpublished corporate strategy report, Manchester Business School, 1974. In addition the company has published a substantial number of special supplements to its annual reports giving details of particular group activities.
2. The Mitchell Cotts Group, company publication providing details of internal activities.
3. J. McGee, Dalgety Ltd., *Case Clearing House of Great Britain and Ireland*, 1972.
4. T. Lester, 'The Inchcape Caper', *Management Today*, July 1974, pp. 75–9, 116, 118, 120.
5. D. Robinson and D. F. Channon, 'The London and Rhodesian Mining Company,' published in J. M. Stopford, D. F. Channon, D. Norburn, *British Business Policy*, Macmillan, London, 1974.
6. M. Maybury, 'Gill and Duffus Group Ltd.', unpublished corporate strategy report, Manchester Business School, 1976.
7. C. Barron, 'How Berisford Trade Up', *Management Today*, November 1976, p. 67–73, 146, 148, 152.
8. See G. Turner, *Business in Britain*, Pelican Books, 1971, p. 309–14. There was also extensive press coverage of the company at the time of the proposed merger with Bovis and significant details of group activities are contained regularly in the house journal *Wavelength*.
9. See J. Wyles, 'How Student princes led Ocean away from the sea,' *Financial Times*, Nov. 9, 1976, p. 17. See also G. Turner, op. cit., p. 318–19.
10. J. R. Buckley, 'The British and Commonwealth Shipping Company,' unpublished corporate strategy report, Manchester Business School, 1976. See also G. Turner, op. cit., p. 319–20.
11. See also D. F. Channon, *British Banking Strategy*, op. cit. p. 134–7.

CHAPTER 6

1. Much of the detail contained in this chapter is drawn from D. M. Booker, 'The Development of Leading Companies in the Property and Construction Industries,' Unpublished MBA dissertation, Manchester Business School, 1974.
2. O. Marriott, *The Property Boom*, Pan Books 1969, Appendix 1. This book provides a most interesting and useful discussion of the early post war development boom through to the mid 1960s and is recommended to anyone interested in studying this industry further.
3. Ibid, p. 45.
4. Booker, op. cit. p. 14.
5. Ibid p. 14–15.
6. Marriott, op. cit., p. 40–1.
7. Channon, *British Banking Strategy*, op. cit., p. 94.
8. Marriott, op. cit., p. 50–1.
9. Ibid, p. 55.
10. Booker, op. cit., p. 32–4.
11. Ibid, p. 34–5.
12. Ibid, p. 36–7.
13. Ibid, p. 46–48, see also A. Jenkins, *On Site*, Heinemann, London, 1971, a history of Taylor Woodrow, and G. Turner, op. cit., p. 295–299.
14. See D. Gradel, 'Trafalgar House Investments', unpublished corporate strategy report, Manchester Business School, 1974.
15. D. Booker, op. cit., p. 67–8.
16. Ibid, p. 68–9.
17. Ibid, p. 69–72.
18. See A. M. Sewell and P. Quinn, 'Grand Metropolitan Limited', Unpublished case study, University of Bradford Management Centre, 1973. See also H. Duffy, 'Grand Mets growing discomfort', *Investors Guardian*, 2 February 1973, p. 5–6.
19. See R. Winsbury, 'The Big Build-up at Trust Houses', *Management Today*, July 1970, pp. 70–9; see also R. Heller, 'The Making of Fortes', *Management Today*, Sept. 1969, pp. 59–65.
20. See D. F. Channon, 'Lex Service Group', Unpublished Case Study, Manchester Business School, 1975, and also A. Davis, 'The Lex Service Group', Unpublished Corporate Strategy Report, Manchester Business School, 1975.

CHAPTER 7

1. Much of the detail in this chapter is drawn from R. I. Milligan, 'The Development of Food Retailing in Great Britain' and C. Ryan, 'Studies in the Structure and Strategy of British Retailing', both of which were unpublished MBA dissertations, Manchester Business School 1975.
2. See R. I. Milligan op. cit., pp. 67–81, see also M. Corina, *Pile it High Sell it Cheap*, Weidenfeld and Nicholson, London 1971.
3. See B. Godfrey and D. J. Martin, 'J. Sainsbury Ltd,' unpublished corporate strategy studies, Manchester Business School 1975, see also JS 100 – *The Story of*

Sainsbury, Company Publication 1969 and R. Milligan op. cit., p. 55-62.

4. See Thomas, 'Fitch Lovells Federal Food', *Management Today*, April 1972. p. 57-65, see also A. Keevil, *The Story of Fitch Lovell 1972*.

5. See James Capel brokers report on *Cavenham 1973* for a comprehensive analysis of the company; see also 'Cavenham Foods Ltd,' F. R. Levene, unpublished MSc project report, University of Bradford Management Centre 1973 and K. van Musschenbroek, 'Big Deal at Cavenham,' *Management Today*, October 1972 p. 109-16.

6. See G. Pottinger, *The Winning Counter*, Hutchinson, London 1971; see also C. Ryan op. cit., p. 52-5.

7. See J. Katz, 'The Debenham Group', unpublished corporate strategy report, Manchester Business School 1975; see also C. Ryan op. cit., p. 42-6.

8. See C. Ryan op. cit., p. 55-61, see also G. Turner op. cit., p. 268-9, *About the John Lewis Partnership*, Company publication 1973 and 'The John Lewis Partnership - Ten Years On', unpublished paper presented at the London School of Economics by Mr. O. B. Miller 1964.

9. See G. Rees, *A History of Marks & Spencer*, see also Lord Sieff, *The Memoirs of Israel Sieff*, Weidenfeld & Nicholson; and R. H. Joseph & J. L. Whyte, 'Marks & Spencers Ltd', unpublished corporate strategy report, Manchester Business School 1975.

10. C. Ryan op. cit., p. 34-7, see also *The History of British Home Stores*, company publication 1971. K. van Musschenbroek, 'The Branding of BHS,' *Management Today*, October 1970, p. 96-101.

11. See C. Ryan op. cit., p. 77-80, see also K. van Musschenbroek, 'Why Woolworths Went Wrong', *Management Today*, September 1969 and J. Mills, *F. W. Woolworth & Co*, unpublished corporate strategy report, Manchester Business School 1976.

12. See C. Ryan op. cit., p. 30-4, see also D. Rudsdale, 'The Boots Company', unpublished corporate strategy report, Manchester Business School 1975.

13. See C. Ryan op. cit., p. 69-73, see also T. Lester, 'W. H. Smith's New Chapter', *Management Today*, Jan 1972, p. 67-75, 129, and S. N. Emery, 'W. H. Smith & Son', unpublished corporate strategy report, Manchester Business School 1975.

14. C. Ryan op. cit., p. 65-9.

15. Ibid p. 46-53, see also Sir Isaac Wolfson, 'The Growth & Development of the Great Universal Stores Ltd', paper delivered at the London School of Economics in which Wolfson reveals how he came to adopt a divisional structure based on that of Sears Roebuck.

16. C. Ryan op. cit., p. 73-7, see also C. Mansell, 'New Cut at John Collier,' *Management Today*, April 1971 pp. 84-9, 130.

17. C. Ryan op. cit., p. 37-42, see also D. Jones & D. F. Channon, 'The Burton Group' in Stopford, Channon & Norburn op. cit.

18. Scotland has its own Cooperative movement with links to the English & Welsh organisation.

19. See *The Cooperative Wholesale Society in Retrospect and Prospect and A Review of the Organisation and Activities of the CWS Ltd*, unpublished internal documents, CWS 1972, see also R. J. Kelshaw, 'The Cooperative Wholesale Society', unpublished corporate strategy report, Manchester Business School 1974.

CHAPTER 8

1. A. W. J. Thomson & L. C. Hunter, *The Nationalised Transport Industries.* Heinemann, London 1973 p. 48.
2. Airline capacity can be measured in capacity ton miles (CTM) which reflects both payload availability and distance flown. For a single aircraft with a payload capacity of 10 tons flying 1000 miles per week, the CTM would be 1000 CTM. Demand is reflected by the load factor or percentage of the CTM capacity actually used.
3. T. Lester, 'Tightened Belts at BEA,' *Management Today*, February 1972, p. 62.
4. BOAC Annual Report, 1950.
5. 'The Financial Problems of the British Overseas Airways Corporation', C5: HMSO 1963.
6. 'British Air Transport in the Seventies' (Cmnd 4018) HMSO 1969.
7. 'Civil Aviation Policy' (Cmnd 4213, HMSO 1969.)
8. Thomson and Hunter, op. cit., p. 48.
9. This section owes much to the work of K. D. Worthing, 'The Strategy and Structure of the Nationalised Landbased Transport Industries,' unpublished MBA dissertation, Manchester Business School, 1974.
10. Extracted from K. D. Worthing, p. 27.
11. YTHC Annual Report, 1968.
12. Thomson and Hunter, op. cit., p. 116.
13. SCNI, Ministerial Control of the Nationalised Industries, HMSO 1968, Volume II, p. 400.
14. R. Kelf Cohen – *Twenty years of Nationalisation*, MacMillan 1969, p. 18.
15. Ibid.
16. Select Committee on Nationalised Industries, *Ministerial Control of Nationalised Industries*, op. cit.

CHAPTER 9

1. I am indebted to the Electricity Council for their help in providing excellent background material themselves and also reproducing bibliographies and synopses of other works on the industry. In particular data was obtained from two Electricity Council publications, *Electricity Supply in Great Britain, a Chronology* and *Electricity Supply in Great Britain, Organisation and Development.*
2. R. Kelf Cohen, *British Nationalisation, 1945–73*, MacMillan, London 1973, p. 39.
3. C. H. Reid, K. Allen and D. J. Harris, *The Nationalised Fuel Industries*, Heinemann, London, 1973 pp. 177–9.
4. Ibid p. 180–4.
5. Report of the Committee of Inquiry into the Electricity Supply Industry, Cmnd 9672, HMSO 1956.
6. *The Electricity Council, Organisation and Development* op. cit., p. 20–4.
7. Reid et al op. cit., p. 204–19.
8. Ibid p. 190–6.
9. Space does not permit a detailed discussion of the industry tariff structure, which has been progressively developed toward a marginal price system. An

excellent overview of this is provided in G. L. Reid et al p. 204–19. An
alternative argument is presented by R. Pryke, *Public Enterprise in Practise*,
MacGibbon and Kee, London 1971, Chapters 9, 16, 17.

10. *The Financial and Economic Obligations of the Nationalised Industries*, 1337, HMSO
1961, p. 8.
11. Reid et al p. 219–24.
12. 'The Gas Industry: Report of the Committee of Enquiry,' Cmnd 6699,
HMSO, 1945
13. Reid et al op. cit., p. 93–100.
14. Select Committee on Nationalised Industries, The Gas Industry, HC 280,
HMSO, 1961 Vol II p. 613.
15. Ibid pp. 600–601.
16. Select Committee on Nationalised Industries, The Gas Industry, HC280,
HMSO, 1961, p. 45 Vol. 1.
17. Financial and Economic Obligations of the Nationalised Industries, Cmnd
1337, op. cit.
18. Gas Council Annual Report 1963/4, p. 19.
19. See White Paper on Fuel Policy Cmnd, 2498, HMSO, 1965.
20. Gas Council Annual Reports.
21. Ibid
22. Gas Council Annual Report 1962.
23. Gas Council Annual Reports.
24. Gas Council, Annual Report 1968–9, p. 15.
25. British Gas Corporation Annual Report, 1974.
26. *Report on Post Office Development and Finance*, HMSO, Cmnd 9576, 1955.

CHAPTER 10

1. See D. F. Channon, *Strategy and Structure of British Enterprise*, op. cit. p.
2. A. D. Chandler, op. cit.
3. M. S. Salter: 'Stages of Corporate Development,' *Journal of Business Policy*,
Vol. 1, No. 1, 1970, pp. 40–51.

Index

286